THE INSTANT
Astrologer

THE INSTANT
Astrologer

FELIX LYLE
AND
BRYAN ASPLAND

BOOK OF INTERPRETATION

St. Martin's Press ≈ New York

Dedicated to the memory of Len Roberts 1950 – 1994

Library of Congress Cataloging-in-Publication Data available on request

ISBN 0-312-19427-7

First St. Martin's Edition: 1998

1 3 5 7 9 10 8 6 4 2

AN EDDISON·SADD EDITION
Edited, designed and produced by
Eddison Sadd Editions Limited
St Chad's House, 148 King's Cross Road
London WC1X 9DH

Phototypeset in New Baskerville BT using QuarkXPress on Apple Macintosh.
Printed and bound in China through Leo Marketing UK.

CONTENTS

HOW TO RUN THE PROGRAM

This program runs on PCs operating systems *Windows 95*, *Windows 98* and *Windows NT*. Once you have installed the program, you can quickly calculate a chart for anyone born between the years 1900 and 2020.

Installation

1. Insert the CD in your CD drive.
2. Click on the **Start** button.
3. Click on **Run**.
4. In the **Run** dialog box type e:setup ('e' is the assumed drive letter of your CD drive. If it is another letter, type in the appropriate letter.)

5. Click on **OK**. *The Instant Astrologer* installs itself automatically. You may be prompted to confirm steps in the installation procedure. Follow these instructions.

The program will guide you through creating birth charts. All you need to do is fill in the blank panels on each screen to create a birth chart, which you can then interpret in the following chapters.

Running the program

1. Click on **Start** (lower left corner of screen).
2. Scroll up to **Programs**.
3. Select **Astro**. The program will load.

Fig. 1 Opening Screen and Chart Wheel Screen

You have two main options:
A. To create a new birth chart, or
B. To retrieve an existing chart from the **Name List**.

To view chart options, see page 9.

A. To create a new birth chart
1. Click on **Data** to reveal a menu.
2. Click on **New Name** from the Data menu. A dialog box appears *(see Fig. 2 opposite)*. Go to Fig. 2.

B. To retrieve a chart already in the Name List
1. Click on **Data** to reveal a menu.
2. Click on **Name List** from the Data menu. A dialog box appears *(see Fig. 5 on page 8)*. Go to Fig. 5.

To calculate a chart comparison bi-grid (to compare two people's birth charts), go to page 12.

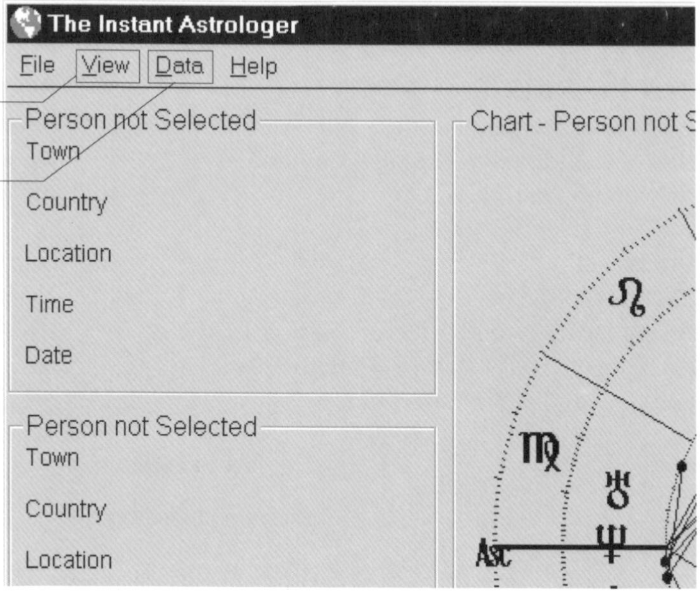

Fig. 2 New Name

*When you have completed each field (empty white panel), either click on the next field, or press the **Tab** key.*

Check if **Daylight Saving Time** was in operation with the relevant local authority (for those born in the UK the program already compensates).

The information in this box explains exactly what you have to do in each field as you work through the screen. If in doubt, check it!

If you make a mistake, the **Clear** button will clear all fields so that you can start again.

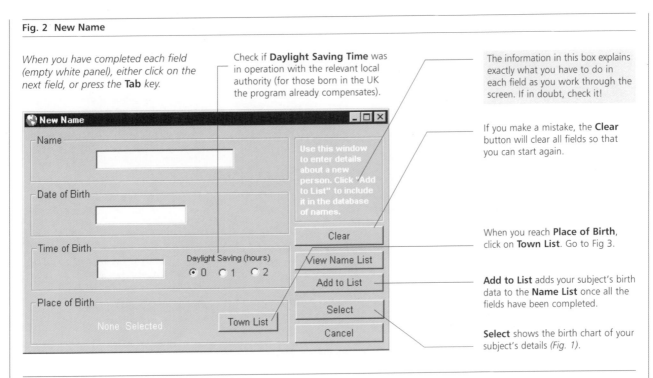

When you reach **Place of Birth**, click on **Town List**. Go to Fig 3.

Add to List adds your subject's birth data to the **Name List** once all the fields have been completed.

Select shows the birth chart of your subject's details *(Fig. 1)*.

Fig. 3 Town List

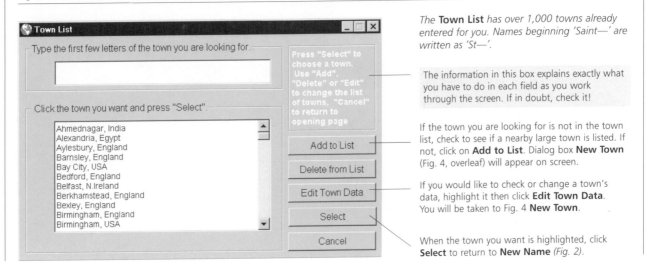

The **Town List** has over 1,000 towns already entered for you. Names beginning 'Saint—' are written as 'St—'.

The information in this box explains exactly what you have to do in each field as you work through the screen. If in doubt, check it!

If the town you are looking for is not in the town list, check to see if a nearby large town is listed. If not, click on **Add to List**. Dialog box **New Town** (Fig. 4, overleaf) will appear on screen.

If you would like to check or change a town's data, highlight it then click **Edit Town Data**. You will be taken to Fig. 4 **New Town**.

When the town you want is highlighted, click **Select** to return to **New Name** (Fig. 2).

Fig. 4 New Town

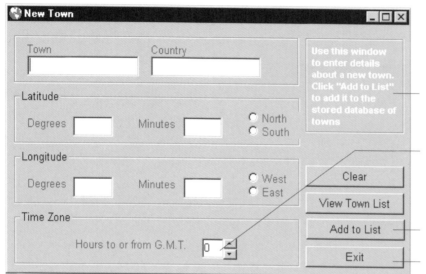

When you have completed each field, either click on the next field, or press the **Tab** *key. You will need to look up the latitude and longitude of the town in an atlas to complete this screen.*

The information in this box explains exactly what you have to do in each field as you work through the screen. If in doubt, check it!

Use the map on page 14 to find the time zone of the birth town. Scroll up or down to select the correct time zone here. This is not necessary for the UK.

When all fields are completed click **Add to List**. This adds your new town to the **Town List** for you to select *(see Fig. 3)*.

Exit returns you to **New Name** dialog box *(Fig. 2)*.

Fig. 5 Name List

The **Name List** *has 100 names already entered.*

The information in this box explains exactly what you have to do in each field as you work through the screen. If in doubt, check it!

Click the name from the list you want, then press **Select**. This returns you to Fig. 1 where the chart will be displayed.

If you cannot find the name you want, this button takes you to **New Name** *(Fig. 2)* to create a new birth chart.

Name List

Type the first few letters of the name you are looking for.

Click the name you want and press "Select".

Adams, Douglas	Borg, Bjorn
Allen, Woody	Boycott, Geoffrey
Andrews, Julie	Branagh, Kenneth
Armstrong, Neil	Braun, Eva
Beatty, Warren	Bruce, Lenny
Becker, Boris	Caine, Michael
Behan, Brendan	Cher
Bergman, Ingrid	Collins, Joan

Press "Select" to view chart. Use "Add", "Delete" or "Edit" to change the list of names, "Cancel" to return to main page.

Add to List

Delete from List

Edit Birth Data

Select

Cancel

Fig. 6 Options from Chart Wheel Screen: Planetary Data

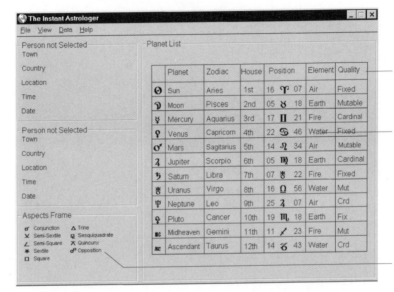

This menu from the chart wheel screen (Fig. 1) gives you two additional information screens for the chart that you have just calculated. The options are **Planetary data** *(right) and* **Grid** *(Fig. 7, below). Return to the chart wheel by choosing* **Chart**.

This is the planetary data screen; it shows the planets' positions in the signs and houses *(see page 11)*.

The last three columns show the overall balance of the signs *(see page 11)*.

This key is a quick reference guide to the symbols used in astrology. You can view Zodiac signs, Planet and Aspect symbols by clicking on **Help**.

Fig. 7 Options from Chart Wheel Screen: Grid

This is the aspect grid screen; it shows the angular relationships between the planets at the time of birth (see page 11).

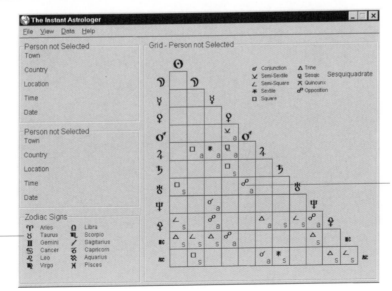

This key is a quick reference guide to the symbols used in astrology. You can view Planet and Aspect symbols and Zodiac signs by clicking on **Help**.

Where a symbol appears in a box in the grid, it shows that a planet is in aspect to another planet or Angle. Here, Mars (♂) is in opposition (☍) to Uranus (♅) *(see chapters 5 and 7)*.

Birth Chart Print Out: This is the birth chart of Diana, Princess of Wales, featured in Chapter 8.

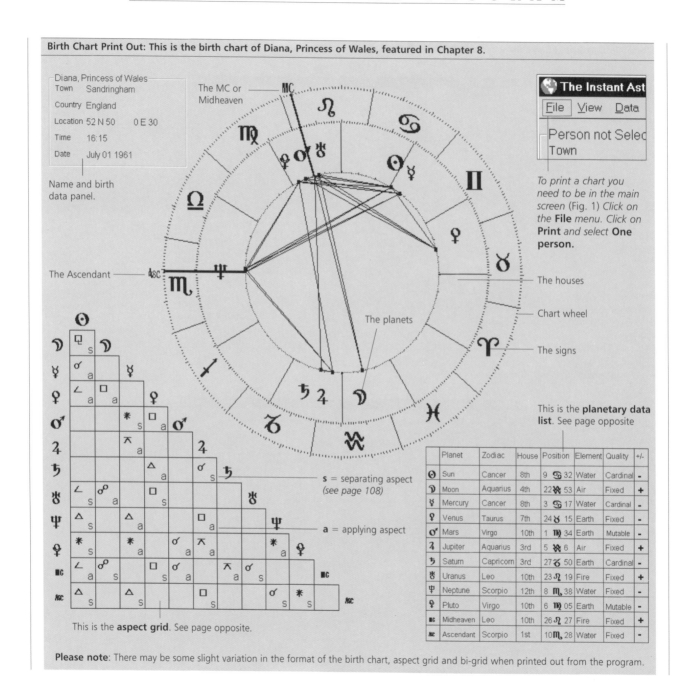

Diana, Princess of Wales
Town	Sandringham
Country	England
Location	52 N 50 0 E 30
Time	16:15
Date	July 01 1961

Name and birth data panel.

The MC or Midheaven

MC

The Instant Ast
File View Data

Person not Selec
Town

To print a chart you need to be in the main screen (Fig. 1) *Click on* the **File** *menu. Click on* **Print** *and select* **One person.**

The Ascendant — Asc

The planets

The houses

Chart wheel

The signs

This is the **planetary data list.** See page opposite

s = separating aspect (see page 108)

a = applying aspect

This is the **aspect grid.** See page opposite

	Planet	Zodiac	House	Position	Element	Quality	+/-
☉	Sun	Cancer	8th	9 ♋ 32	Water	Cardinal	-
☽	Moon	Aquarius	4th	22 ♒ 53	Air	Fixed	+
☿	Mercury	Cancer	8th	3 ♋ 17	Water	Cardinal	-
♀	Venus	Taurus	7th	24 ♉ 15	Earth	Fixed	-
♂	Mars	Virgo	10th	1 ♍ 34	Earth	Mutable	-
♃	Jupiter	Aquarius	3rd	5 ♒ 6	Air	Fixed	+
♄	Saturn	Capricorn	3rd	27 ♑ 50	Earth	Cardinal	-
♅	Uranus	Leo	10th	23 ♌ 19	Fire	Fixed	+
♆	Neptune	Scorpio	12th	8 ♏ 38	Water	Fixed	-
♇	Pluto	Virgo	10th	6 ♍ 05	Earth	Mutable	-
MC	Midheaven	Leo	10th	26 ♌ 27	Fire	Fixed	+
Asc	Ascendant	Scorpio	1st	10 ♏ 28	Water	Fixed	-

Please note: There may be some slight variation in the format of the birth chart, aspect grid and bi-grid when printed out from the program.

Chart Printout

The printout displays all the essential components for interpreting a birth chart: the signs, the planets, the houses, the Angles and the aspects. The Book of Interpretation explains each of these components in detail. Follow the chapter references below, then consult Chapter 8 on how to interpret all these components.

The Signs

Acting as a backdrop to the planets is the zodiac belt – an imaginary band in the heavens around which the planets appear to move as viewed from Earth. The zodiac is divided into twelve sections of 30°, each with its own name and symbol. These are the zodiac signs in the outer ring of the birth chart wheel. Each sign colours the way the planetary energies in a chart are released.
See Chapter 2 THE SIGNS OF THE ZODIAC

The Planets

The planets (in astrology these include the Sun and Moon) are the building blocks of the birth chart. Each planet has its own symbol, or glyph, and is associated with a specific type of energy, a basic inner drive. The planets' positions in the chart are shown in the 'Planetary Data' list in degrees and minutes of the sign they occupy at the moment of birth.
See Chapter 3 THE PLANETS

The Houses

The twelve houses in the birth chart represent spheres of experience. They show the areas of life where the planetary energies are most likely to be expressed. The houses take their cue from the Ascendant, which marks the beginning, or cusp, of the first house. The remaining houses are counted anti-clockwise on the inner ring of the birth chart wheel. The house occupied by each planet is also shown in the 'Planetary Data' list.
See Chapter 4 THE HOUSES

The Ascendant

The Ascendant marks the exact degree of the sign rising on the eastern horizon at the time and place of birth. This point sets the overall tone of the chart as it represents your personal 'window' on life, both in terms of how you view the world and how the world sees you. Its opposite point is the Descendant.
See Chapter 4 THE HOUSES; *Chapter 6* ASPECTS TO THE ANGLES

The MC

The MC, also known as the Midheaven, is the degree of the sign directly overhead at the moment of birth. It shows your most conscious goals and your worldly ambition. Its opposite point is the IC. The Ascendant–Descendant and the MC–IC axes, known as the Angles, are among the most sensitive points in the chart.
See Chapter 4 THE HOUSES; *Chapter 6* ASPECTS TO THE ANGLES

The Aspects

At the heart of birth chart interpretation lie the angular relationships between the planets, known as the aspects. Shown in the grid in the printout, the aspects reveal how the energies of the planets interact.
See Chapter 5 THE ASPECTS; *Chapter 7* ASPECT PATTERNS AND CHART SHAPES

Overall Balance

While each sign has a 'colour' of it own, it also shares characteristics with other signs. These similarities enable the planets in the signs to be grouped in a way that gives an overall impression of an individual's personality 'type'. The most important groupings, The Elements, Qualities and Polarities are shown on the printout under 'Planetary Data' for easy reference. The Polarities are entered under the column headed +/–.
See Chapter 2 THE SIGNS OF THE ZODIAC

Fig 8 To Create a Chart Comparison 'Bi-grid'

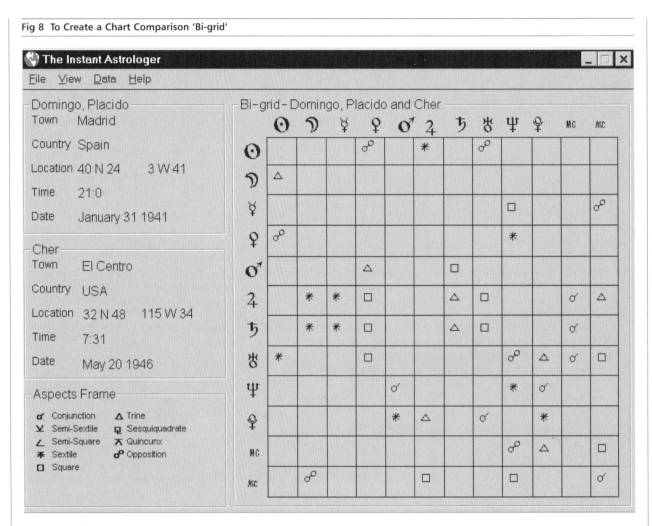

To create a chart comparison bi-grid, first calculate the birth chart for person one by following steps on pages 6–8, and add it to the list. Then calculate the birth chart for person two by again following steps on pages 6–8. Click on **View** and select **Bi-grid** to compare them. In order to make a comprehensive comparison, you should print out both birth charts (see page 10) as well as the bi-grid.

Click on **View**. Then Click on **Bi-grid** to show the aspect comparison grid (above).

Use the **File** menu to print out a bi-grid chart. Click on the **File** menu. Click on **Print** and select **Two persons**.

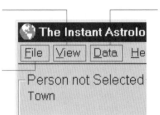

Click on **Data**. Then Click on **Swap Names.** This option allows you to swap between two people's charts, grids and planetary data. It also enables you to swap who you view as person one and person two on the bi-grid.

Fig 9 Bi-grid Chart Print Out: This is the aspect bi-grid for Louise and George featured in Chapter 9

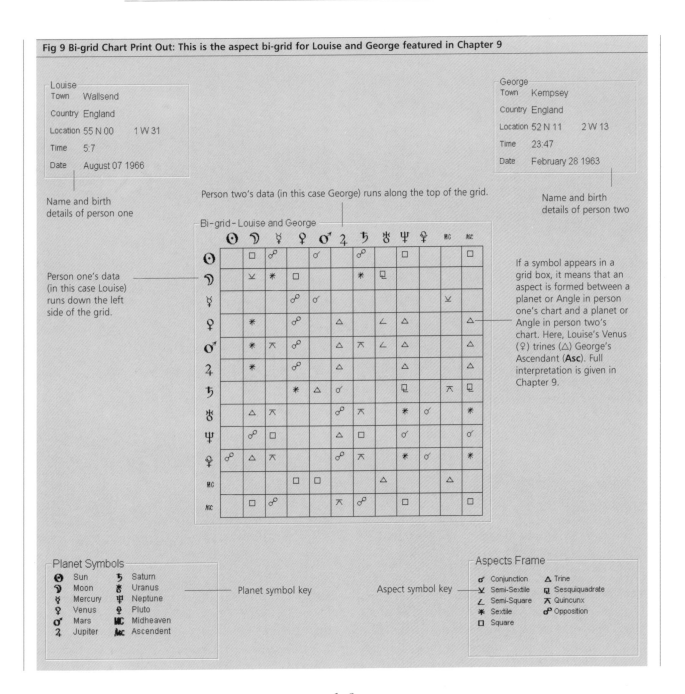

Louise
Town   Wallsend
Country   England
Location   55 N 00   1 W 31
Time   5:7
Date   August 07 1966

George
Town   Kempsey
Country   England
Location   52 N 11   2 W 13
Time   23:47
Date   February 28 1963

Name and birth details of person one

Person two's data (in this case George) runs along the top of the grid.

Name and birth details of person two

Bi-grid – Louise and George

Person one's data (in this case Louise) runs down the left side of the grid.

If a symbol appears in a grid box, it means that an aspect is formed between a planet or Angle in person one's chart and a planet or Angle in person two's chart. Here, Louise's Venus (♀) trines (△) George's Ascendant (**Asc**). Full interpretation is given in Chapter 9.

Planet Symbols

☉	Sun	♄	Saturn
☽	Moon	♅	Uranus
☿	Mercury	♆	Neptune
♀	Venus	♇	Pluto
♂	Mars	MC	Midheaven
♃	Jupiter	Asc	Ascendent

Planet symbol key

Aspects Frame

♂	Conjunction	△	Trine
⌄	Semi-Sextile	⬓	Sesquiquadrate
∠	Semi-Square	⊼	Quincunx
✳	Sextile	☍	Opposition
□	Square		

Aspect symbol key

Fig 10 Time Zone Map

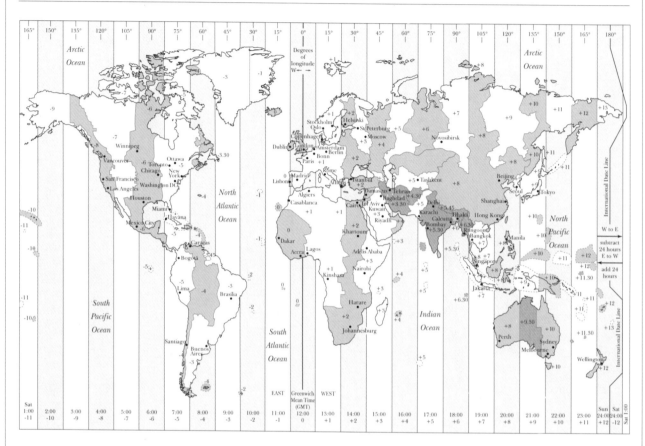

Time Zones

+ = hours 'to' or ahead of Greenwich Mean Time   − = hours 'from' or behind Greenwich Mean Time

Note: Some countries utilize Daylight Saving Time, advancing their clocks by one hour for part of the year. These time changes are not shown in the Time Zone map. For people born in the UK, Daylight Saving – and Double Daylight Saving during the 1940s – is automatically calculated by the program; for other countries you will need to consult either the ACS American Atlas or the ACS International Atlas (*see reading list on page 223*), or contact the appropriate authority.

CHAPTER 1

INTRODUCTION TO
THE BOOK OF
INTERPRETATION

Astrology is nothing if not resilient. After hundreds of years of vilification at the hands of mainstream science, it is still alive, kicking and, indeed, prospering as never before. Yet it continues to stir rabid controversy, because in an age that demands empirical proof, astrology's central tenet – that the relative positions of the planets somehow have an effect on human behaviour – has no demonstrable basis in scientific fact. All the same, a growing number of people are turning to astrology for guidance in their everyday lives. Recent research shows that in the US alone, an estimated 20 million people regularly consult an astrologer. This estimate was supported by a 1990 Gallup poll, which found that over forty-five per cent of Americans held some belief in astrology.

At the popular end of the market, the national and regional press is awash with Sun-sign columns dispensing advice to readers on how best to profit from the planetary movements in the heavens. Belief in the stars' influence on human affairs is not confined to the general public. A United Nations study into the international repercussions of astrology revealed that no less than twelve governments made decisions on national policy on the basis of astrological prediction.

Who can forget the international uproar triggered by the disclosure that Nancy Reagan, wife of former US President Ronald Reagan, frequently consulted the stars before a major political event? Perhaps not surprisingly, the United Nations condemned the use of astrology by political leaders by concluding that 'this is not the most responsible way to conduct national or international affairs'.

The sceptics' viewpoint

Astrology's increasing popularity is viewed by many with disbelief. Countless scientists, for instance, have argued that science has long since swept away many of astrology's presumptions – most notably the notion that the planets have any physical influence on our lives. In their book, *The Gemini*

Syndrome, astronomers Dr Roger Culver and Dr Philip Ianna set out to disprove astrology by demonstrating that, while the Sun and Moon affect us strongly, the gravitational force and electromagnetic fields of the planets in our solar system are so weak as to have a negligible effect on our behaviour. To illustrate their point, the two scientists calculated that the gravitational pull of Mars on a baby is approximately 500 times less than that of the hospital where it was born.

Other surveys have also failed to produce results in favour of astrology. In 1974, for instance, the National Council for Geocosmic Research (NCGR) carried out one of the most comprehensive 'hindsight' tests ever undertaken. Scrutinizing the astrological birth charts of over 2,000 suicide cases, researchers failed to find a single planetary pattern that would enable them to predict such an outcome. Given these findings – and they are by no means the only ones – what is it about astrology that draws perfectly rational and intelligent people to embrace it? How *does* it work? And what can it tell us about human character?

How does astrology work?

Is astrology a science or an art? Or is it simply a bundle of superstitions carried over from a primitive age? The simple answer to these questions is that nobody really knows – there is no known mechanism by which astrology can be shown to work. There are, however, a number of theories that have been suggested. Some try to explain the planetary effects on our lives in scientific terms, in the form of some as yet to be discovered physical force. A variation of this idea is found in modern 'chaos' theory – as developed by theoretical physicists – which argues that even the most massive systems can be seriously affected by the smallest of physical causes.

Others believe that astrology works on a more metaphysical plane, at a level where human consciousness and the universe merge to form part of a seamless, interconnected whole. Yet others maintain that astrology is not about cause and effect at all, but as astrophysicist Michael Shallis explains it, 'consists of an acausal correspondence between an apparently random moment in time [such as the birth of an individual] and the exact but relative positions of the planets at that time.' This idea, incidentally, was first mooted by the eminent Swiss psychologist Carl Jung in his theory of synchronicity.

Finally, there are those who are convinced that astrologers gain their insights by paranormal or occult means, such as ESP, discarnate spirits or Old Nick himself. The plain truth of the matter is that, however elegant or plausible some of these theories might be, they all miss the point. To understand how astrology works, it is necessary to understand what it is – and to do this we have to look briefly at its origins.

Astrology has its roots in a cultural tradition that is thoroughly alien to our modern age, dominated as it is by the twin 'gods' of materialism and consumerism. Our ancient ancestors viewed the Earth and the heavens in a very different light. To them, the cosmos was a living entity infused with subtle but potent forces that had a direct bearing on the welfare of the tribe or group. Their gods took many forms, among which were the Sun, the Moon and the planets visible to the naked eye. They invested these gods with powers which were derived from a combination of detailed empirical experience and the deepest recesses of the human psyche. Astrology, or astronomy – for the two were one and the same thing – was, in fact, a sophisticated cosmology in which the vagaries of an uncertain world were given meaning through the 'actions' of the gods-as-planets. This was not the cold, sterile cosmology of modern science, which observes and measures the physical universe, but can never comprehend its purpose. It was a cosmology based on the Ancients' inner experiences projected on to external reality; to understand it was to step into it body and soul and thereby take one's place in a purposeful universe.

Nowadays, of course, industrialized, urban society has almost completely lost this bridgehead between inner and outer reality. Until fairly recently, astrology had lost it as well, for like the scientific paradigm that displaced it, it had become solely concerned with external reality. But, thanks mainly to the insights of psychology, the planets in astrology have become 'internalized', and are now seen in terms of archetypes – timeless symbols of the psyche that not only connect us to the rest of humanity, but can direct us towards our own particular purpose.

So to return to the question of what astrology is, the answer is that it is part science, in that it incorporates empirically observable phenomena – the movements of the planets through the heavens; it is a form of art because, like any language, it communicates through symbols that need to be interpreted; it can also involve 'divination' in as much as that by steeping ourselves in its symbolism, it is possible to gain profoundly intuitive insights. But it also embraces psychology, mythology, metaphysics, and more or less anything else that anyone studying the subject cares to include.

This is why it is virtually impossible to explain to an outsider how astrology works, because it is not a specific discipline governed by a strict methodology. Admittedly, the calculation of a chart is based on scientifically derived data, but the way that data is interpreted is determined as much by the astrologer doing the interpretation as it is by the conventional meanings of the symbols themselves.

Perhaps this explains why many scientists and other sceptics who dismiss astrology without ever having studied it lose all sense of rationality when attacking the subject. Orthodox science uses the power of the mind to explore the workings of external reality, while at the same time denying that the consciousness of the observer plays any part in what is being observed. In fact, many scientists refuse to accept that there is such a thing as consciousness, preferring to reduce the mind to a series of biochemical reactions. In astrology, however, consciousness is everything. It uses external reality as a means of gaining access to and understanding the power of the psyche. In short, astrology deals in experience-centred reality in a way that current mainstream science never can. And scientists believe astrology is a delusion?

A map of our potential

This brings us to the second question – what can astrology or, more precisely, a birth chart tells us about an individual?

The birth chart is commonly described as a blueprint of our potential. In essence, it is a map of the heavens drawn up for the exact time and place of birth. But, just as each of us is an unique individual, so is each birth chart. No one will share the identical 'layout', not even a twin, because the way the planets and other sensitive points in the chart interlink with each other from any given standpoint on Earth changes with every minute that passes. Once this map has been drawn up, the process of 'reading' the symbols can begin. There are four essential reference points to chart interpretation, all of which are explained in detail in the relevant chapters – so we will confine ourselves to a brief overview here:

• **The planets.** These represent particular kinds of energy which are expressed as instinctive psychological drives or urges. For example, Venus is a symbol of our need for harmony and union, and shows how we go about the business of forming close relationships in our lives. It is worth mentioning here that in astrology 'planets' is used as a shorthand for all the celestial bodies in a chart, including the Sun and Moon. Just to confuse matters further, these last two are also sometimes jointly referred to as the 'Lights' or 'Luminaries'.

• **The signs of the zodiac.** At any given moment in time, each planet will be found to 'occupy' one of the twelve signs of the zodiac. Each sign acts as a lens, modifying the way the planets' energies are expressed. Returning to our example, if Venus is placed in the sign of Aries, our love affairs and close friendships will be coloured by the spontaneous and fiery qualities characteristic of this sign. Venus in Taurus, on the other hand, will manifest its energies in a slower, more sensual manner, and so on.

• **The houses.** The twelve houses are mathematically derived divisions of the birth chart circle. They show specific areas of life where all the planetary activity, coloured by the signs, is likely to find an outlet.

• **The aspects.** These are angular relationships that the planets form relative to each other – as seen from Earth – and to other points in the chart. The aspects are considered to be the nucleus of the birth chart. They signify dynamic meeting points between two or more different types of energy within the psyche, which will bring either stability or tension to those areas of life indicated by the planets, signs and houses that are implicated in the aspects.

At this point, it is worth clarifying what a chart can and cannot reveal. One of the main arguments raised by astrology's detractors is that if our destinies are in some way encoded in the planet's positions at the moment of birth, then there can be no free will – our lives are fated and we have no choice but to act out our pre-ordained roles. To be fair, astrology has not helped itself in this matter, because it often resorts to using the language of fate. Typically, astrologers talk of the 'influence' of a planet or a sign, or the 'effect' an aspect can have, in a way that is undeniably deterministic.

The trouble is that, although astrology has moved on from the bad old days when the consensus was that the planets really did influence our lives, it has not changed its terminology. Instead of describing planets in terms of their influence, astrologers should talk of the way they correspond to certain patterns of behaviour. As we have already seen, the birth chart is purely symbolic and a planet is just a symbol of a certain type of psychological energy. The symbol itself has no inherent power, and certainly cannot determine what will happen to us, how we will live out our lives, or what our allotted lifespan might be.

Moreover, a birth chart makes no value judgements, and therefore cannot distinguish between a saint or a sinner, success or failure, fame or ignominy. It cannot even reveal the sex of an individual. What it can do, though, is show us the potential psychological energies we have at our disposal, in what balance, and at what times in our lives we can make maximum use of them. But everyone of us has the free will to do exactly as we please with these energies. We may deliberately ignore them, or unconsciously repress them; we may choose to resist them or submit to them; or we may decide to learn how to harness them productively and move our lives forward, with a new level of understanding. As the astrological adage assures us, 'the stars incline, but never impel'.

Once the birth chart is understood as a map of our potential, it becomes clear that the task of the astrologer is to make sense of this inner landscape, to define the lie of the land and signpost the various routes open to us on our journey of self-realization. This is a challenging undertaking, not least because the way the planetary energies are expressed can take many forms.

For example, Saturn symbolizes, among other things, the principles of structure and stability, fear and repression. Its position in the chart by sign and house placement and the aspects it makes, when weighed against all the other features in the birth chart, will provide general clues as to how dominant the Saturnian energies in the personality might be. But looked at on its own, it is extremely difficult, if not impossible, to know precisely how, and in what balance, Saturn will manifest in an individual's life without determining how he or she has developed or inhibited the natural tendencies indicated in the chart.

This can only be established in detail by talking to the individual concerned. Contrary to a lot of people's perception of astrology, birth chart interpretation is not a guessing game; it is a dialogue. And for beginners to make sense of the keyphrase meanings of the planets and aspects given in this book, or any other for that matter, it is strongly recommended that they discuss the accuracy of the suggested interpretations with the person whose chart is being scrutinized. A pre-judged viewpoint, based upon a 'dry', textbook study of a chart cannot possibly yield a deep understanding of such personal influences as family background or early upbringing. The chart is a starting point for an astrologer's investigations, not the final solution.

Some popular misconceptions

Related to the whole issue of free will versus fate is the fundamental misconception that astrology can somehow help us pinpoint our ideal partner. The reality is that there is no astrological equivalent of a magic wand for the perfect relationship and no planetary significators for harmony and longevity in love, because we all have widely differing and divergent needs.

All the same, chart comparison – which is dealt with in the final chapter of this book – is an immensely valuable tool, because what it can address is not whether a relationship will work but how it will work. In short, chart comparison concerns itself with the 'type' of relationship, not its validity. Perhaps one partner may find fulfilment through being dominated, while another finds emotional security through being with someone who is financially successful. A couple may function best with lashings of passionate sex, or by spending large chunks of time apart from each other.

The permutations are virtually limitless, but the point is made. There is ultimately no recipe for a successful relationship between two people, only the experience, be it good, bad or indifferent. It is not the business of astrologers to allow personal feelings and prejudices to interfere with their judgement of the dynamics of a relationship or, to put it bluntly, to decide whether a particular relationship is 'worthwhile'. What chart comparison can do is to show how a couple will interact, where the strengths and weaknesses of the relationship lie, where pleasure may be found, as well as areas of potential of conflict.

Another misconception that is commonly held by those not familiar with astrology – and even by some professionals – is that people born near the beginning or the end of a sign – in other words, on the cusp – are somehow invested with the qualities of both signs. This is an area of some controversy, but we subscribe to the view that the first and last degrees of a sign actually appear to strengthen, rather than dilute, the qualities associated with it, as if a planet placed here is resisting the pull of the neighbouring sign.

About this book

The principle behind *The Instant Astrologer* is to provide an astrological program, designed to be both highly accurate and simple, with a basic interpretation book for beginners. As there is no benchmark for what constitutes a beginner's guide to astrology, this has involved making some tough and, it has to be said, arbitrary choices as to what to include and what to leave out. But we had to draw the line somewhere. Overall, we believe – and hope – that what is offered here is more than enough for anyone new to the subject to handle. In the book, we also decided to keep descriptions of the astronomical and mathematical variables behind the calculation side of astrology to a minimum. For anyone

interested in following up this side of astrology, there is a reading list at the end of the book.

Wherever possible, we have tried to present the material in a simple and manageable way. In trying to explain the inner psychological dynamics associated with the signs, houses, planets and aspects, it is impossible in a book of this scope to give anything more than a thumbnail sketch. Besides, nothing that is written in this book is cast in stone. It is not our intention to present the meaning's given over the following pages as fixed definitions; they are merely guidelines.

A planet's position in a chart does not predispose a person to express either its positive or its negative side. Astrology cannot deal in such black-and-white definitions because, in reality, most people will express a mixture of both the positive and negative traits that correspond to a particular planetary energy. So we have aimed to present what we believe to be some of the more common positive and negative manifestations of the planets, leaving you to explore the shades in between.

Practice is everything in astrology, and to help deepen your understanding of chart interpretation, we have included the birth data of a selection of celebrities – past and present. These are all people whose lives have been reasonably well documented, so by comparing their outer circumstances to factors in their charts, you should be able to get a sense of the inner person. A word of caution, though. The details provided in the software's celebrity file is generally regarded as 'A' class data – in other words, it has been confirmed by an authoritative source. However, we cannot personally confirm the accuracy of the time of birth. Since it is not unknown for celebrities to lie about their age, we can only assume the data is genuine.

♈ ♉ ♊ ♋ ♌ ♍ ♎ ♏ ♐ ♑ ♒ ♓

CHAPTER 2

Aries Taurus Gemini Cancer Leo Virgo Libra Scorpio Sagittarius Capricorn Aquarius Pisces

THE
SIGNS
OF THE
ZODIAC

Imagine the Earth at the centre of a vast celestial sphere, containing the Sun, the Moon and all the planets of our solar system. Although in reality it is the Earth that rotates around the Sun, the route that the Sun appears to follow on its journey across the heavens – as viewed from Earth – is a path called the Ecliptic. As the other planets in our solar system orbit the Sun on roughly the same plane as Earth, they, too, appear to take more or less the same route as the Sun – Pluto being the notable exception, with an orbit that deviates over 8^0 in latitude either side of the Ecliptic. Acting as a backdrop to this celestial highway is a narrow circular band known as the 'zodiac belt', which contains the twelve constellations – groups of so-called 'fixed' stars – that bear the names of the astrological signs.

Astrology divides the zodiac belt into twelve equal sections of 30^0, with each section corresponding to a sign of the zodiac. However, due to a tiny, but progressive, wobble in the Earth's axis, the zodiac belt 'slips' fractionally each year against the backdrop of the twelve constellations, with the result that the zodiac signs are now 'out of synch' with the zodiac constellations.

Astrology has compensated for this unfortunate slip up by devising two ways of gauging the planets' movements around the zodiac. One incorporates the Earth's wobble by measuring the planets' positions against the backdrop of the fixed constellations – the sidereal zodiac. The other ignores the 'wobble effect' altogether and simply measures the planets positions in relation to the point where the plane of the Celestial Equator – the Earth's equator projected into space – intersects the plane of the Ecliptic – the Sun's apparent path – on the first day of spring. This point always coincides with the Sun's entry into Aries, the first sign of the zodiac. The tropical zodiac, as this method of measuring the planets is known, is the one favoured by Western astrologers, and is used in the computer program that accompanies this book.

Although popular astrology has made even

sceptics aware of their Sun sign, in birth chart, or 'natal', astrology it is the position of all the planets in the signs they occupy at the time of birth that contributes towards our unique astrological signature. The role the signs play in chart interpretation is to act as a lens, or a channel, that subtly influences the manner in which any planet passing through them radiates its natural energy.

The Sign Groupings

With its obsession for order and symmetry, astrology, does not just look at each sign in isolation, but groups them according to certain characteristics. These groups act like a series of intersecting cogs and gears, making each sign integral to the functioning of the whole. Traditionally, astrologers have classified the twelve signs of the zodiac into three main categories: the Elements (Fire, Earth, Air and Water); the Qualities (Cardinal, Fixed and Mutable); and the Polarities (Positive and Negative). These groupings are still used by astrologers today, and understanding the way they interlink makes the core meanings of the signs easier to grasp.

The Elements

The first group – the Elements – divides the twelve signs into four groups of three signs each: the Fire signs (Aries, Leo and Sagittarius); the Earth signs (Taurus, Virgo and Capricorn); the Air signs (Gemini, Libra and Aquarius) and the Water signs (Cancer, Scorpio and Pisces). Signs allocated to the same Element are believed to share basic psychological characteristics.

As the Earth revolves round the Sun, it appears as if the Sun, the Moon and other planets move against the background of fixed stars known as the zodiac belt. In astrology, this imaginary belt is divided into twelve equal sections giving us the signs of the zodiac.

The Qualities

The second group – the Qualities – divides the signs into three groups of four signs each: the Cardinal signs (Aries, Cancer, Libra and Capricorn); the Fixed signs (Taurus, Leo, Scorpio and Aquarius) and the Mutable signs (Gemini, Virgo, Sagittarius and Pisces). Signs sharing the same Quality act and react to life in a similar way, although this is strongly coloured by the Element to which each sign belongs.

The Polarities

The third group – the Polarities – divides the signs into two groups of six signs: the Positive signs (Aries, Gemini, Leo, Libra, Sagittarius, Aquarius) and the Negative signs (Taurus, Cancer, Virgo, Scorpio, Capricorn and Pisces). Like a lot of symbolism in astrology, the Positive and Negative signs are also characterized as 'masculine' or 'feminine' energies, and are believed to correspond to the classic extrovert-introvert typology used in psychology.

THE ELEMENTS

FIRE

The Spark of Life

THE FIRE SIGNS: ♈ ARIES, ♌ LEO, ♐ SAGITTARIUS

Fire is concerned with raw energy. It symbolizes the inspirational world of pure spirit, free of hidden depths and dark subtleties. The Fire signs embody the idea of 'the spark of life', the will to live and the primal energy that ignites and sustains all existence.

The nature of Fire: Fire is optimistic. It believes in, and creates, its own luck. Consequently, Fire types tackle life in an uncomplicated fashion, confronting obstacles they meet head on, with an almost childlike innocence. Disarmingly direct and honest, even when serving their own interests, Fire types need space to express themselves freely and spontaneously. They are usually immensely assertive, and often pursue their goals with passion and conviction.

Fire signs are rarely short of confidence, and people with a generous spread of planets in this Element are renowned for their powers of self-motivation and for their ability to 'fire up' others with enthusiasm. Just in case this all sounds too good to be true, the down side is that Fire lacks consistency, a sense of caution and the patience to deal with detail.

Fire-dominant types: In a birth chart, an excess of planets in Fire signs often reveals itself as restless enthusiasm. In fact, these types are often so full of energy – always wanting something to happen – that they never know when to stop. On the other hand, they can also be domineering and arrogant, with a breathtaking ability to forget that others have needs as well. At their worst, these types can be over-confident, vain and ruthless – in short, unrestrained egomaniacs.

Fire-lacking types: For those with few or no planets in fire signs, pragmatism is likely to take preference over passion. They often suffer from low vitality, and a tendency to despondency, caving in easily in the face of adversity. And they can be something of a kill-joy, inclined to expect the worst. Although they can take a long time to recover from major setbacks, they are often able to draw on endless reserves of patience.

THE ELEMENTS

EARTH

The Container of Life

EARTH SIGNS: ♉ TAURUS, ♍ VIRGO, ♑ CAPRICORN

Earth is concerned with the realm of the senses – the physical world that surrounds us. It symbolizes the environment in which growth takes place. The Earth signs embody the concept of containment – plant a seed and Earth will protect and nurture it, bringing it to fruition.

The nature of Earth: Unlike Fire, Earth is a stabilizing influence. Its focus is on using available resources to achieve practical ends. People with a healthy smattering of planets in Earth signs have little difficulty in adapting to the limitations of physical reality. Often blessed with physical stamina and self-discipline, they will usually persevere when others give up. Earth types may not be fired with a strong sense of vision, but they compensate for this shortcoming with a fine instinct for what can and cannot be done. In short, Earth enables dreams to become a reality.

Earth signs have a highly developed sense of stewardship, and can be relied upon to take care of the affairs on which the other more flighty and fluid signs have difficulty concentrating. As might be expected, Earth also has a strong affinity with Nature, and people with planets in these signs may devote their energies to supporting or working for environmental issues.

Earth-dominant types: An over-emphasis of planets in Earth signs often indicates an instinct for maintaining the status quo against the instability of change. At best these types make stout defenders of traditional values. At worst they can be highly acquisitive, concerned only with indulging their fondness for money, food, sex, and all the pleasures of the flesh.

Earth-lacking types: Those with few or no planets in Earth signs in their chart often find it difficult to keep their feet on the ground, or to get to grips with the practical essentials of everyday life. They may also have problems settling down, or finding fulfilling work. Lacking the 'grounding' of Earth, they are also likely to suffer from destabilizing mood swings, and can have an unhealthy disregard for their daily bodily needs.

THE ELEMENTS

AIR

The Breath of Life

THE AIR SIGNS: ♊ GEMINI, ♎ LIBRA, ♒ AQUARIUS

Air is concerned with the realm of ideas, perception and the rational mind. It symbolizes the winds of change that bring fresh opportunities for growth. The Air signs embody the concept of dissemination – exchanging and spreading information.

The nature of Air: Air is the Element of creative thought. That does not mean that people with this Element strong in their charts are astrology's eggheads; they simply view the world from an objective perspective – detached from the swirling undercurrents of emotions and feelings. This gives them a 'switchboard' mentality for processing vast amounts of information, which they can then turn into abstract concepts or theories. At their best, their active, analytical minds can make sense of the relationship between 'things'.

Air types are usually sociable, for they need to exercise their minds through the constant exchange of ideas. While this makes them natural communicators, it is no guarantee that what they have to say has much substance. The lack of emotional depth that characterizes this Element means that many Air types feel more at ease when skimming along on life's surface.

Air-dominant types: People with an excess of planets in Air signs in their charts, are usually extremely restless. Their overactive minds make them hungry for new experiences, but they rarely settle long enough to form genuinely intimate relationships. With their heads firmly lodged in the clouds, keeping a grip on the day-to-day affairs of life might prove a challenge too far, unless they match their huge reserves of mental energy with self-discipline.

Air-lacking types: People with few or no planets in Air signs often struggle to articulate their thoughts or ideas. They may also lack the social graces that mark the Air signs as the masters of small talk, and they can find it difficult to get along with others easily or to adapt to new ideas. At worst, these types find it hard to distance themselves from, or anticipate the effects of, their actions.

THE ELEMENTS

WATER

The Flow of Life

THE WATER SIGNS: ♋ CANCER, ♏ SCORPIO, ♓ PISCES

Water is concerned with emotion and feeling. It symbolizes the ocean from which life is believed to have begun. The Water signs embody the concept of intuition – the process by which the world is perceived directly, by-passing rational or conscious thought.

The nature of Water: Of all the Elements, Water is the most profound, and the most difficult to define. It seeps into areas of life that are inaccessible to the other Elements, which is why it is associated with subconscious emotional forces. Those born under these signs are generally highly sensitive, and either wear their emotions on their sleeves or try to hide them from view. Their subtle attunement to their surroundings means that they often have a nebulous sense of self, leaving them unable to distinguish between their own and others' feelings.

On the positive side, Water types are protective, nurturing and compassionate, with a fine understanding of the emotional currents to which we are all prey. But raw exposure to emotionally charged atmospheres makes them defensive. As a result, the need for privacy, to shut out the excesses of the outside world, is usually very marked.

Water-dominant types: People with a surfeit of planets in Water signs often feel emotionally 'all at sea'. The harsh realities of human existence can at times overwhelm them, and they tend to over-dramatize their emotions. Unless they find an outlet for their extremely sensitive natures, they can become self-absorbed and fearful of what life holds in store. They may seek to escape from the rough-and-tumble of the outer world through a life of solitude, drink or drugs.

Water-lacking types: A lack of planets in Water indicates people who are cut off from their feelings, dismissing their value altogether. They are also likely to show little sympathy for others' emotional needs. To the outer eye they may appear self-contained, but this usually masks inner feelings of emptiness. Ironically, these types often look to emotionally 'rich' partners or friends to fill the void.

THE QUALITIES
The Cardinal Signs

♈ ARIES, ♋ CANCER, ♎ LIBRA, ♑ CAPRICORN

The Cardinal signs are reckoned to be the 'initiators' of the zodiac, a description which owes everything to the fact that the Sun enters a Cardinal sign on the first day of each season: spring (Aries), summer (Cancer), autumn (Libra) and winter (Capricorn). From the psychological standpoint, these signs are viewed as enterprising self-starters, with each one colouring a planetary impulse in a way that corresponds to the sign's particular Element. Aries, for instance, generates new momentum by force of will (Fire), while Cancer sets out to meet the world on an emotional level (Water) by building a secure environment – a role that it can skilfully play anywhere, not just in the home. Libra's impetus is directed towards creating harmonious relationships (Air) with a view to furthering its own ends, while Capricorn is motivated by the desire to build solid foundations for material gain or worldly achievement (Earth).

The Cardinal signs can also be described as pioneering. They are at their best searching out new, exciting areas of life that they can 'conquer'. People with an excess of planets in Cardinal signs may be highly self-motivated with huge reserves of 'get up and go', but they also tend to lack the persistence to see their vision through to completion. They also tend not to suffer fools gladly, and have little or no sympathy for those who do not function at the same pace as they do. As a result, they can easily become impatient, intolerant, and, occasionally, even ruthless.

The opposite is true of people with few or no planets in Cardinal signs. Lacking in any initiative of their own, they often have to rely on others to get projects off the ground.

The Fixed Signs

♉ TAURUS, ♌ LEO, ♏ SCORPIO, ♒ AQUARIUS

The Fixed signs are considered to be the 'safe hands' of the zodiac. While the Cardinal signs dash off into the unknown, starting new enterprises and then dropping them to pursue the next dream, the Fixed signs step in and transform the raw product into the finished article. Stability and endurance are their watchwords; they do not tend to falter or switch allegiances, nor do they make decisions lightly. Once committed, they usually stick to their chosen path through thick and thin.

Planets in Fixed signs consolidate the energy of the Cardinal signs according to their Elements. Taurus, for instance, will focus its considerable storehouse of energies on steadily securing material stability (Earth), whereas Leo is more inclined to concentrate on wielding the reins of power, or at least getting itself noticed (Fire). Scorpio looks to manipulate situations in order to maintain emotional stability (Water), and Aquarius will try to hold on to its ideas by bending others to its point of view (Air).

Persistence, strength of purpose and endurance under pressure are qualities much to be admired. But too many planets in Fixed signs in a chart often manifests as an inability to change when circumstances require it. When this happens, it is all too possible for the stubborn or, at worst, wilful behaviour, for which these signs are notorious to come to the fore.

When there is a shortage of planets in Fixed signs, there is a corresponding lack of determination. These types may be full of ideas, but they are essentially rudderless, lacking in application, and often cave in rather too easily.

The Mutable Signs

♊ GEMINI, ♍ VIRGO, ♐ SAGITTARIUS, ♓ PISCES

Also known as 'Common' signs – on account of their role as a bridge between the Fixed and Cardinal signs – the Mutable signs are the 'chameleons' of the zodiac, for whom adaptability is a byword. Where the Fixed signs resist change, the Mutable signs positively embrace it; where the Cardinal signs lose interest in their vision, the Mutable signs are capable of injecting fresh life into it. Resourceful, versatile and usually extremely flexible, these signs are viewed as genuine all-rounders.

As with the other Qualities, each Mutable sign is shaped by its own Element. Gemini reveals its mutability through constantly adapting its understanding of the world to accommodate new ideas (Air); Virgo is always fine-tuning its awareness of how the material world works to make itself more effective (Earth); Sagittarius seeks to slake its thirst for meaning through exploration of one kind or another (Fire); while Pisces seeks to adjust itself to the ever-changing emotional influences within and around it (Water).

Too much mutability, however, creates instability, and people with a surplus of Mutable signs in their charts tend to dissipate their energies through a scatter-gun approach to life. These types are essentially restless spirits who need a sense of direction in order to translate their many talents into concrete achievements. On the other hand, a lack of Mutable signs indicates people who find it hard to adapt to the inevitable changes that life throws at them. As a result, they can be narrow-minded, inflexible and unappreciative of the natural resources at their disposal.

THE POLARITIES

POSITIVE SIGNS: ARIES, GEMINI, LEO, LIBRA, SAGITTARIUS, AQUARIUS
NEGATIVE SIGNS: TAURUS, CANCER, VIRGO, SCORPIO, CAPRICORN, PISCES

The Polarities group alternate signs of the zodiac as Positive or Negative, which simply means that their energies operate like opposite 'charges', or 'poles', of a battery or magnet.

The Positive Signs
Air and Fire signs are Positive. A series of studies carried out by the eminent psychologist Professor Hans Eysenck, in conjunction with astrologer Geoff Mayo, found that the general characteristics of the Positive signs broadly matched those for the extrovert personality. Positive signs are naturally more impulsive, buoyant, communicative and sociable than the Negative signs, but rarely show the same levels of sensitivity or the same depth of understanding of emotional subtleties. Moreover, the Positive signs tend to crave excitement and are therefore inclined to direct their energies outwards into the world around them.

The Negative Signs
Earth and Water signs are Negative. The Eysenck-Mayo studies showed that the Negative signs lean towards introversion and prefer to draw on their own resources rather than to look for external stimuli. These signs are generally more receptive, sensitive and nurturing than their Positive brethren. However, they are also likely to be much more cautious, retiring and stand-offish, with a tendency to keep their feelings under tight control. By no means all signs show the same level of Positive or Negative qualities. The studies showed that Aries and Sagittarius were the most flagrantly extrovert signs, whereas Taurus and Virgo were the most introverted.

WHEELS WITHIN WHEELS

The basic traits of each sign arise largely from the fact that each is a unique blend of Element, Quality and Polarity *(see chart, right)*. For instance, Aries is the only Positive, Cardinal, Fire sign; Taurus the only Negative, Fixed, Earth sign, and so on.

In chart interpretation, astrologers look to see how the distribution of the planets in the signs affects the balance of the sign groupings. An excess or lack of planets in a particular Element, Quality or Polarity is seen as a significant indicator of the way we approach life at a fundamental level.

	FIRE	EARTH	AIR	WATER
CARDINAL	Aries	Capricorn	Libra	Cancer
FIXED	Leo	Taurus	Aquarius	Scorpio
MUTABLE	Sagittarius	Virgo	Gemini	Pisces
	POSITIVE	NEGATIVE	POSITIVE	NEGATIVE

♈ ♉ ♊ ♋ ♌ ♍ ♎ ♏ ♐ ♑ ♒ ♓

THE SIGN MEANINGS

THE SIGN GROUPINGS REVEAL SOME OF THE SIGNS' BASIC CHARACTERISTICS. THE FOLLOWING SECTION IN THIS CHAPTER DEALS WITH THE INDIVIDUAL MEANINGS OF EACH SIGN, SOME OF WHICH ARE SUMMARIZED AS KEYWORDS.

No one knows for certain how the signs of the zodiac came to acquire the individual characteristics that astrology attributes to them. These meanings have evolved over thousands of years, and will almost certainly continue to do so in the future, as successive generations of astrologers bring fresh insights to the subject. One recent practice, for instance, is to view the zodiac signs as a 'cycle of life', starting with Aries as the point of conception through to dissolution in Pisces. As the chart *(right)* shows, each sign symbolizes a different stage of progression or development from infancy through to maturity. This cycle helps to understand how the signs fit into the overall scheme of the zodiac.

On the following pages, we give a brief sketch of some of each sign's traits, an overview of how these modify some of the planets and a description of the sign's symbolism. Also included is an at-a-glance panel which shows each sign's basic attributes, as well as the colour, and parts of the body that are traditionally associated with it.

Each sign is also said to be 'ruled' by, or have an affinity with, a particular planet. While these rulerships are included in each panel, their significance is explained in the introduction to each planet in the next chapter.

Capricorn worldly wisdom and achievement

Aquarius collective consciousness

Sagittarius broadening horizons

Scorpio emotional/ sexual union

Pisces transcendence/ dissolution

Libra awakening social conscience

Aries conception/ beginnings

Virgo adjustment to external reality

Taurus physical development

Leo awakening ego

Gemini mental development

Cancer emotional development

ARIES

• **ASSERTIVE** • **WILFUL** • **INDEPENDENT** • **SELF-CENTRED** • **ENTHUSIASTIC**
• **IMPATIENT** • **HONEST** • **RECKLESS** • **COMBATIVE** • **ARGUMENTATIVE**
• **ENERGETIC** • **DECISIVE** • **DOMINEERING** • **PASSIONATE**

As the first sign of the zodiac, Aries is associated with the high-octane energy and enthusiasm of youth, casting it as the 'child' of the zodiac. Like any growing child, Aries wants to find its feet and, in its quest for independence, it will frequently lock horns with conventional attitudes, and resist pressure from those more experienced than itself to do things any other way than its own. Such headstrong passion can produce impressive results in the world at large, and often drives courageous Aries to the very top.

However, in Aries' strength lies its weakness. Its tendency to do everything at full throttle has given this sign a reputation for behaving like unguided missiles. It is certainly true that unless Aries has a clear plan of action, it can fall prey to some of its less appealing traits. In particular, its lack of patience, consideration or caution can drop it, and those around it, into very deep water.

On the positive side, perhaps Aries' most endearing feature is its directness. You know where you stand with the Ram, even though you might not always like what it has to say. But for all the competitive spirit attributed to this sign, it is arguably Aries' inability to dissemble that distinguishes it from the other signs of the zodiac.

Planets in Aries: In general, Aries quickens the pulse of planets that fall within its sphere of influence. In particular, the Sun and Mars – the archetypal 'male' planets – are said to prosper in this sign, gaining in vigour, sharpness of mind and strength of purpose. The notable exceptions are Saturn, who tends to dampen Aries' irrepressible spirit, and Venus, whose instinct for compromise can clash with this sign's impulse to do things its own way.

The Ram symbolizes Aries' instinctive and forceful approach to life, as well as its readiness to rush headlong into a challenge.

ARIES AT A GLANCE	
SYMBOL:	The Ram
CORE MEANING:	To initiate
RULER:	Mars
ELEMENT:	Fire
QUALITY:	Cardinal
POLARITY:	Positive
COLOUR:	Red
PARTS OF THE BODY:	Head, brain, eyes, adrenal glands,

TAURUS

• **STEADFAST** • **PATIENT** • **STABLE** • **METHODICAL** • **DELIBERATE** • **STUBBORN**
• **PRODUCTIVE** • **PASSIVE** • **RESTRAINED** • **AFFECTIONATE** • **POSSESSIVE**
• **SENSUOUS** • **SELF-INDULGENT** • **GENEROUS** • **GRASPING**

The phrase 'slow and steady wins the race' could have been coined to describe the Taurean approach to life. Quick and adaptable this sign may not be, but what it lacks in speed, it certainly makes up for in thoroughness, leaving few things to chance. Maddening though this cautious line is to other signs, Taurus will have it no other way.

The clue to this sign's intransigence lies deep within its psyche. As its symbol, the Bull, implies, Taurus is driven by powerful, lusty instincts which, once roused, are difficult to control. One way of containing these urges is to create a stable environment. When it feels secure, a contented Bull rewards those around it with love, tenderness and loyalty.

The trouble is that once this sign finds stability, it wants to keep it that way for ever. As a creature of habit, Taurus would rather stay in its cosy, self-contained routines than face the prospect of change. But change is inevitable, and wayward Bulls who fight it often end up clutching at straws. On a more positive note, Taurus' earthy nature often finds its expression in a delight of the physical pleasures of life. And, more than any other sign, Taurus can teach us about the wonders of the world of the senses.

Planets in Taurus: As might be expected planets in Taurus are slowed down by coming into contact with this sign, but in exchange they acquire patience, endurance and deliberation. The Moon, for instance, acquires an emotional steadiness and strength that it naturally lacks. Mars, on the other hand, finds its impulsive nature frustrated, although it gains in stamina. Venus, the ruler of Taurus, can either manifest as artistic talent or a desire for an easy life.

The Bull is a symbol of Taurus's strong instinctual nature, which can be expressed as bestial indulgence or fertile creative power, or both.

> **TAURUS AT A GLANCE**
>
> SYMBOL: The Bull
> CORE MEANING: To nourish
> RULER: Venus
> ELEMENT: Earth
> QUALITY: Fixed
> POLARITY: Negative
> COLOUR: Green
> PARTS OF THE BODY: Neck, throat, larynx,
> vocal cords, thyroid

♊

GEMINI

• **VERSATILE** • **CURIOUS** • **SHALLOW** • **STIMULATING** • **COMMUNICATIVE**
• **RESTLESS** • **SOCIABLE** • **QUICK-WITTED** • **FICKLE** • **DEXTEROUS** • **INGENIOUS**
• **DIFFUSIVE** • **INCONSISTENT** • **CHATTY** • **ARTFUL** • **FLIPPANT**

Bright, sociable and communicative one day, sullen and moody the next, Gemini, the Twins, is unquestionably the most mercurial sign of the zodiac. The fact is that, while we are all made up of many 'selves' somehow masquerading as one person, Gemini is the living embodiment of the split personality. This is not to say that all those whose planets are touched by this sign are rampant Jeckyll-and-Hydes, but there is no denying that Gemini seems positively to thrive in a see-saw existence of contrast and paradox.

Variety is another word for it but, no matter, the point is that this Air sign is a free spirit trapped in a physical world that makes heavy demands on it. Gemini's way of dealing with it is to stay on the move and keep talking. Adaptable, versatile and highly inquisitive, this sign can mesmerize anyone innocent enough to listen to it. The trouble is this ingenious, and at times slippery, sign never really knows when it has hit upon the answers to all its incessant questioning. But it probably does not matter. In need of an ever-changing environment, it will pick up the threads of another conundrum and follow them until the next challenge comes along.

GEMINI AT A GLANCE
SYMBOL: The Twins
CORE MEANING: To understand
RULER: Mercury
ELEMENT: Air
QUALITY: Mutable
POLARITY: Positive
COLOUR: Yellow
PARTS OF THE BODY: Shoulders, arms, hands, respiratory system, thymus

Planets in Gemini: Any planet located in Gemini will function at a much faster rate and, in most cases, on a light-hearted level. The Moon in this sign, for example, tends to rationalize the emotions – often on a superficial, even trivial, level. Like the Moon, Mercury in Gemini can deal in mindless gossip, but it can also adapt to new ideas at lightening speed. Jupiter, on the other hand, is less easy in this sign, as it emphasizes depth of knowledge as opposed to breadth – Gemini's favoured dimension.

👫 The Twins signify Gemini's dual nature, and its challenge to get to grips with the world of opposites – for example, between light and dark, belief and cynicism, intuition and reason.

CANCER

• **PROTECTIVE** • **TENACIOUS** • **IMAGINATIVE** • **SENSITIVE** • **NOSTALGIC** • **TOUGH** • **CLANNISH** • **TOUCHY** • **CLINGING** • **POSSESSIVE** • **SHREWD** • **CARING** • **MANIPULATIVE** • **INTUITIVE** • **DEVIOUS** • **FEARFUL** • **DEPENDENT**

Just like the crab, this sign's symbol, Cancer has a tough exterior that houses a soft underside. Such vulnerability to life – for that is how it instinctively perceives it – makes Cancer the most defensive sign in zodiac. And with good reason. Through Cancer, we enter the watery world of human emotions. Instinct, intuition, gut-feeling, call it what you will, this level of relating to the environment makes Cancer extremely sensitive to the moods and emotional undercurrents around it.

Cancer draws its strength from the close emotional ties it forms to its past, family, friends, possessions – even country. When it knows its place in the world, Cancer can be as self-assured and resourceful as any sign. But its particular gift to the rest of the zodiac is to nurture and protect those around them. When it feels emotionally adrift, however, Cancer will withdraw into itself and protect its own interests instead. In this mode, Cancer displays all the maturity of an insecure child. It may take this sign the best part of a lifetime to find the independence of spirit to drop its defences and use them only when they are needed. And when it does, it has an underwater world of rare beauty with which to bedazzle the rest of humanity.

> **CANCER AT A GLANCE**
>
> SYMBOL: The Crab
> CORE MEANING: To protect
> RULER: The Moon
> ELEMENT: Water
> QUALITY: Cardinal
> POLARITY: Negative
> COLOUR: Silver
> PARTS OF THE BODY: Breasts, chest, alimentary and digestive system, sternum

Planets in Cancer: Any planet that makes its home in Cancer will be sensitized by this sign. Astrology also associates Cancer with all aspects of mothering. As a result, most planets – Uranus and Pluto being the notable exceptions – acquire a protective edge in this sign. For women with the Sun or the Moon in Cancer, love, affection and compassion come naturally. For men, the Luminaries here often play havoc with their emotions – and their machismo – and can signify a lifelong search for Mother.

The Crab symbolizes Cancer's hard exterior, which it uses to protect its vulnerable emotions, while the claws denote its tenacity or possessiveness.

♌ LEO

• **SELF-ASSURED** • **SINCERE** • **GENEROUS** • **OPTIMISTIC** • **CONSTANT** • **DIGNIFIED** • **SPONTANEOUS** • **ARROGANT** • **INTOLERANT** • **SLOPPY** • **DEMONSTRATIVE** • **DOMINEERING** • **SELF-OBSESSED** • **POMPOUS** • **LAZY** • **AUTOCRATIC** •

Leo's association with the Lion – a universal symbol of power and authority – seems to have handed it the mantle of royalty on a plate. This sign's infuriating habit of lording it over others certainly lives up to the part, but it is worth remembering that the Lion's realm is the animal kingdom, and all the untamed instincts that implies. The truth is that Leo's link with kingship lies in its heroic and all-too-human conflict between noble intentions and raw passion.

In this epic struggle, in which Leo acts out for all of us the light and dark sides of human nature, Fate has equipped this sign with the necessary qualities to meet the challenge. Pride, dignity and courage – and a rich sense of drama – are all traits this sign possesses in abundance. And when the force is with it, Leo's self-belief, as it puts everything into achieving its heart's desire, can be nothing short of inspirational.

Like any player in the spotlight, Leo needs an audience. While those who admire its act will be generously rewarded with warm-hearted loyalty, negative feedback can shade Leo's sunny nature into arrogance, spite or overbearing behaviour. But, once it accepts that the recognition it craves is not a birthright, but has to be earned, Leo's chances of leaving something to posterity will be hugely enhanced.

Planets in Leo: Any planet in Leo glows with a radiance and steadiness, often with the focus firmly on the individual. On the other hand, planets in Leo often highlight brittle self-esteem and the search for personal identity. In contrast to Cancer's link with the mother, Leo symbolizes the father. For both sexes – and women in particular – the Sun and Moon in this sign can signify an often unconscious quest for Father's approval.

In the Lion, strength and dignity combine with powerful emotions, symbolizing Leo's need to master its instinctual passions.

LEO AT A GLANCE

SYMBOL: The Lion
CORE MEANING: To radiate
RULER: The Sun
ELEMENT: Fire
QUALITY: Fixed
POLARITY: Positive
COLOUR: Gold
PARTS OF THE BODY: Heart, upper back, spleen, spinal cord, aorta

---

VIRGO

• DISCERNING • EFFICIENT • OBSERVANT • CONSCIENTIOUS • MODEST • PRECISE • ANALYTICAL • DEPENDABLE • ORDERLY • CRITICAL • ANXIOUS • PEDANTIC • FUSSY • UNDEMONSTRATIVE • PURITANICAL • NARROW-MINDED

It says a great deal about traditional attitudes to feminine sexuality that Virgo, the Virgin – the only female symbol of the zodiac – should be scripted as astrology's prude. The fact is, the original meaning of 'virgin' had little to do with chastity, but signified a free woman who was beholden to no one. And herein lies Virgo's secret.

In seeking to come to terms with an uncertain world, Virgo has to weigh the accepted way of doing things, with all its imperfections, against its own inner promptings of what is right. In this search for correctness, Virgo can sometimes sacrifice inner content for technical proficiency. But it can also use its powers of discrimination, together with an immense capacity for digesting information, to make itself and the world more efficient and effective.

The trouble is that Virgo's obsession with 'getting it right' often leads it down blind alleys, where concern for detail obscures the overall picture. Such cul-de-sacs can cause Virgo to give up its quest for purity altogether, and slide into meek conformity. Or it can resort to self-righteous criticism, carping at others' faults, while shamelessly practising double standards. When Virgo learns to sort out the wheat from the chaff in its own life, however, its humility, honest self-appraisal and, above all, integrity, can be a lesson to us all.

Planets in Virgo: Virgo's need to dissect life into its components suits some planets more than others. Mercury, for example, enjoys detailed work, while Saturn stabilizes the Mutable quality of this sign and sharpens its critical side. The more impulsive, expansive energies of planets such as Mars, Jupiter and Uranus, however, tend to be frustrated by Virgo's caution – although Jupiter brings philosophical depth to this sign's search for knowledge.

The Virgin is an ancient symbol of fertility, which for Virgo indicates the need to use all available material resources to maximum effect.

VIRGO AT A GLANCE

SYMBOL: The Virgin

CORE MEANING: To discriminate

RULER: Mercury

ELEMENT: Earth

QUALITY: Mutable

POLARITY: Negative

COLOUR: Brown

PARTS OF THE BODY: Intestines, abdomen, lower dorsal nerves

♎

LIBRA

• CONGENIAL • DIPLOMATIC • CO-OPERATIVE • PERFECTIONIST • CHARMING
• ROMANTIC • FAIR-MINDED • SOCIABLE • AESTHETIC • INSINCERE
• INDECISIVE • DISHONEST • FRIVOLOUS • INDOLENT • VAIN

Libra's symbol – the Scales – identifies it as the sign of justice. While it's certainly true that this sign's strong sense of fair play can be seen in its ability to consider all sides of a case, and to keep warring factions from shredding each other, the reality is that life does not always work along such idealistic lines – as Libra well knows.

Somewhere deep in the Libran psyche there is a titanic struggle between the desire to please itself and the need for approval, with the result that this Cardinal sign may spend considerable time sitting on the fence devising clever strategies on how to take the initiative by appearing to cave in. Nowhere is this more apparent than in the arena of relationships – reputedly Libra's strong suit – where this sign's penchant for going its own way is often at war with its desire to keep the peace.

Such contradictions can paralyse Libra, and force it to be economical with the truth – especially of the emotional kind – or to blame others for its own failings. This apparent lack of honesty has saddled Libra with a reputation for being the zodiac's most insincere charmers. But in its defence, Libra can argue that, in seeking to balance irreconcilable opposites, it is only trying to keep everyone happy.

Planets in Libra: Most planets in Libra emphasize the social aspect of this sign – the desire to get along with others. Warlike Mars, however, is a notable exception, as it can veer between inaction and bouts of open hostility. Libra also imparts a love of style, beauty and sophistication to planets located here – except for Saturn, for whom Libra's concern with appearances is seen as frivolous. The Luminaries and Venus have no such reservations and gaily display this sign's lighter, flirtatious side.

♎ The Scales symbolises Libra's challenge to find a balance between the 'self' and 'not-self' – between personal desires and the needs of others.

LIBRA AT A GLANCE

SYMBOL: The Scales

CORE MEANING: To balance

RULER: Venus

ELEMENT: Air

QUALITY: Cardinal

POLARITY: Positive

COLOUR: All pastels

PARTS OF THE BODY: Lumbar region, buttocks, kidneys, endocrine system

---

SCORPIO

• **PROFOUND** • **PENETRATING** • **IMAGINATIVE** • **SUBTLE** • **FEARLESS** • **DEEP** • **LOYAL** • **HEALING** • **SELF-DESTRUCTIVE** • **JEALOUS** • **SUSPICIOUS** • **VINDICTIVE** • **RESENTFUL** • **CONTROLLING** • **SECRETIVE**

Driven by an intensity of purpose, Scorpio approaches life with total commitment, or not at all. As far as this deep, secretive and utterly impenetrable sign is concerned, the impulse to immerse itself in all it does – particularly in close relationships – stems from an unshakeable need to feel a strong bond of emotional involvement in anything or anyone it values. But a deeply buried fear of becoming a hostage to fortune or other people's ambitions, drives Scorpio to control its immediate environment – and the people in it – with an icy grip.

This confusing and thoroughly manipulative dance of passionate advancing followed by frozen withdrawal can develop into an obsession with sex and power. But once Scorpio is stirred by the deep emotional surges that push it along a certain course of action, nothing can stop it, not even the relative rights or wrongs of what it is doing. Only after a series of challenging and, at times, painful life experiences, which wash away the past and force it to look deep inside itself, does Scorpio find the answer to its inner needs. And with this transformation can come a profound understanding of the underlying value of life and its peak experiences.

Planets in Scorpio: Any planet in Scorpio acquires this sign's emotional intensity and fearlessness, but, unless other factors in the chart indicate otherwise, the strength of these qualities will often only emerge in private, or when stung into action. Mars strengthens resolve and intensifies sexual jealousy although, like Venus and Pluto, it will mercilessly exploit other people's weaknesses while giving little of itself away. Scorpio gives Mercury a laser-like mind that can get to the heart of a problem.

The Scorpion represents this sign's need to transform its dark, brooding power through symbolic death and rebirth.

SCORPIO AT A GLANCE

SYMBOL: The Scorpion
CORE MEANING: To transform
RULER: Pluto; co-ruled by Mars
ELEMENT: Water
QUALITY: Fixed
POLARITY: Negative
COLOUR: Maroon
PARTS OF THE BODY: Sex organs, anus, genito-urinary system, prostate gland

---

SAGITTARIUS

• **ADVENTUROUS** • **PHILOSOPHICAL** • **EXPANSIVE** • **UTOPIAN** • **ASPIRATIONAL**
• **WISE** • **GENEROUS** • **OUTSPOKEN** • **TACTLESS** • **BOASTFUL** • **MORALISTIC**
• **INCONSIDERATE** • **UNDISCIPLINED** • **UNREALISTIC** • **UNRELIABLE**

As this sign's symbol, the half-human, half-horse Centaur suggests, Sagittarius has a distinctly dual nature. One half represents reason – the higher mind probing the universe, searching for meaning – while the other symbolizes instinctual passion. This latter side of Sagittarius simply wants to 'horse around', occasionally in a thoroughly dissolute and licentious manner. The big dilemma for this spirited, changeable sign, therefore, is whether it's ruled by the head of a man or the rear end of a horse.

The wild nature of Sagittarius comes across in its love of freedom and refusal to conform to social conventions. This side of Sagittarius would much rather gamble with the laws of chance than apply itself to the serious business of life. Fun though this can be, it begins to pall when Sagittarius indulges its fondness for sermonizing to all around it on how to run their lives. No matter how true its aim, this 'do as I say, not as I do' aspect of Sagittarius marks it as

the zodiac's biggest hypocrite. Fortunately, however, the other side of this sign is much more principled and disciplined. And when Sagittarius focuses on its ability to explore horizons beyond our immediate environment, its gift to the rest of the world is to make us aware of the deeper social, moral and spiritual issues that underpin life.

Planets in Sagittarius: This sign needs constant mental and physical stimulation, which gives a restless edge to planets here, notably the Luminaries, Mercury, Mars and Uranus. Saturn, on the other hand, often checks this urge. Planets such as Venus, Jupiter and Neptune tend to stimulate Sagittarius' idealistic side, although Venus in this sign also has a reputation for avoiding emotionally binding relationships.

The Centaur with its bow and arrow symbolizes Sagittarius' challenge to raise our understanding of the half-man, half-beast nature of humanity.

SAGITTARIUS AT A GLANCE

SYMBOL: The Centaur
CORE MEANING: To give meaning
RULER: Jupiter
ELEMENT: Fire
QUALITY: Mutable
POLARITY: Positive
COLOUR: Purple, deep blue
PARTS OF THE BODY: Hips, thighs, pelvis, sacrum, hepatic system

---

♑

CAPRICORN

• **PATIENT** • **PERSEVERING** • **ENTERPRISING** • **INDUSTRIOUS** • **CONSTRUCTIVE**
• **AMBITIOUS** • **ORGANIZED** • **FAITHFUL** • **CONVENTIONAL** • **CALCULATING**
• **DICTATORIAL** • **PESSIMISTIC** • **MISERLY** • **COLD**

Capricorn learns from an early age that we live in an inherently unstable world. For this self-contained sign – whose symbol, the Mountain Goat, is said to represent this sign's lofty ambitions – life favours those who develop the discipline and determination to succeed. Much of this Earth sign's attitude to the world around it is shaped by practical necessity. While this may seem an unduly materialistic view of the world, to Capricorn the principle is as obvious as it is universal: only the best placed get to make a name for themselves.

In pursuit of its goals, Capricorn will stick with the established way of doing things, taking the long-term view that success comes through forward planning, good organization, hard work and, of course, the right contacts. Not surprisingly, Capricorn's habit of valuing people according to their position, or money, has earned it a name for being a hard-nosed social climber. At some stage in life, however, this sign may start to question where all its cautious

CAPRICORN AT A GLANCE

SYMBOL: The Mountain Goat
CORE MEANING: To achieve
RULER: Saturn
ELEMENT: Earth
QUALITY: Cardinal
POLARITY: Negative
COLOUR: Dark grey, black
PARTS OF THE BODY: Skeletal system, knees, skin

climbing is leading. This is, after all, a Cardinal sign, and therefore a force for social change – albeit within the limits of tradition. But if Capricorn loses sight of the bigger picture, and its ability to enjoy life, by simply serving its own ends, it will find life on the mountain top a solitary experience.

Planets in Capricorn: All planets in Capricorn tend to emphasize this sign's reserved nature and the need for control. As a result, 'people-oriented' planets, such as the Moon and Venus, suffer from the Capricorn chill factor, whereas 'action-oriented' planets, like the Sun and Mars, are less inhibited. For all its sober reputation, Capricorn can 'act the goat' as well as any sign, especially if Mercury or Jupiter are placed in this sign.

🐐 Often depicted as a Sea-Goat, this pictograph symbolizes Capricorn's need to remember its link with the ocean – the source of wisdom and all life.

AQUARIUS

• SOCIABLE • COMMUNICATIVE • ALTRUISTIC • PROGRESSIVE
• INDEPENDENT • RATIONAL • DETACHED • ECCENTRIC • DOGMATIC
• IMPRACTICAL • WILFUL • ERRATIC • CRANKY • UNPRINCIPLED

It may seem unfair on Aquarius to be cast as the zodiac's flagbearer for social progress, especially as its actions often fail to live up to the radicalism this sign supposedly embraces. All the same, there is an undeniable altruistic streak coursing through its veins which can be seen in its readiness to listen and offer advice or assistance to anyone in need. But however far-sighted its solutions may be, Aquarius shows a profound reluctance to deal with the darker human instincts, such as greed or envy. Consequently, its lack of real understanding of the deep emotional urges to which we are all prey makes it somewhat aloof in its one-to-one dealings.

On the surface, Aquarius' rational, detached approach to life can appear to work well. Following the principle of 'who has pays', Aquarius will usually give when it can without expecting others to do the same in return. However, for all the social conscience astrology attributes to this sign, Aquarius is no less immune than the rest of us from putting its own interests first – often perversely expecting others to adapt to its way of thinking. But when Aquarius learns to reconcile its own individualistic views with the needs and expectations of society – or any group for that matter – it can become the true source of enlightenment it is meant to be.

Planets in Aquarius: Planets coloured by Aquarius often reflect the contradictory nature of this sign's Fixed-Air nature. Mercury and Jupiter in Aquarius, for instance, can be both sociable and intolerant, while Mars can be resolutely 'fixed' one moment and wildly unorthodox the next. Conversely, because Aquarius inclines towards friendship rather than close emotional ties, the 'feeling' planets, such as the Moon and Venus, are 'rationalized' by this sign.

The Water Bearer symbolizes the knowledge that is available for the benefit of all when this sign tunes into the intuitive side of its mind.

AQUARIUS AT A GLANCE

SYMBOL: The Water Bearer
CORE MEANING: To illuminate
RULER: Uranus; co-ruled by Saturn
ELEMENT: Air
QUALITY: Fixed
POLARITY: Positive
COLOUR: Electric blue
PARTS OF THE BODY: Lower legs, ankles, circulatory system

PISCES

• **SENSITIVE** • **RECEPTIVE** • **COMPASSIONATE** • **IMAGINATIVE** •
• **SELF-SACRIFICING** • **IMPRESSIONABLE** • **PASSIVE** • **SLIPPERY** •
• **ESCAPIST** • **ACQUIESCENT** • **CONFUSED** • **OVER-EMOTIONAL** •

Time and again astrology writes off Pisces as a head-in-the-clouds dreamer, hopelessly ill equipped for the harsh realities of life. True, this Mutable-Water sign lives in a fluid environment, in which the boundaries that separate external reality from inner fantasy – 'what's mine' from 'what's yours' – are constantly shifting. From this perspective, it is easy to see why Pisces can become so confused and vulnerable, and why this most sensitive, compassionate – and manipulative – of signs so often ends up fleeing outer reality or becoming a passive victim of circumstance.

However, this free-flowing nature can also work in Pisces' favour. When it allows its powerfully receptive mind to 'go with the flow', it seems privy to creative possibilities far beyond the reach of other signs. And Pisces' famed ability to see the 'unity in all things', and to blend, chameleon-like, with its surroundings, makes this the sign of the consummate artist and performer. As always with Pisces, there is a fine line between going for the impossible and knowing when to stop. The challenge for impressionable Pisces is to be clear about its motives, and not to allow its infinite capacity for self-deception – or to be swayed by others – to confuse real with imaginary feelings and needs.

Planets in Pisces: Although planets in this sign become highly sensitized, the ability to discriminate is weakened. For example, Venus here can be selflessly loving, but often lets itself down by falling hopelessly in love with unsuitable people. Mercury in Pisces heightens the imagination, but can also be exceedingly gullible. Because of this sign's highly emotional and sensitive nature, men who have the Sun or Mars in Pisces may try to camouflage inner feelings of vulnerability by being aggressively 'male'.

The Fishes swimming in opposite directions signify Pisces' need to balance the conflicting demands of its inner world with material reality.

> **PISCES AT A GLANCE**
>
> SYMBOL: The Fishes
> CORE MEANING: To transcend
> RULER: Neptune; co-ruled by Jupiter
> ELEMENT: Water
> QUALITY: Mutable
> POLARITY: Negative
> COLOUR: Aquamarine
> PARTS OF THE BODY: Feet, toes, lymphatic system, pituitary gland

| Sun | Moon | Mercury | Venus | Mars | Jupiter | Saturn | Uranus | Neptune | Pluto |

THE
PLANETS

Excluding Earth, the planets of our solar system, together with the 'Luminaries' – the Sun and the Moon – form the building blocks of astrology. The ancients viewed the planets as living 'gods', whose every action reverberated through the lives of their mortal subjects. Although we now have a very different view of the cosmos, the myths have survived – handed down from generation to generation. Even today, their symbolism speaks clearly to us: red Mars, the indomitable god of war (aggression); Venus the beautiful goddess of love (harmony); Jupiter, the thundering king of the gods (expansion); Saturn the grim reaper, patrolling the perimeter of the ancient universe (restriction).

The Planets as Archetypal Energies

Modern astrology has adapted these myths to the concept of archetypes. The planets-as-gods are associated with psychological energies or impulses that we all express in one way or another. Many of these impulses are rooted in our unconscious, and can be traced back to mankind's beginnings. Depending on their birth chart dynamics – and each chart is a unique mosaic of human potential – these planetary energies may be weak, strong, or indifferent; they may flow freely, be frustrated or dominate the whole chart; alternatively, their effects may be harmonious or discordant.

Traditional astrology did not concern itself with psychology. It dealt with purely practical matters – the affairs of everyday life. In this context the planets were interpreted in a much more simplistic fashion than they are today. They were basically either 'benefic' (favourable) or 'malefic' (evil), and there were few, if any, grey areas. With the psychological approach to astrology, this black-or-white view of life has largely disappeared. In psychological astrology, the planets are believed to 'influence' us on both the inner, or motivational, level and the outer, behavioural, level.

Clearly, these two strands are closely intertwined, but they can also be treated, and understood, quite separately. For instance, a strong Saturnian influence may inwardly signify a strong predisposition to feel easily rejected or intimidated. Externally, however, it may well register as a steely determination to achieve worldly success.

Before looking at how the planets are modified by each sign and house, it is worth explaining a number of principles that underpin the planets' meanings:

• **As above, so below:** One of the traditional philosophical beliefs that is still common astrological currency today is the 'law of correspondences'. According to this principle, everything in the cosmos is interconnected so that what happens above in the heavens is reflected here below on Earth. Applying this principle to the planets, astrology maintains that the energies symbolized by a planet do not just correspond to our psychological make-up; they manifest in all forms and spheres of life. In other words, we are just as likely to encounter these planetary energies in the world at large – through the people that we meet or the experiences that we attract – as we are to express them ourselves.

• **Personal, social and generational planets:** At a fundamental level, each planet's 'sphere of influence' is determined by the time it takes to complete a cycle of the zodiac. The faster moving bodies – the Sun, Moon, Mercury, Venus and Mars – spend relatively little time in each sign, and are therefore referred to as the inner or 'personal' planets, since they are thought to correspond to psychological drives or impulses that are specific to the individual. As Jupiter and Saturn have much slower orbits – roughly twelve and twenty-nine years respectively – their impact is reckoned to be more

'social', in the sense that they reflect background influences that shape our expectations of life. The so-called 'outer' planets – Uranus, Neptune and Pluto – move so slowly through each sign that they are seen as indicators of impersonal or generational trends. The exception to this rule is when any of these planets is prominent in a chart, in which case their energies can be projected in a personal way.

• **Planetary symbolism:** Each planet is represented by a symbol – known as a glyph – which encapsulates the planet's essence. Each glyph is made up of a combination of three basic shapes: the circle, the crescent and the cross. The circle is the symbol for pure spirit and represents eternity, the realm of infinite possibilities. The circle also corresponds to the Sun, the vital force that pervades all creation. The crescent is the symbol for pure soul and contains the blueprint that gives form to all life. This shape corresponds to the Moon and the cyclical nature of life, death and rebirth. The cross symbolizes the four elements of the material world, and corresponds to the physical body and its sensations – in fact, all matter.

• **Planetary strengths and weaknesses:** Planets are commonly described as being 'strong', 'well placed', 'dominant', 'weak' or 'afflicted'. What causes these conditions to vary is discussed in other chapters, so we need only to consider the general conventions governing planetary strengths and weaknesses. A planet is considered to be strong when it occupies a

♃   ♄   ♅   ♆   ♇

'sympathetic' sign, or when it 'rules' the Ascendant, Sun or Moon sign (*see box below*); it is strongly placed when it is close to the Ascendant or MC, or in its natural or 'essential' house; it is weak when it forms few or no aspects, or falls in an 'unsympathetic' sign; it is dominant when it is strongly placed in the chart, but has to battle with a series of challenging aspects; finally, it is afflicted when it is both weak and its expression is hindered by similarly challenging aspects.

PLANETARY STRENGTHS AND WEAKNESSES

According to an ancient system, each planet has a special affinity with two or three signs of the zodiac. Planets are regarded as 'strong' in the signs that most enable their energies to flow freely. They are said to 'rule' or 'govern' these signs and consequently to be in their 'dignity'. The sign in which a planet is believed to be capable of expressing its highest potential is said to be its 'exaltation'.

At the other end of the spectrum, there are signs in which each planet's potential is thought to be distinctly obstructed. A planet in the sign opposite to the one that it rules is considered to be at its weakest or in its 'detriment', whereas a planet in the sign opposite to its exaltation – known as its 'fall' – can experience considerable frustration.

Before the arrival of the outer planets – Uranus, Neptune and Pluto – upset the symmetry of the old order, the Sun and the Moon were given rulership of Leo and Cancer respectively, while the remaining five planets each governed a pair of signs. Since their discovery, the outer planets have gradually been incorporated into the system of rulerships, although there is still considerable disagreement over their signs of exaltation and fall. In fact, some astrologers still stick with the traditional seven-planet system of rulerships, while others only work with the revised order. A common practice – and one that we recommend to beginners – is to use both systems, which means that Scorpio, Aquarius and Pisces have two rulers each. (The exaltations and falls in brackets in the chart below are only provisional.)

Planet	Dignity	Detriment	Exaltation	Fall
Sun	Leo	Aquarius	Aries	Libra
Moon	Cancer	Capricorn	Taurus	Scorpio
Mercury	Gemini Virgo	Sagittarius Pisces	(Virgo)	(Pisces)
Venus	Taurus Libra	Scorpio Aries	Pisces	Virgo
Mars	Aries Scorpio	Libra Taurus	Capricorn	Cancer
Jupiter	Sagittarius Pisces	Gemini Virgo	Cancer	Capricorn
Saturn	Capricorn Aquarius	Cancer Leo	Libra	Aries
Uranus	Aquarius	Leo	Scorpio	(Taurus)
Neptune	Pisces	Virgo	(Cancer)	(Capricorn)
Pluto	Scorpio	Taurus	(Pisces)	(Virgo)

THE SUN
The Essential Self

• VITALITY • WILL • IDENTITY • CENTREDNESS • RECOGNITION • PRIDE •
• ILLUMINATION • ENLIGHTENMENT • CREATIVITY • PURPOSE •
• DIRECTION • MEANING • FUTURE • AUTHORITY •

In the Ancient World, the Sun was seen as a ceaseless wanderer, rising each day to dominate the heavens, before descending into the deep of the night. There he would repeatedly fight the demons of the underworld in a cosmic battle between light and dark, good and evil. It is small wonder that solar eclipses held such terror for our ancestors.

In the birth chart, the Sun also symbolizes an endless journey – the voyage of self-discovery; only, here, the struggle is an internal one in which the Sun, representing the awakening consciousness of the individual, wrestles with the darkness of the unconscious elements of the psyche. In essence, this tussle is born out of the Sun's essential nature, for wherever it shines it casts a shadow, which in psychological terms signifies the unintegrated or unacknowledged part of ourselves.

Indeed, Jungian psychology describes this struggle as the process of individuation – the urge to integrate all the disparate parts of the self into a 'centred whole'. Another way of looking at it might be to say that the Sun represents our capacity for enlightenment. It is essentially a symbol of destiny, and represents a lifetime's quest to discover our true potential and the indestructible 'I' that lies at the core of our being. For this reason, it is inextricably linked with our search for a sense of identity and purpose, for we must become one with our individuality and our heart's desire if we are to realize our solar potential.

As the heart of the psyche, the Sun represents vitality and the will to live. Its function is to fill our lives with meaning and a sense of direction. It is the active, motivating influence behind our conscious aims, the life-force which drives us to express the creative impulse that lies within us all. As the ruler of the heart, the Sun also shows a great deal about our natural approach to love. While Venus symbolizes our need for harmony and relationship, it is the Sun that expresses love in its purest form, unqualified and undemanding. This is the self-love that enables us to love others for what they are, as opposed to the love of self, which has little regard for others, and is a distortion of the solar function.

A well-placed Sun in a chart reveals itself through exuberance, dignity and strength of character, according to the qualities of the sign in which it is placed. The urge to achieve is often accompanied by tremendous will power and a natural sense of authority. However, where a strong Sun radiates light and warmth, a dominant Sun tends to blind and scorch, and can be ruthless, arrogant, and extremely self-centred, promising much but delivering little. A weak or ill-placed Sun, by contrast, often registers as low vitality and a lack of will and self-confidence.

Because of its association with the active, creative force of life, the Sun is seen as an essentially masculine energy. It is also a symbol of the paternal archetype, both in terms of how we experience 'father', or the dominant male influence in early life, and how this affects the way we access the masculine energy within us later on. The traditional view is that men express their solar energy more readily than women, simply because they are more set on finding their individual identity, whereas women are more inclined to pour their energies into nurturing those around them. In a woman's chart, therefore, the Sun is said to indicate the kind of qualities she looks for in a man in order to become whole. Nowadays, of course, an increasing number of women feel empowered to explore their solar energy in their own right.

In the world at large, the Sun rules fatherhood; enlightenment; the monarchy, rulers and leaders; creative individuals; all forms of energy that continually transmute into ever higher forms.

Symbolism

The astrological glyph for the Sun is a circle, the symbol of eternity, with a dot in the centre, representing the divine spark that is within each individual. It is through the power of the Sun that we have the potential to find inner illumination and to define ourselves in relation to the universe.

THE SUN IN PERSPECTIVE

The Sun is is considered to be strong or weak in:

- **Leo** (Dignity): The Sun rules fiery Leo, the sign of creative power and leadership, where its energy is believed to shine at its most radiant and steady. Both sign and planet are associated with vitality and authority, and in this respect compliment each other perfectly.
- **Aquarius** (Detriment): In Aquarius, unlike Leo, the emotions are cool and the emphasis is on raising individual consciousness in relation to the needs of society or the group as opposed to expressing individuality for its own sake.
- **Aries** (Exaltation): because of its affinity with Fire, the Sun is exalted in the sign of the Ram, where the need to meet life's challenges through the assertion of will is paramount.
- **Libra** (Fall): This sign's connection with relationship – to find oneself through others – is at odds with the solar impulse, which is to discover one's unique potential.

THE SUN THROUGH THE SIGNS

• THE ESSENTIAL 'I' • YOUR SENSE OF IDENTITY • YOUR WILL AND PURPOSE IN LIFE • YOUR LEVEL OF VITALITY AND SELF-CONFIDENCE • CONSCIOUS SELF-EXPRESSION • YOUR BLIND SPOT

ARIES Energetic and direct, with a strong sense of individuality; enjoys a challenge and initiating action; hates giving up; needs to learn patience and moderation.

TAURUS Patient and determined, with lusty physical appetites; values stability and possessions; dislikes upheaval and being rushed; needs to learn to be more adaptable.

GEMINI Alert and communicative, with a 'switchboard' capacity for learning; thrives on variety and novelty; resents mental drudgery; needs to learn the value of commitment.

CANCER Emotional and intuitive, with a strong sense of personal attachment; loves familiarity; dislikes confrontation and emotional quagmires; needs to learn to be less touchy.

LEO Warm and generous, with a flair for dramatisation; flourishes when centre stage; dislikes authority and being ignored; needs to learn to soften pride and accept criticism.

VIRGO Conscientious and methodical, with a fine eye for detail; loves to be of service and to create order; hates not 'being in the know'; needs to learn self-worth and to trust feelings.

LIBRA Gregarious and considerate, with a strong social sense; yearns to please and to be pleased; recoils from injustice and disharmony; needs to learn to handle conflict firmly.

SCORPIO Strong-willed and self-contained, with a talent for probing; prizes loyalty and total involvement; deplores indifference and superficiality; needs to learn to be more open.

SAGITTARIUS Optimistic and sincere, with an insatiable thirst for 'exploration'; cherishes freedom and aiming high; hates detail and hypocrisy; needs to learn discipline.

CAPRICORN Resourceful and persevering, with a strong sense of duty; believes fervently in tradition and order; distrusts the untried and untested; needs to learn compassion.

AQUARIUS Companionable and quirky, with a humanitarian streak; loves originality and independence; shuns practicalities; needs to learn to accept 'dark side' of emotions.

PISCES Sympathetic and impressionable with a powerful imagination; values giving, escaping and mystery; resents drab reality and suffering; needs to learn to be less self-pitying.

THE SUN THROUGH THE HOUSES

• SHOWS IN WHAT AREA OF LIFE YOU SEEK TO ESTABLISH YOUR IDENTITY
• WHERE YOU CAN SHINE • YOUR CREATIVE NATURE • WHERE YOU LOOK FOR
RECOGNITION • WHAT YOU 'PUT YOUR HEART INTO'

I FIRST A strong need to make one's mark; a talent for self-promotion; completely absorbed in own interests; seeks to gain recognition for creative abilities; inflated opinion of oneself.

II SECOND Self-identity enhanced through material security; enjoyment of physical pleasures; may attach great importance to possessions or looks; can be overly acquisitive.

III THIRD Seeks credit for knowledge and mental abilities; possible excess mental energy; may gain recognition through communication skills; can be intellectually arrogant.

IV FOURTH Derives a strong sense of identity through the home; needs a secure environment to pursue goals; may struggle to break free from early conditioning; can be easily slighted.

V FIFTH Takes great pride in abilities and achievements; a powerful urge to enjoy and give pleasure; may gain recognition through creative talents; can be recklessly self-confident.

VI SIXTH Seeks to grow through meaningful work; needs to be appreciated for usefulness; may gain recognition through hard work and service to others; can be obsessed with health.

VII SEVENTH Seeks a sense of self through partnerships; needs to balance personal goals with others' demands; tends to give power away to partners; can make powerful enemies.

VIII EIGHTH Needs to find identity through emotional security; seeks self-transformation through intimate relationships or life-or-death situations; drawn to illuminate society's taboos.

IX NINTH Sets out to develop potential through experiences that broaden the mind; may look for self-definition through moral or spiritual values; can be a restless spirit.

X TENTH Seeks fulfilment through taking on responsibility; driven by the need to be seen as important; may place career or social position above all else; career shaped by parent(s).

XI ELEVENTH Links personal identity to group activities; idealism may find an outlet through political or humanitarian issues; a natural socialite or networker.

XII TWELFTH Seeks recognition through service to a higher ideal; likely to need periods of solitude; may sacrifice personal identity to collective needs; inner feelings of inferiority.

THE MOON
The Instinctual Self

• **RECEPTIVITY** • **INSTINCT** • **HABITS** • **MOODS** • **NURTURE** • **MOTHERING** •
SANCTUARY • **HOME** • **ROOTS** • **THE PAST** • **MEMORY** • **PROTECTIVENESS** •
DEFENSIVENESS • **IMAGINATION** • **NOURISHMENT** • **DIET**

To the ancients, the Moon's phases – crescent, full and new – symbolized the never-ending cycle of birth, death and rebirth. So perhaps it is not surprising that the Moon in astrology is associated with the ebb and flow of everyday life – which in psychological terms corresponds to the watery and changeable realm of human emotions.

In many ways, the astrological Moon is the polar opposite of the Sun. Where the Sun concerns itself with the archetypal male principle in both men and women through 'action' – the will directed towards conscious goals – the Moon governs the female principle of 'reaction' – our unconscious attunement to our surroundings. In other words, the Moon holds dominion over the passive, or receptive, side of the personality – our 'gut' instincts and feelings. But, as with all opposites, astrologers see the Moon as the Sun's inseparable companion. Just as by night, the Sun makes his presence felt by lending his light to the Moon, while by day the Moon exerts her invisible influence through her gravitational pull on

Earth, the interplay between lunar and solar energies in the birth chart is believed to cast light on the way we develop from infancy into a fully fledged adult.

In fact, astrology holds that our sapling years, when we are bound to Mother's apron strings, are ruled by the Moon. For this reason, the Moon is linked to the process of nurturing – beginning in the womb – which plays such a profound role in shaping our emotional security. Indeed, the Moon's position in the birth chart says much about our experience of childhood – especially, the way we experienced Mother (whoever she, or even he, might have been) and our early home environment. Later in life, the Moon's association with nurture is reflected in the way we take care of our physical needs, in particular our eating habits. For the Moon not only shows how our early conditioning affects the way we nurture ourselves, it shows how we absorb what life throws at us. In a woman's chart, it is also said to reveal what kind of mother she might in turn become herself.

In adulthood, the Moon continues to hold sway over our emotional life in a number of ways. On one level, it reveals our attitudes to our past, not just childhood, but our family and ancestral roots, even our native country. From this, it can also show what impact our early years have on our adult relationships. A positively expressed Moon often indicates someone who is emotionally 'grounded', responsive to others' needs and who adapts well to new surroundings.

Those with difficult Moon placements, however, may find it hard to grow up emotionally, being held back by behavioural patterns that rightfully belong to childhood. Alternatively, they may be plagued by a sense of not belonging anywhere, which makes it difficult for them to settle or commit themselves to relationships. It's not surprising, therefore, that many astrologers see the Moon as the archetypal 'inner child' that we all carry within us, irrespective of age.

The way in which the Moon manifests herself in the outer world is as varied as she is changeable. The enormous gravitational power of the Moon often finds its counterpart expression in the birth chart. A strongly placed Moon astride the Ascendant, for instance, is believed to denote tremendous personal magnetism, whereas a Moon perched on the Midheaven bestows the ability to tune into the public's needs and moods. Because the Moon can be so magnetic and appealing – if sometimes manipulative – those in whose birth charts she makes a strong showing may find themselves drawn to careers that bathe in the 'limelight'.

In the world at large, the Moon rules photography; motherhood; the nursing and caring professions, especially childcare; and the public.

Symbolism

The Moon's glyph, the crescent, is seen by many astrologers as the container of life. In essence, it represents the fertile womb offering itself up to be impregnated by the Sun's seed. This union of male and female principles is the key to all physical life.

THE MOON IN PERSPECTIVE

The Moon is considered strong or weak in :
- **Cancer** (Dignity): The Moon's natural affinity with the watery sign of Cancer is very clear. Both are associated with nurture, emotional security and an active imagination, making this sign the perfect home for the Moon.
- **Capricorn** (Detriment): The sensitive Moon feels ill at ease in the harsh and unforgiving environment of Capricorn. Often, the serious, brooding and self-preoccupied side of this sign squashes the Moon's sympathetic tendencies.
- **Taurus** (Exaltation): The Moon thrives in earthy Taurus because of this sign's reputation for being in touch with the senses, and all that means in terms of nourishment and overdoing it.
- **Scorpio** (Fall): One might imagine that the Moon would be in her element in emotionally intense Scorpio but, because of this sign's mercilessly vindictive and manipulative side, she is reckoned to reveal her darkest qualities here.

THE MOON THROUGH THE SIGNS

• **SHOWS HOW YOU REACT INSTINCTIVELY** • **HOW YOU RESPOND TO YOUR SURROUNDINGS** • **THE WAY YOU SEEK SECURITY AND PROTECTION** • **YOUR SENSE OF FAMILY** • **HOW YOU NURTURE AND LOOK FOR EMOTIONAL SUSTENANCE**

ARIES A tendency to react hastily; a fiery temper that quickly burns itself out; thrives in competitive environments; a childlike sense of wonderment; responds poorly to authority.

TAURUS Emotionally stable; requires outlets for pressing physical needs; can be loyal to the point of stubbornness; becomes easily habit-bound; responds poorly to change.

GEMINI Open-minded and adaptable; susceptible to sudden and frequent changes of mood; tends to make light of 'heavy' emotions; responds poorly to restrictive routines.

CANCER Great emotional strength; highly responsive to others' moods; gains security by cultivating a sense of family; forms deep attachments; responds poorly to being uprooted.

LEO A playful disposition; strong but stable, emotions; tends to be self-centred and bossy; repays love and appreciation with loyalty; responds poorly to loss of dignity.

VIRGO A sensitive, caring nature; finds it hard to express emotions; fears the unknown; nurtures by being useful; sets high standards; responds poorly to being undervalued.

LIBRA Even-tempered and mild-mannered; finds it hard to be emotionally honest; tends to compromise own needs for the sake of peace and quiet; responds poorly to confrontation.

SCORPIO Given to powerful all-or-nothing responses; bears deep grudges when crossed; has an uncanny awareness of others' weak points; responds poorly to being exposed.

SAGITTARIUS Reacts enthusiastically to anything that smacks of adventure; a strong instinctual nature; often fails to finish what it starts; responds poorly to being pinned down.

CAPRICORN Self-reliant and dutiful; feels comfortable when in control; hides feelings of insecurity behind a cool facade; distrusts deep intimacy; responds poorly to lack of purpose.

AQUARIUS Prone to unpredictable mood swings; feels more at home with friendship than deep involvements; can become cut off from own needs; responds poorly to possessiveness.

PISCES Sensitive to emotional undercurrents; a frail grasp of own emotional needs; nurtures through empathy; a strong self-indulgent streak; rich fantasy life; responds poorly to criticism.

THE MOON THROUGH THE HOUSES

• **Shows in what area of life you find nurture** • **where you find sanctuary from life's difficulties** • **Where you look for a sense of inner security** • **Natural-born talents that are rarely remarked upon**

I   **FIRST**   A magnetic personality; wears its heart very much on its sleeve; highly tuned sensitivities and instincts; possibly highly insecure (childlike emotions); easily influenced.

II   **SECOND**   Acquires a sense of security through emotional attachment to possessions; may spend money impulsively; fluctuating financial fortunes; a love of nature.

III   **THIRD**   Mental energies ebb and flow; a voracious appetite for knowledge; perceptions are coloured by moods; absorbs information by osmosis; a natural communicator.

IV   **FOURTH**   Sense of belonging is derived from family and cultural roots; sensitive to surroundings; views the home as a sanctuary; a need for privacy; a fascination for the past.

V   **FIFTH**   Seeks emotional fulfilment through children or creative pursuits; a fluctuating self-image; an instinct for entangled love affairs; often fickle in love; a natural performer.

VI   **SIXTH**   Seeks comfort in routine and attention to detail; possible interest in health issues; needs to feel emotionally involved in work; easily stressed; a natural caring instinct.

VII   **SEVENTH**   Looks for sustenance in one-to-one relationships; a constant need for company; apt to place partners' needs and feelings first; emotionally exploitable; strong aesthetic sense.

VIII   **EIGHTH**   Emotional responses are magnified by unconscious urges; a subtle awareness of what motivates others; may use money as a source of emotional comfort; a flair for business.

IX   **NINTH**   Strong 'gut' convictions; seeks comfort in belief systems; a tendency to be intolerant; may be drawn to foreign cultures; an aptitude for tuning into future trends.

X   **TENTH**   Public acclaim bestows a feeling of security; ambition obscures a childlike need for approval; may follow family footsteps in career; an instinct for knowing what the public wants.

XI   **ELEVENTH**   A strong need for nurturing friendships; ideals and long-term goals may wax and wane; an active social life; needs to find an individual purpose; a natural listener.

XII   **TWELFTH**   Susceptible to strong emotions; reticent about feelings; a periodic need to 'get away from it all'; deep-seated phobias; working with the afflicted; mediumistic abilities.

MERCURY

The Principle of Awareness

• **THOUGHT PROCESSES** • **LEARNING** • **SPEECH** • **WRITING** • **KNOWLEDGE**
• **UNDERSTANDING** • **CURIOSITY** • **RESTLESSNESS** • **REASON** • **GOSSIP**
• **ELOQUENCE** • **COMMERCE** • **HEALING** • **COMMONSENSE** • **CUNNING**

Mercury, the smallest and swiftest planet in the solar system, occupies a unique place in mythology. Of all his guises, which include liar, thief, orator, trickster, musician, gymnast and patron of the healing arts, merchants and travellers – his main function was to act as the messenger of the gods. In this capacity he was the only figure, god or man, who could travel freely between the human realm, the underworld, where Hades ruled supreme and Olympus, home of the gods. This freedom of mobility tells us something of Mercury's role in astrology, for he symbolizes the ability of the human mind to carry the torch of consciousness into the different levels of the psyche, particularly the unconscious, giving us the opportunity for greater self-awareness and integration. In his highest expression, he is a symbol of the unity of mind and spirit that flows throughout the universe

Mercury represents our mental patterning – how we seek knowledge of the world and organize our perceptions of reality so that they can be interpreted and communicated. Essentially, he signifies our ability to make connections – to see the relationship between 'things', and between ourselves and the world. His 'influence' begins early in life when we gradually become conscious of ourselves as separate individuals, and start to build bridges to overcome this gap. We do this primarily by learning to walk and talk, both functions that are traditionally associated with Mercury.

In the body, Mercury's bridge-building capacity corresponds to the nervous system, which processes messages received from the outside world and from within the body itself, enabling the body's organs to send messages to each other. Some of this information reaches consciousness, and some of it doesn't, which shows that Mercury operates on the conscious as well as unconscious level. Revealingly, if the nervous system is irreparably damaged the result can be paralysis or loss of speech – in other words, a loss of the Mercury function.

In the birth chart, Mercury's sign, position and aspects to the other planets reveal our mental frequency – how we think, learn and communicate, our manner of speech and how we adapt and change our attitudes to our environment. He also describes what we find mentally stimulating, and the type of work that most suits our temperament. When he is strong or well-placed in a chart, Mercury invariably reveals himself through a nimbleness of mind or body.

Mercurial types are usually quick-witted, and versatile with an impish sense of humour and an inquiring mind. They can also be articulate, knowledgeable and, reflecting Mercury's connection with mind–body co-ordination, extremely dexterous. Given such a menu of talents, it is not surprising that this planet has a reputation for being a skilled operator in the world of commerce. When weak or afflicted, however, Mercury indicates changeability, superficiality, indecision, nervous restlessness and, if this planet's knavish side is given full rein, downright deceitfulness. There can also be difficulties with self-expression.

In the world at large, Mercury rules all forms of speech and writing, including the media and the rapidly expanding network of telecommunications; all database systems; the transport and distribution industries; a nation's infrastructure, such as roads, canals, airports and ports; all forms of commerce; schools, students and teachers; and clerical work.

Symbolism
Mercury's glyph is the only one that includes all the primary shapes – the circle of spirit, with the semi-circle of soul above and the cross of matter below, symbolizing receptivity through the triumph of spirit over matter.

This glyph is similar to Mercury's *caduceus* – a winged baton with two intertwined serpents around the shaft – that had the power to resolve conflicts and disputes. A symbol of wisdom, the *caduceus*, has been adopted by the medical professions as their emblem, suggesting the natural healing powers of the mind.

MERCURY IN PERSPECTIVE

Mercury is considered strong or weak in:
- **Gemini/Virgo** (Dignity): Mercury has a natural affinity with the openly communicative medium of Air, and is therefore said to prosper in Gemini – the most 'airy' of all the signs. By contrast, Virgo's analytical, discriminating, but well-grounded approach gives this planetary prankster much needed methodicalness.
- **Sagittarius/Pisces** (Detriment): Mercury sits uneasily in flighty Sagittarius and nebulous Pisces. Both signs, ruled by Jupiter, present a too unruly and unstructured environment for Mercury, who is more concerned with detailed breadth of knowledge than the depth of understanding sought by both these signs.
- **Virgo** (Exaltation): One tradition maintains that Mercury has no sign of exaltation, while another gives it to Virgo, a sign he rules.
- **Pisces** (Fall): The same applies here as with Mercury's sign of exaltation.

MERCURY THROUGH THE SIGNS

• **YOUR MENTALITY** • **HOW YOU COMMUNICATE** • **YOUR POWERS OF OBSERVATION**
• **YOUR NERVOUS ENERGY** • **THE WAY YOU ACCESS YOUR UNCONSCIOUS MIND**
• **HOW YOU ACQUIRE AND USE KNOWLEDGE** • **WHAT TURNS YOU ON**

ARIES Mentally combative; quick to react with a sharp wit; communicates forcefully and to the point; dislikes dishonesty; leaps before thinking; a creative problem solver.

TAURUS A shrewd and practical thinker; believes only what it sees; takes time to form opinions; sticks by decisions; literal-minded; strong sense of form; good concentration.

GEMINI A restless and inquisitive mind; needs a high level of mental stimulation; quick-witted and articulate; needs outlets to prevent mental congestion; extremely versatile.

CANCER Mental impressions are coloured by emotions; absorbs information intuitively; able to tune into others' thought processes; over-personalizes views; inclined to worry.

LEO Flamboyant thinker; capable of great concentration; authoritative communicator; poor grasp of details; inclined to 'know it all'; insensitive to others' views; good at selling ideas.

VIRGO An orderly mind; predisposed to analyse; piercingly perceptive; tends to lose sight of overall picture and get bogged down in detail; likes to test ideas; a natural researcher.

LIBRA Fair-minded and able to see both sides of an argument; prefers diplomacy to blunt honesty; likes to balance opposites; can be paralysed by indecision; management skills.

SCORPIO A penetrating and self-contained thinker; keen observer of hidden motives; sharp tongued; can lose objectivity when emotionally involved; secretive; the mind of a detective.

SAGITTARIUS A lively mind with a philosophical bent; ideas may lack substance; bigoted views; prone to hypocrisy; a flair for seeing the overall pattern in events.

CAPRICORN An organized and thorough mind; enjoys translating ideas into reality; instinctively takes a sceptical viewpoint; distrusts novelty; possible business acumen.

AQUARIUS Has the ability to think both laterally and logically; can be original and inventive; tends to dissociate thought processes from feelings; inclined to hold autocratic views.

PISCES An intuitive, flexible mind; highly impressionable; a vivid imagination; can seemingly pluck ideas out of nowhere; capable of great self-deception; needs to focus energies.

MERCURY THROUGH THE HOUSES

• WHAT AREA OF LIFE STIMULATES YOUR MIND • WHAT INTERESTS YOU • WHAT FIRES YOUR IMAGINATION • WHAT AROUSES YOUR CURIOSITY • WHERE YOU OPEN YOURSELF TO NEW EXPERIENCES • TYPES OF COMMERCIAL ACTIVITY

I **FIRST** Likes to be seen as bright and alert; the urge to make oneself heard; will be drawn to any occupation that is mentally stimulating; a sharp observer; may have a gift for mimicry.

II **SECOND** An astute awareness of the power of knowledge and communication; often indicates an acute grasp of the value of things; may have a gift for wheeling and dealing.

III **THIRD** Eager to learn; quick on the uptake; can be extremely alert to surroundings; often has many interests; needs to acquire depth of knowledge; may have a gift for communicating.

IV **FOURTH** Mental outlook influenced by family background; often has to work hard to gain self-awareness; enjoys working from home; may have a gift for real-estate.

V **FIFTH** Delights in expressing intellectual powers; drawn to mentally stimulating people; a playful mind; dramatic self-expression; may have a gift for speculative ventures.

VI **SIXTH** Needs to establish well-organized routines and to watch stress levels and diet; information overload affects mental health; may have a gift for working in 'caring' professions.

VII **SEVENTH** Seeks a 'marriage of minds' in close relationships; self-awareness gained or held back through partners; benefits from joint ventures; may have a gift for arbitration.

VIII **EIGHTH** Is drawn to intense mental contacts with others; can denote strong sexual fantasies; often fascinated by the mysteries of the mind; may have a gift for counselling.

IX **NINTH** A philosophical mind; fascinated by anything that broadens one's understanding of human nature; interested in prevailing attitudes; may have a gift for teaching.

X **TENTH** Sees knowledge as way to self-advancement; a jack-of-all-trades mentality; changeable career path; possible flair for commerce; may have a gift for public speaking.

XI **ELEVENTH** Idealistic thinker; often shows an interest in political or social issues; seeks mental stimulation from wide circle of friends; a natural networker; may have a gift for debating.

XII **TWELFTH** Thinking is strongly influenced by unconscious drives; powerful imagination; expression is often confused; may have a gift for helping people with learning difficulties.

♀

VENUS

The Principle of Attraction

• RELATIONSHIP • HARMONY • PEACE • BEAUTY • TASTE • STYLE • CHARM
• PLEASURE • APPEARANCE • DESIRE • INTIMACY • UNION
• SHARING • ARTISTRY • RIVALRY • VANITY

Although she takes her name from the Roman goddess of sensual love and beauty, Venus's flirtation with all things amorous and beautiful stretches back into the haze of antiquity. She first appears nearly 6,000 years ago in the cosmology of the Sumerians as Inanna, a fertility goddess skilled in the arts of love. Several transmutations later, she re-emerges as the Greek goddess Aphrodite whose legendary beauty made her irresistible and cast her as a symbol of seductive feminine power.

In modern astrology, Venus's association with the joys – and tears – of sex remains. Along with Mars and, to a lesser degree, Jupiter and Pluto, she is considered to be a symbol of sexuality. In a woman's chart, Venus is believed to represent what she puts out romantically and sexually. At her best, she signifies an independent woman who knows her own worth, and who is loving without being compliant. In a man's chart, Venus is said to indicate the type of woman that he finds physically desirable and, as with the Moon, the often unacknowledged feminine side of his own personality.

In matters of the heart, the Venusian impulse is to find common ground with a partner. When positively expressed, it manifests itself as an ability to make adjustments in a relationship and to bring out the best in a partner without self-compromise. Negatively, Venus shows herself as a tendency to keep the peace at any price by glossing over differences and fulfilling others' needs at our own expense. In the bedroom, a positive Venus brings harmony, intimacy and sensuality into the physical side of a relationship, and her sexual artistry can help to prevent the flame of desire from fading.

However, every planet has its wild side and when Venus is let off her leash she can display distinctly unpleasant attributes. It is often forgotten that in her many mythological guises, Venus was a war goddess who sought victory in battle as well as love. In fact, she can be jealous, competitive and, when crossed, extremely vengeful. She can also set out to attract admirers out of mere vanity, or for purely personal gain. History is littered with the corpses of those who have fallen under the spell of provocative

Venusian archetypes: the seductive siren, the artful coquette and the ice queen are all manifestations of Venus's ability to incite the passions and play havoc with the feelings of her hapless victims.

As in mythology, however, Venus in the birth chart is not all about the vicissitudes of love. As Aphrodite, she also presided over the arts, and her gift to mankind was culture. Consequently, the astrological Venus is not just concerned with personal adornment. She reveals our creativity in the way we seek to beautify and refine our environment – and her position in the birth chart can often indicate artistic talent. On the flip side, Venus is often characterized by the hedonist or the glamour puss – idle pleasure seekers, who dedicate themselves to the 'good life' or being seen in the most fashionable places.

In day-to-day life, Venus describes our ability to establish harmonious relationships with anyone we have to rub shoulders with on a regular basis. When strongly placed, on the Ascendant or in her own signs, for instance, she frequently manifests as considerable personal charm and an ability to put people at their ease. On the down side, besides an often ill-concealed 'bitchy' streak, Venus also has impossibly high expectations of others, and suffers hugely when friends or colleagues fail to deliver.

In the world at large, the Venusian principle can also be seen at work in peace movements, diplomatic initiatives, women's rights, girl power, the beauty industry, artists of all kinds, interior design and public relations. Some astrologers maintain that, as Venus rarely gives without expecting something in return, she also governs all means of exchange, including money.

Symbolism

The glyph for Venus shows the cross of matter surmounted by the circle of spirit, signifying that through the union of the four elements life can be transformed from matter into spirit.

VENUS IN PERSPECTIVE

Venus is considered to be strong or weak in:

- **Taurus/Libra** (Dignity): Venus is reckoned to display the most unfettered side of her romantic and aesthetic nature in Libra. By contrast, the more indulgent, acquisitive and sexual side of her nature is believed to prosper in sensual Taurus.
- **Scorpio/Aries** (Detriment): In Scorpio, feelings become intensified to such an extent that Venus's desire for harmony is undermined. In Aries, Venus's equilibrium is unbalanced by the egocentric quality of this sign.
- **Pisces** (Exaltation): Venus thrives in watery Pisces where love can reach its highest expression through self-sacrifice.
- **Virgo** (Fall): Although Venus in Virgo indicates marked artistic taste or ability, she is considered to be held back by this sign's tendency to repress the feelings in matters of the heart.

VENUS THROUGH THE SIGNS

• **SHOWS HOW YOU SET OUT TO ATTRACT OTHERS** • **WHAT YOU EXPECT OF LOVE**
• **WHAT YOU ARE LIKE IN A RELATIONSHIP** • **HOW YOU GET ON IN COMPANY**
• **HOW YOU REACT WHEN YOU FEEL SHORT-CHANGED** • **YOUR SENSE OF STYLE**

ARIES Ardent and impulsive; highly idealistic in love; honest in affections; needs to balance desire for intimacy with need for independence; may be too uncompromising.

TAURUS Calm and gentle; prefers to allow others to do the chasing; highly sensual; needs tangible signs of commitment before feeling secure; may be too passive and stubborn.

GEMINI Engaging and adaptable; tends to prefer variety to deep emotional contacts; loves to flirt; looks for a strong mental rapport; may be too changeable and superficial.

CANCER Sentimental and tender; makes strong emotional attachments; finds it hard to 'let go'; highly sensuous and imaginative; may be too sensitive and 'crabby'.

LEO Playful and indulgent; needs to lionize the partner and feel adored in return; loves glamour and grand gestures; can be generous to a fault; may be too self-centred and vain.

VIRGO Cool and controlled; enjoys the physical side of love, but tends to keep feelings on a tight rein; admires quality and order; may be too fussy and buttoned up.

LIBRA Charming and accommodating; needs to be liked; inclined to mask true feelings to keep the peace; apt to blame others for own failings; may be too unrealistic.

SCORPIO Intense and passionate; needs to experience love as 'all or nothing'; seeks a sense of mystery; loves secrecy; may be too manipulative and jealous.

SAGITTARIUS Spontaneous and lusty; easily aroused, but can find initial enthusiasm difficult to sustain; likely to make wild promises; may be too hypocritical.

CAPRICORN Undemonstrative and cautious; looks for constancy and stability in love; can use personal contacts for social advancement; may be too cold and unfeeling.

AQUARIUS Relaxed and approachable; puts emphasis on friendship in close relationships; often finds deep emotions hard to handle; may be too rational and naive.

PISCES Quiescent and elusive; needs to temper yearning for love with discrimination; has to guard against emotional dependence in love; may be too exploitable and idealistic.

VENUS THROUGH THE HOUSES

• **SHOWS IN WHAT AREA OF LIFE YOU CAN FIND FULFILMENT** • **WHERE YOU SEEK PLEASURE** • **THE COMMON GROUND YOU LOOK FOR IN THE PEOPLE YOU MEET** • **WHERE YOUR DESIRES MAY BE THWARTED** • **YOUR CREATIVE POTENTIAL**

I FIRST A non-confrontational approach; an ability to find compromises; seeks popularity; natural artistic talent; can lack self-discipline; may expect success without effort.

II SECOND A love of physical comforts; can be acquisitive; an eye for beauty; good for handling people in financial transactions; may be undone by extravagant tastes.

III THIRD A natural learner; the ability to mediate; a flair for language(s); skill in commerce; many interests; may be too inclined to say what others want to hear.

IV FOURTH A profound desire for peace; strong sense of family values; artistic taste; needs to make the home a beautiful place; may be too dependent in relationships.

V FIFTH Powerful creative instincts; an irresistible sense of style; fulfilment through children; rich, eventful love life; may be over-concerned about desirability.

VI SIXTH A talent for learning practical or technical skills; often drawn to health and beauty professions; may struggle to find balance between work and pleasure.

VII SEVENTH Looks for sense of worth through relationships; tends to over-idealize the partner; natural public relations skills; may need to stand up for own rights.

VIII EIGHTH Seeks to share at the deepest level; inharmonious love life; 'fated' or transformative relationships; flair for business; may find desires constantly thwarted.

IX NINTH A taste for adventure and new experiences; often attracts publicity; love of knowledge and diverse cultures; may find one-to-one relationships too restricting.

X TENTH Desires public admiration; often denotes a charismatic image; takes pride in profession; family pressure to shine in career; may find life lonely at the top.

XI ELEVENTH Likes to share ideals as an active part of a group; sets high standards of friendship; a flair for entertaining; may be obsessed with being in the 'right crowd'.

XII TWELFTH Secretive about affairs of the heart; lacks discrimination in relationships; finds inner peace through selfless service; may experience many disappointments in love.

MARS

The Principle of Assertion

• **SELF-ASSERTION** • **INDEPENDENCE** • **INDIVIDUALITY** • **ACTION** • **ANGER**
• **AGGRESSION** • **CHALLENGE** • **COMPETITION** • **CONFLICT** • **COURAGE**
• **RESISTANCE** • **STRENGTH** • **FRUSTRATION** • **INITIATIVE** • **PASSION**

Mythology has it that when the all-powerful god Jupiter gave birth to Minerva, his wife Hera was so incensed she conceived Mars, the god of war. Born out of spiteful anger, Mars came to be associated down the ages with unbridled hostility. Traditional astrology labelled him the 'Lesser Malefic', believing him to be a significator of violence, treachery, pestilence and, of course, strife. Modern astrology, however, takes a less judgmental view, preferring to see Mars as a symbol of raw energy that is neither 'good' nor 'bad'.

At the instinctive level, Mars represents self-assertion. Some astrologers go as far as to say that he represents the impulse to be born, manifesting as the push down the birth canal. In childhood, he is the stage at which we strike out on our own and begin to find our feet in the world. It is Mars who drags us away from the bosom of the family and drives us to affirm our independence. Without his services as defender of our emerging individuality, our instinct to survive, let alone carve out a life for ourselves, would be seriously impaired.

But Mars is not just concerned with standing up for ourselves; he also represents what we want from life. Physically, he reveals our energy levels and strength; psychologically, he corresponds to what motivates us, our basic drive. His position in the birth chart shows how we try to subjugate the world to our will and whether we have the stamina to match. At his best, Mars, like the Sun, fires us with the courage and initiative to forge ahead in life, conferring the ability to act quickly and decisively, and to get things done efficiently.

On the other hand, Mars can spill out as selfishness, impatience, foolish recklessness or frustrated aggression. At his most inflamed, he stumbles into mindless brutality. This can be especially true if the need to assert our individuality is constantly thwarted early in life, preventing us from fighting for what we instinctively want. When this happens, there is a danger that Mars will turn inwards and fester as feelings of impotence or anger which, later on in life, can resurface as overbearing or bullying behaviour.

Clearly, Mars is a highly volatile, some would say primitive, energy that works best when it is consciously focused, which is why this planet is linked with competitive sport. Indeed, in his purest expression, individualistic Mars relishes testing his strength and courage through competition of all kinds, not so much out of a desire to dominate those around him , but because he needs to see how far he can push himself in all that he does. On account of this egocentric concern with his own prowess, Mars does not have a good reputation when it comes to co-operation, especially in relationships.

In matters of the heart, Mars is seen as a symbol of thrusting male sexuality playing opposite to Venus, who represents the feminine. For this reason, Mars in a man's chart is said to show how he feels about and expresses his masculinity, while in a woman's chart he is believed to show qualities she finds desirable in a man. In practice, however, both planets preside over our sexuality and, although they represent opposite principles – Venus seeking union where Mars strives for independence – they are energies that manifest in both sexes and ideally work in tandem. Both in our relationships and within our psyches, Venus has the potential to civilize Mars, raising him from the level of selfish instinct to being conscious of his actions. In turn, a strong Mars helps us to stand up for what we want and prevents us from being exploited by others.

In the world at large, Mars also corresponds to the military; fire-arms and explosives; all forms of coercion; machines and mechanics; technicians; engineers; fire; inflammations, accidents and surgical operations.

Symbolism

The traditional astrological glyph for Mars ($\male$), as opposed to the stylized version used today ($\mars$), is the cross of matter sitting on the circle of spirit, suggesting that Mars has the power to create matter from abstract spirit or to debase pure energy, reducing it to its grossest state.

MARS IN PERSPECTIVE

Mars is considered to be strong or weak in:
- **Aries/Scorpio** (Dignity): The initiatory energy of Mars is ideally suited to forthright Aries, the sign of beginnings. In Scorpio, Mars's survival instincts and cutting edge are at their strongest, investing him with discipline and determination.
- **Taurus/Libra** (Detriment): Mars sits somewhat uncomfortably in the signs that Venus rules. In passive Taurus, his vibrant energy is generally incompatible with this sign's measured pace, whereas in Libra his impulsiveness is constrained by the need for compromise.
- **Capricorn** (Exaltation): Mars is considered to prosper in Capricorn, where his storehouse of energy can be marshalled towards achieving long-term ambitions.
- **Cancer** (Fall): In the quintessentially female sign of Cancer, the forceful, direct energy of Mars is diluted, forcing him to learn subtleness instead.

MARS THROUGH THE SIGNS

• SHOWS HOW YOU SET OUT TO GET WHAT YOU WANT • YOUR 'FIGHT OR FLIGHT' INSTINCT • CONSCIOUS AND UNCONSCIOUS MOTIVES • YOUR SEX DRIVE • YOUR COMPETITIVE SPIRIT • HOW YOU LET OFF STEAM

ARIES Reckless and fiercely independent; impulsive sex drive; brash confidence often masks feelings of inferiority; loves to take the upper hand; inconsiderate; lacks perseverance.

TAURUS Purposeful and determined; conserves energy; powerful sex drive; may focus single-mindedly on pursuit of wealth; creative or artistic talent; often has a lazy streak.

GEMINI Quick and well-developed critical faculties; a razor-sharp wit; sexually open-minded; highly-strung; constantly generates new ideas; has problems knowing what it wants.

CANCER Tenacious, but diffidence makes self-assertion difficult; tends to bury anger; fluctuating sex drive; fiercely protective; needs a loving environment to stabilize emotions.

LEO Loves to be 'king of the castle'; self-confident to the point of arrogance; fearlessly competitive; steady sex drive; craves respect; gallant; can be overbearing and inflexible.

VIRGO Watchful, acting only after assessing correct procedures; controlled sex drive; lacks vitality; sides with the underdog; sense of self strengthened through specialist knowledge.

LIBRA Measured action; asserts self through personal charm; delicate sex drive; forceful powers of persuasion; often forces will on others; angered by injustice; strong vain streak.

SCORPIO Deep reservoirs of energy; never gives up once a goal is set; likes to win against the odds; intense sex drive; enjoys power games; keeps intentions hidden; intensely jealous.

SAGITTARIUS A bold, crusading spirit; demands unfettered freedom of movement; can waste energy through lack of defined goals; adventurous sex drive; hugely tactless.

CAPRICORN Pursues desires relentlessly; likes to plan action with military precision; strong but cautious sex drive; gives and expects obedience; may trample on others.

AQUARIUS Unpredictable, although enjoys 'bucking the system'; the desire to act rationally may override passions; experimental sex drive; needs to learn the value of teamwork.

PISCES Subtle pursuit of goals; will fight for 'good causes'; subtle sex drive; energy levels are strongly affected by moods; outer show of strength masks vulnerability.

MARS THROUGH THE HOUSES

• **SHOWS IN WHAT AREA OF LIFE YOU SEEK TO ASSERT YOURSELF** • **WHERE YOU CONCENTRATE OR SCATTER YOUR ENERGIES** • **WHERE YOU ARE MOST INDEPENDENT OR TERRITORIAL** • **WHAT MAKES YOU ANGRY**

I FIRST Brimful of energy; the urge to impose oneself on one's environment; strong physical presence; extremely territorial and self-centred; needs to learn when to soften its approach.

II SECOND Energy directed towards material gain; seeks to assert the right to dispose of resources as sees fit; fights tooth and nail for what it values; tends to spend money rashly.

III THIRD A forceful communicator; needs to channel mental energies towards practical ends; an overactive mind that needs to find ways to 'switch off'; possible interest in education.

IV FOURTH Family conflicts; intensely protective of loved ones; upbringing steeped in competition or aggression; anger that is slow to surface; possible building or DIY skills.

V FIFTH Needs to establish supremacy; loves a challenge for the sake of it; sees love as a conquest; pride in athletic prowess; possible work with children; a compulsive gambler.

VI SIXTH Seeks to take initiative at workplace; fighting for employment rights; pushing oneself to the limit; challenging work routines; possibly attracted to the healing professions.

VII SEVENTH Likely to find drives constantly thwarted; issues on who wears the trousers in relationships; may look for forceful partners; a penchant for litigation; makes enemies easily.

VIII EIGHTH Learning to handle powerful basic drives; instinctively seeks to test strength through challenging situations or relationships; a talent for research; may be drawn to the occult.

IX NINTH A quest for constant adventure; fighting for convictions; a love of contests; the search for a meaningful outlook; can be insufferably opinionated; half-baked ideas.

X TENTH The urge to be seen as assertive; fighting for public recognition; inexhaustible energy; the need for an active occupation; frustrated ambition; a ruthless streak.

XI ELEVENTH Caught between the urge to be leader of the pack and need to work in a team; needs clear-cut aims; working tirelessly to achieve goals; competitive friendships.

XII TWELFTH Weak boundaries between own and others' drives; self-doubt; the search for a higher sense of purpose; covert activities; festering resentments; sex drive on a leash.

4

JUPITER
The Principle of Expansion

• EXPANSION • FAITH • LUCK • BELIEFS • TRAVEL • EXPLORATION •
• OBESITY • WASTE • SLOPPINESS • EXAGGERATION • WEALTH •
• MEANING • INSIGHT • INFLATION • BIGOTRY • GREED •

As befits the largest planet in the solar system with the greatest number of satellites, Jupiter in astrology plays a larger-than-life role, governing all areas concerned with expansion – be it the mind, the wallet or the girth. Traditionally, he was known as the 'Greater Benefic', largely on account of his role as harbinger of good fortune and bestower of largesse. Indeed, his legacy of good-natured optimism is enshrined in our language today: the word 'jovial', meaning genial, is derived from the Latin name for Jupiter – Jove.

In mythology, Jupiter was the king of the gods, renowned for his varied roles and his exuberant exploits – many of them sexual. Like the ancient sky god, the astrological Jupiter takes on many guises in our day-to-day affairs. He is the magistrate dispensing wise justice, the authority in the field of education, the priest preaching moral values, the explorer pushing back the frontiers of knowledge, the gambler riding his luck or the successful entrepreneur. On a somewhat less exalted plane, Jupiter is the acquaintance who bowls us over in the street as we are going quietly about our business, and drags us off for a strong brandy when we are already late for an appointment. And ever the optimist, he always sees the glass as half full, never half empty, for he is an exhausting delight who knows no half measures.

In the birth chart, Jupiter shows us how we strive to reach upwards and outwards, growing beyond the sphere of our personal world to experience life to the full. This world view is the 'big picture' in which we all play a part, however small. Jupiter's role is also to turn experience into meaning, and to fashion his insights into a body of knowledge, or set of beliefs, that feed our expectations of life and our ideals – whether these concern God, Mammon, or moral or philosophical principles. In this respect, Jupiter also shows how we revitalize ourselves when our batteries are low, how we reconnect with whatever belief system that embodies our understanding of the world and, more specifically, our place in it.

When strongly positioned in the chart, Jupiter invariably makes his presence felt through an

4

optimistic outlook and a sense of abundance – as if our hopes are mirrored by our environment and our background. Whatever our circumstances, a strong Jupiter seems to pull us out of the mire so that we always appear to land on our feet. However, in reality, it is the world reflecting our self-confidence back on ourselves.

So where is the catch? Jupiter's biggest problem is a tendency to take everything to excess. As he expands any planet that he touches in a chart, he tends to exaggerate difficult areas out of all proportion. Among his most spectacular failings are complacency and over-optimism, which can register as inflated self-importance, unrealistic expectations or wasted opportunities.

Moreover, while he has a flair for the majestic overview, Jupiter has a very poor grasp of detail. All too often, he is quick to pass judgment without looking at the facts of a case, and can sometimes cut corners dangerously thin. Perhaps it is no surprise that he features strongly in charts of major man-made accidents. Jupiter can also be exceptionally greedy, his appetite for the good things in life knowing no bounds. Morally, too, he is often quick to grab the high ground and hurl critical thunderbolts at others without examining his own behaviour first. However, a well-placed Saturn usually helps to counteract the inflationary tendencies of a rampant Jupiter.

In the world at large, Jupiter presides over the clerical profession; religious faith; philosophy; philanthropy; politics; the spirit of the law; travel; exploration; economic growth and inflation.

Symbolism

The glyph for Jupiter resembles the number four, but is in fact made up of the cross of matter surmounted by the crescent of soul. Jupiter's natural direction is uplifting, always attempting to transmute the grosser energies of matter into a more refined form.

JUPITER IN PERSPECTIVE

Jupiter is considered to be strong or weak in:
- **Sagittarius/Pisces** (Dignity): Jupiter's rulership of Sagittarius emphasizes his philosophical side – the urge to turn experience into a coherent belief system. In Pisces, Jupiter's generosity of spirit is given full throttle, expressing itself through compassion and sensitivity to others.
- **Gemini/Virgo** (Detriment): Jupiter does not blend easily with flighty Gemini, as this sign's restless curiosity works against the planet's hunger for depth of understanding. In meticulous Virgo, Jupiter is believed to be constricted by this sign's concern for detail.
- **Cancer** (Exaltation): Jupiter's exaltation in Cancer implies that his sympathetic nature can find its highest expression through nourishing and protecting loved ones.
- **Capricorn** (Fall): Although this pairing highlights worldly ambition, Jupiter's love of freedom is restricted in conventional Capricorn.

4

JUPITER THROUGH THE SIGNS

• YOUR EXPECTATIONS OF LIFE • HOW YOU SEARCH FOR MEANING IN LIFE
• YOUR GENEROSITY OF SPIRIT • YOUR SPIRITUAL OR MORAL IDEALS
• HOW YOU HARNESS OR CHALLENGE PREVAILING CULTURAL BELIEFS

ARIES Forward looking; sees life as a series of limitless opportunities; loves to lead from the front; has supreme faith in own abilities; can be breathtakingly arrogant; takes unnecessary risks.

TAURUS Hedonistic; sees life as a treasure trove of sensual experiences; a strong sense of beauty; prefers traditional values; may attract and dispose of wealth easily; highly acquisitive.

GEMINI Jack-of-all-trades; sees life as a vast information network; a social commentator; can get carried away by the sound of its own voice; changeable beliefs; tends to scatter energies.

CANCER Sympathetic; sees life as a charity to alleviate suffering; powerful imagination; enjoys home comforts; immensely patriotic; highly sentimental; emotions may cloud reason.

LEO Flamboyant; sees life as a stage for demonstrating abilities; supremely self-confident; inspirational leader; naturally creative; excessive pride; enjoys holding court.

VIRGO Generally modest; sees life as a mosaic of interconnected parts; extremely practical, with good technical skills; well-honed critical faculties; lacks self-confidence.

LIBRA Conformist; sees life as a team game to be played fairly; a romantic adventurer; marked artistic streak; seeks popularity and being with the 'in-crowd'; easily swayed.

SCORPIO Resourceful; sees life as a search for self-mastery; fascinated by the nature of power; tends to over-emphasize sex; deep convictions; consumed by passion; self-absorbed.

SAGITTARIUS Optimistic; sees life as a perpetual search for meaning; strong faith in own luck; far-sighted; often tolerant, but may hold dogmatic beliefs; lacks focus; boastful.

CAPRICORN Quietly confident; sees life as a serious business; believes in tradition and and discipline; takes great pride in reputation; success through hard graft; self-righteous.

AQUARIUS Sociable; sees life as a 'world community'; open minded but often holds wildly impractical beliefs; good-humoured; tolerant so long as everyone else agrees.

PISCES Idealistic; sees life as a dream; powerful spiritual yearnings; strong sense of vision but lacks direction and discipline; deep love of glamour; escapist urges; exploitable.

4

JUPITER THROUGH THE HOUSES

• **SHOWS IN WHAT AREA OF LIFE YOU FIND A SENSE OF PURPOSE** • **WHAT KIND OF EXPERIENCES BROADEN YOUR UNDERSTANDING OF LIFE** • **WHERE THINGS FALL INTO PLACE MOST EASILY** • **WHERE YOU TAKE LIFE MOST FOR GRANTED**

I **FIRST** Seeks to take charge; a larger-than-life personality; can generate enthusiasm and confidence in others; seductive charm; comes across as dignified or over-bearing.

II **SECOND** The urge to give ideals concrete form; a love of material comforts; an eye for beauty; money-fixated; may be undone by extravagant tastes or financial risk-taking.

III **THIRD** Natural mental abilities; the eternal student; a flair for language(s); may have a talent for commerce; a wide range of interests and contacts; intellectual arrogance.

IV **FOURTH** A profound desire for peace; strong family ties and values; the search for the 'ideal home'; often over-dependent in relationships; a late developer; artistic taste.

V **FIFTH** The urge to live life to the full; big-hearted and theatrical in love; a natural exhibitionist; powers of leadership; an affinity with children; over-confident and self-satisfied.

VI **SIXTH** The search for meaningful work; a tendency to take on too many commitments; an over-indulgent lifestyle; concern for health can turn into hypochondria; healing abilities.

VII **SEVENTH** The search for the perfect partner; disappointments through high expectations of others; may invest partners with larger-than-life qualities; many social contacts.

VIII **EIGHTH** Seeks union through (many) deep sexual experiences; able to turn a crisis into an opportunity for growth; looks for hidden meanings; financial benefits through others.

IX **NINTH** The search for truth and meaning in life; a strong need to develop intellectual potential; an inflated belief in one's mission; wanderlust; possible gift for teaching.

X **TENTH** A powerful drive to make something of life; a talent for organizing and delegating; a 'big' reputation – for integrity or hypocrisy; strong sense of drama may denote acting ability.

XI **ELEVENTH** The search for a collective goal or ideal; active social life may hamper more serious pursuits; may seek to expand influence through friends in high places.

XII **TWELFTH** The search for a higher ideal; may drift through life believing 'something will turn up'; strong escapist tendencies; frail beliefs; looks to support or be supported.

ħ

SATURN

The Principle of Limitation

• STRUCTURE • DISCIPLINE • RESISTANCE • EXPERIENCE • NECESSITY
• DELAY • AMBITION • RESPONSIBILITY • THRIFT • CAUTION
• CONTROL • TIME • AUTHORITY • WISDOM • FEAR • DENIAL • HARDSHIP

In traditional astrology, Saturn was regarded as little short of evil. The 'Greater Malefic', as he was chillingly called, was associated with loss, hardship, delay, loneliness and death. A more grim repertoire is hard to imagine, but, given Saturn's mythology, it is hardly unwarranted: having castrated his father, Uranus, to seize control of the world, Saturn then devoured his own children in order to hold on to the reins of power. Nowadays, thanks largely to the more rounded insights of psychology, astrology's view of Saturn is somewhat less jaundiced, and he is seen to have a beneficial side as well.

On the psychological level, Saturn's position in a chart reveals those fears and anxieties that, through negative early conditioning, make us feel deeply inadequate. Because these raw feelings are given the stamp of disapproval, we try to camouflage them by putting on a brave face, or by building elaborate defence mechanisms to keep them at bay. But no matter how well we appear to hide them, these feelings somehow will not go away. Commonly, they re-emerge as personality traits that we despise in others, or they can manifest as obstacles, seemingly beyond our control, that inhibit us from achieving our most cherished ambitions.

Indeed, Saturn is all around us. He has a genius for accentuating those parts of ourselves that we most dislike. He is the person who makes our hackles rise on sight, the oppressive parent who thwarts our innermost desires or the authority figure who picks on us, seemingly for the sake of it. As psychologist-astrologer Liz Greene points out, it is when we are at our most oversensitive and defensive, and when we most fiercely blame others for our shortcomings, that we are revealing the side of Saturn psychology calls our 'Shadow'.

But it is vital not to see Saturn as all gloom and doom, because he has important lessons to teach us. At his most constructive, he imparts worldly wisdom gained through hard experience. In confronting what we least like in life, he can show where we most need to work on ourselves. 'As ye sow, so shall ye reap' could easily be his mantra. In many ways he is The Lord of Karma – the principle of cause and effect – insisting that we take responsibility for our thoughts and deeds. Often his lessons seem cruel, but they are necessary because, in contrast to Jupiter who looks for the infinite possibilities in everything, Saturn teaches us to operate within our limitations.

In fact, wherever we turn, Saturn brings us face to face with necessity, especially with the need for structure in our lives. In the human body, Saturn is associated with the skeleton or framework for the tissues, and the skin or 'outer limit' that physically separates us from the external world. Without either we would simply be unable to function, let alone exist – and so it is in every area of our lives that Saturn touches. He helps us to define our place in the world; he teaches us the rules we must play by if we want to translate our dreams into tangible results; and he shows us the value of planning, organization, discipline and endurance – virtues that are frequently lacking when Saturn is poorly placed in a chart.

But, as always with this demanding taskmaster, a balance needs to be struck. A strong Saturn may help us to mature into responsible, socially aware adults, but can also imprison us in the world of form at the expense of inner content. Too much structure and order narrows the mind, stifles creativity, and leads to a dependence on tradition and procedure. When this happens, Saturn is playing his most deadly role, condemning us to a living death in which we deny our potential full expression.

In the world at large, Saturn's domain extends to all rules and regulations; the applied sciences; governments, authority figures and law enforcement agencies; the letter of the law; prisons; economic recession; teachers and exams; time and old age.

Symbolism

The glyph for Saturn is the cross of matter rising above the crescent of soul. His symbol is a reminder that, as far as this planet's interests are concerned, the demands of the material world take precedence over spirituality.

SATURN IN PERSPECTIVE

Saturn is considered to be strong or weak in:
- **Capricorn/Aquarius** (Dignity): In Capricorn, Saturn finds the perfect outlet for his insistence on structure and order, whereas his rulership of Aquarius reflects his sense of social responsibility.
- **Cancer/Leo** (Detriment): No-frills Saturn is unimpressed by Leo's showmanship, and can exacerbate this Fire sign's insecurities about being ordinary. In Cancer, Saturn intensifies a natural tendency to worry, especially about loneliness and rejection.
- **Libra** (Exaltation): Although Saturn in Libra can indicate a fear of commitment, in its highest form, it emphasizes a serious attitude to relationships and the responsibilities that come with them.
- **Aries** (Fall): None of the Fire signs is comfortable with Saturn, least of all Aries, whose boldness and spirit of enterprise can be severely restricted when this planet is placed here.

SATURN THROUGH THE SIGNS

• SHOWS HOW YOU RESPOND TO RESTRICTION • YOUR FEARS AND INNER FEELINGS
OF INADEQUACY • HOW YOU CAN LEARN TO WORK WITHIN YOUR LIMITATIONS
• QUALITIES YOU NEED TO DEVELOP TO OVERCOME SHORTCOMINGS

ARIES Cautious and reserved; needs to develop self-reliance; may struggle to find motivation; keeps temper on ice; egocentric; may lack assertiveness; fears being impotent.

TAURUS Materialistic; needs to develop determination; can be frugal to the point of self-denial; mulishly stubborn; may lack spontaneity; fears financial dependence or uncertainty.

GEMINI Logical; needs to develop versatility; distrusts the irrational and airy-fairy theories; precise or inhibited expression; may lack adaptability; fears not being taken seriously.

CANCER Protective; needs to develop compassion; can get stuck in the past; tends to repress sensitivity; melancholic; self-absorbed may lack buoyancy; fears emotional rejection.

LEO Self-conscious; needs to develop self-assurance; arrogant and autocratic; hides light under a bushel; easily slighted; may lack humility; fears being seen as ordinary.

VIRGO Modest; needs to develop self-confidence; conscientious and hard-working; pedantic and hypercritical; may lack sensitivity to others; fears getting it wrong, the unknown.

LIBRA Coolly objective; needs to develop tolerance; feels unpopular and undesirable; strong sense of justice; may lack the ability to accept own failings; fears real intimacy in love.

SCORPIO Controlled; needs to develop sympathy; focuses ruthlessly on objectives; deep feelings of jealousy or envy; may lack forgiveness; fears emotional dependence.

SAGITTARIUS Philosophical; needs to develop mental discipline; tends to feel under-educated; enthusiasm tinged with cynicism; may lack restraint; fears restriction.

CAPRICORN Determined; needs to develop self-reliance; can be highly organized and disciplined; rigid adherence to tradition; may lack originality; fears failure, disapproval.

AQUARIUS Unpredictable; needs to develop independence; inclined to hold rigid opinions; distrusts radical change; may lack initiative; fears standing out from the crowd.

PISCES Moody; needs to develop self-discipline; can feel intensely vulnerable; needs solitude; self-effacing; may lack courage of convictions; fears 'going with the flow'.

♄

SATURN THROUGH THE HOUSES

• **Shows in what area of life you feel most inhibited** • **Where you must live within your limitations** • **Where you overcompensate for feelings of inadequacy** • **Where you have to work hardest**

I **FIRST** A cautious approach to life; feels environment is unsupportive; undervalues own abilities; vulnerable to criticism; pessimistic outlook; achievement through slow progress.

II **SECOND** A fear of poverty; meanness of spirit; low self-worth; hard work for small returns; may reject material values altogether; benefits through long-term investments.

III **THIRD** Feels insecure about ability to learn and communicate; possible early learning difficulties; narrow-mindedness; excessively logical; difficult relations with sibling(s).

IV **FOURTH** An absence of family support; distrusts emotional closeness; repressed emotional development; immature; may seek popularity to compensate for feeling unloved.

V **FIFTH** Poor sense of own identity; often feels insignificant; creativity suppressed or frequently frustrated; works and plays hard; may unconsciously seek rejection in love.

VI **SIXTH** Feels abilities are undervalued; frustrated search for rewarding work; extremely conscientious; administrative abilities; critical of work colleagues; psychosomatic disorders.

VII **SEVENTH** Difficulty in forming intimate relationships; fear of rejection; tends to blame others for own faults; may marry for status or wealth; a preference for older partner(s).

VIII **EIGHTH** Inhibited emotional expression out of fear of being let down by others; may suppress sexual instincts; unhappy loves; finds it hard to share responsibilities or resources.

IX **NINTH** A lack of adventurousness; a rigidly conventional outlook; may feel inadequate about mental abilities; frustrating search for a personal faith or creed; fear of travel.

X **TENTH** Marked determination to succeed; hard earned public acclaim; seeks to uphold the *status quo*; often feels uncomfortable in the limelight; heavy parental expectations in career.

XI **ELEVENTH** Likes to be 'leader of the gang'; may lack social graces; few but enduring friendships; often prefers to keep own company; frustrated hopes or ideals.

XII **TWELFTH** Harbours sense of impotence; plagued by self-doubt; tends to feel different or isolated from the rest of humanity; may sacrifice material ambitions to higher cause.

URANUS

The Principle of Liberation

• FREEDOM • NON-CONFORMISM • IDEALISM • REFORM • REVOLUTION
• INTUITION • ENLIGHTENMENT • ORIGINALITY • REBELLION
• UNPREDICTABILITY • SHOCK • DEVIANCY • BREAKDOWN • ANARCHY

With Uranus we enter the twilight zone of the 'transpersonal planets' – so called because their sojourn in each sign is so long that their effects are believed to manifest on a collective rather than a personal level. This certainly describes the nature of events surrounding Uranus's discovery in 1781. At that time, the old political and economic order was in a state of turmoil, threatened by mass rebellion and populist reforms in Europe and America and by the first stirrings of the Industrial Revolution. Even astrology was thrown into confusion, because the discovery of this planet demolished the old seven-planet cosmology at a stroke. Understandably, astrologers of the day considered Uranus to be a thoroughly disruptive influence, and over time this overview seems to have held true, although with important modifications.

Maintaining the link with revolutionary change, modern astrology associates Uranus with radical idealism. More specifically, he symbolizes the power of the mind to reach into the realm of 'universal ideas' and apply them to the physical world. This is not Mercury's realm of the rational mind, but belongs to that part of the intuitive mind that is capable of grasping whole concepts in a single, blinding flash of insight.

At his best, Uranus is to be found in the vanguard of social and technological progress, among the movers and shakers whose visionary reforms, discoveries and innovations have revolutionized the world. But in his deviant form, he touches those whose intentions are less than humanitarian – the demagogue who exploits utopian ideals for personal advantage, or the dictator who ruthlessly stamps his callous vision of society on his people. But this is not Uranus's concern. His insights are abstract, impersonal, free from moral imperatives, and it is up to us how we decide to use them.

In the birth chart, Uranus is the inner voice that tells us there is more to life than the established way of doing things. His position therefore signifies the urge to break free from what we perceive to be the restrictions of everyday life. When Uranus is dominant in the chart, the impulse to live according to this inner calling can be urgent enough to override the process by which most of us learn to conform.

Uranian individuals are hard to miss for, by definition, they stand out from the crowd. Some live their lives quietly as harmless eccentrics; some constantly rebel, refusing to abide by any convention; others find themselves being the mouthpiece for a group or generation, demanding change or freedom in their sphere of activity. But for those of us who feel more at home with Saturn's safe conformity, Uranus often springs into our lives uninvited, through an external agent – an individual or an event that somehow forces us to re-evaluate our lives and cut away the deadwood. In this respect, Uranus is the arch-enemy of Saturn, because he strips away the stifling or fossilized structures within the personality – and society – to pave the way for change and new growth.

Even though Uranus offers a fast track out, such upheaval is rarely welcome because he invariably turns our world inside out. As often as not, he demands that we let go of all the trappings of material success and security for which we have so painstakingly worked, because it is our attachment to these that prevents us from feeling truly alive. Yet no matter how painful these rude awakenings are, their function is to shake us out of our cosy complacency and offer us the chance of greater self-awareness and fulfilment in a way that can be truly liberating.

In the world at large, Uranus represents all innovative and state-of-the-art technologies; radical political, economic and social reform; the theoretical or cutting-edge sciences; rebels and revolutionaries; anarchy; civil liberties.

Symbolism

The glyph for Uranus is seen by some astrologers as the cross of matter above the circle of spirit, flanked by two crescents of soul, symbolizing this planet' search for a higher truth through exploring the nature of existence.

URANUS IN PERSPECTIVE

Uranus is considered to be strong or weak in:
- **Aquarius** (Dignity): Astrology has rather half-heartedly given Uranus the rulership of Aquarius, mainly because both sign and planet are linked with radicalism and innovation. But many astrologers argue that Aquarius is too Fixed for such an unstable influence as Uranus.
- **Leo** (Detriment): Leo's egocentric nature conflicts with Uranus's transpersonal approach, and his placement here reflects this sign's inherent wilfulness.
- **Scorpio** (Exaltation): Some astrologers argue that Uranus's concern with seeking out the underlying principles of life naturally links it to Scorpio, but others point out that this sign's Element is Water, whereas Uranus's is Air.
- **Taurus** (Fall): There is a good case for assigning Uranus to Taurus here, as this sign's stick-in-the-mud approach to life makes it incompatible with Uranus's change-oriented bias.

URANUS THROUGH THE SIGNS

• SHOWS HOW YOU DEAL WITH OUTMODED PATTERNS OF BEHAVIOUR • YOUR APTITUDE FOR RADICAL THOUGHT AND ACTION • YOUR READINESS TO ROCK THE BOAT • THE URGE TO BREAK FREE • YOUR VISION OF THE FUTURE

ARIES The urge to create new possibilities expressed through: bold initiatives; ruthless individualism; disregard for the past; compulsive need for change; intuitive insights.

TAURUS The urge to find inventive ways of resolving practical issues expressed through: dogged persistence; a preference for predictable change; the need for financial independence.

GEMINI The urge to open up new channels of communication expressed through: ruthless logic; pent-up mental energy; a fascination for new ideas and methods; lack of deep insight.

CANCER The urge to establish emotional independence expressed through: breaks with family tradition; dealing with turbulent inner emotions; developing intuition.

LEO The urge to be seen as unique expressed through: original creative ideas; championing radical causes; exaggerated self-importance; wilful behaviour; autocratic tendencies.

VIRGO The urge to overhaul outmoded practices expressed through: concern for the environment; dissatisfaction with lifestyle; the need for radical reform; dogmatic principles.

LIBRA The urge to explore new ways of relating expressed through: rebelling against accepted social values; the acceptance of mutual responsibility; the right to love 'freely'.

SCORPIO The urge to investigate life's mysteries expressed through: exposure of society's taboos; insight into the dark side of human nature; the tenacity to get to the truth.

SAGITTARIUS The urge to discover new belief systems expressed through: exposing religious humbug; freedom of speech; exploring new horizons; wacky theories or cults.

CAPRICORN The urge to restructure society expressed through: radical conservatism; cutting out waste and corruption; revitalizing traditional values; practical vision.

AQUARIUS The urge to find a 'brave new world' expressed through: the need to pull together; understanding collective issues; progressive reforms; equal rights for all.

PISCES The urge to formulate new concepts of reality expressed through: fresh insights into the nature of consciousness; revolutionary art forms; new spiritual values; impractical idealism.

URANUS THROUGH THE HOUSES

• **SHOWS IN WHAT AREA OF LIFE YOU SEEK FREEDOM OF EXPRESSION** • **WHERE YOU CAN OPEN UP TO THE NEED FOR CHANGE** • **WHERE YOU TEND TO DEVIATE FROM THE NORM** • **WHERE YOUR REBELLIOUS STREAK CAN CAUSE MOST DISRUPTION**

I **FIRST** Strongly individualistic (erratic) behaviour; a need for constant excitement; lacks sensitivity to others; may confuse the unorthodox for originality; flashes of brilliance.

II **SECOND** Breaking with conventional material values; tends to find possessions restrictive; sudden, unexpected financial gains and losses; unusual talents; off-beat lifestyle.

III **THIRD** A highly-strung, inventive mind; intolerant of prejudice; a tendency to speak one's mind (tactless); erratic – capable of brilliant insights or hopelessly impractical ideas.

IV **FOURTH** Unstable home environment – possible break-up or many changes in residence; sees self as the cuckoo in the nest; may rebel against background; unorthodox parents.

V **FIFTH** Heightened need to express unique talents; unconventional – often self-centred – attitudes to love; sudden infatuations that end abruptly; seeks excitement through taking risks.

VI **SIXTH** The search for novel forms of work; disruptive relations at work; nervous disorders through an inability to relax; working with innovative technologies or therapies.

VII **SEVENTH** Difficulty in maintaining conventional relationships; conflict between the need for intimacy and space; attracting partners who force one to make drastic changes.

VIII **EIGHTH** Breaking free from close emotional attachments; uninhibited or experimental (cold) approach to sex; need for excitement can trigger life-transforming crises.

IX **NINTH** A fascination for new or radical ideas; likely to reject conventional religions and philosophies; difficult to teach – prefers to learn from personal experience; eventful travels.

X **TENTH** Unusual vocation; looks for success on own terms; problems with authority figures; chequered career; an agent for change in society; can reject *status quo* for the sake of it.

XI **ELEVENTH** Tension between the need for independence and finding a group identity; radical, and often impractical, ideals; may place social contacts above personal friendships.

XII **TWELFTH** Early conditioning may make it difficult to express individuality openly; the need to liberate oneself from past influences; the search for 'enlightenment'; highly intuitive.

NEPTUNE

The Principle of Transcendence

• INSPIRATION • REFINEMENT • IDEALIZATION • CONFUSION • IMAGINATION •
INFILTRATION • DISINTEGRATION • UNCONSCIOUSNESS • SELF-SACRIFICE •
GLAMOUR • DISSOLUTION • DECEPTION • RENUNCIATION • ILLUSION

As the Greek god Poseidon, Neptune was ruler of the oceans, a sea god prone to attacks of tempestuous rage. His sovereignty of the seas, however, holds the key to his role in astrology, for Neptune takes us from Uranus's air-bound realm of collective ideas and submerges us in the watery depths of collective feeling.

Traditionally, Neptune is associated with loss and confusion on all levels, but his psychological function is to dissolve the boundaries that imprison us in our separate identities and merge us with the Whole, whatever we understand that to be. Typically, Neptune's influence in the outer world can be seen in the football crowd, the angry mob or the religious congregation – in fact, any large gathering or movement where individual identity is given over to the collective.

At his most superficial, Neptune has an abiding love of all things glamorous. The glitzy world of fashion, high society and rock and roll all belong to his world of here-today-gone-tomorrow glimmer and gloss. Neptune also infiltrates all aspects of popular culture – music, clothes, film and art – because they are all essentially expressions of group feeling. It is through this kind of identification with the ground swell of the collective that we derive a sense of being connected to something greater than ourselves which, in however small or trivial a way, enables us briefly to escape the humdrum realities of daily life.

In the birth chart, Neptune's role may be best described as one of refinement. Just as the movement of the sea wears away the sharp edges of a stone, so Neptune dissolves the coarser and less developed sides of our personality. In so doing, he breaks down our ego-boundaries, gently nudging us to transcend the limitations placed on us by external reality. As he opens us up to alternative realities, he heightens sensitivity and the perceptions, and leads us into the shimmering world of dreams, seductively inviting us into a realm of unlimited possibilities. In his highest expression, he symbolizes the ultimate act of purification or self-sacrifice – giving one's life to a lofty ideal, or forsaking one's needs for the betterment of others. This process holds considerable fear for many, especially those gridlocked in the better-the-devil-you-know mentality of Saturn, and so the natural instinct is to repress Neptune's influence altogether. But, like water seeping through the tiniest crack, Neptune has a nasty habit of insinuating his way into our lives and, if he is not recognized, he will leave us feeling isolated and disillusioned, adrift from the undertow of the collective.

However, as his association with loss and confusion suggests, nothing about Neptune is ever quite what it seems. While he can tempt us with visions of ecstasy, he is above all the master of illusion and makes no guarantees that by following his call we will find our nirvana. Indeed, far from promising bliss – spiritual or otherwise – a prominent Neptune in a chart can distort our grip on reality to such an extent that we lose all sense of who we are, leaving us 'all at sea' at the mercy of powerful unconscious currents. At his most afflicted, Neptune can be extremely unstable, bringing self-deception, loss of will power, gullibility, dishonesty and a flight from reality through drugs, alcohol or idle fantasy. Ultimately, however, Neptune teaches us about the illusory nature of reality, and that the only route to ecstasy lies within us, for the outside world can never satisfy our longing to be reconnected with the Divine.

In the world at large, Neptune holds sway over infectious diseases; all forms of propaganda; anaesthetics, opiates, sleep and all forms of altered states of consciousness; hallucinations, including dreams; film making and the cinema; artistic inspiration; shipping; oil; chemical gasses; leaks; mysticism; spiritual redemption.

Symbolism

Often drawn as a trident, Neptune's glyph consists of the cross of matter projected upwards so that it penetrates the crescent of soul. This symbol corresponds to the interface between spirit and matter – the realm where alternative states of consciousness intrude into physical reality.

NEPTUNE IN PERSPECTIVE

Neptune is considered to be strong or weak in:
- **Pisces** (Dignity): Like Neptune, Pisces is associated with loosening the grip of the ego. On the one hand this can lead to the highest expression of love – self-sacrifice – and on the other to confusion and a lack of assertiveness.
- **Virgo** (Detriment): Virgo's obsession with the particulars of life runs counter to Neptune's urge to 'go with the flow'. As a result, the spiritual dimension of Neptune is muted, displaced by a more practical approach to life.
- **Cancer** (Exaltation): Neptune's sign of exaltation is far from agreed, but the consensus seems to be that the emotional and caring side of Cancer is most attuned to this planet's highest expression.
- **Capricorn** (Fall): This sign's concern with materiality can distort Neptune's inflationary energies leading to greed and corruption.

NEPTUNE THROUGH THE SIGNS

• **Shows how you set out to fulfil your dreams** • **How you open your perceptions to other realities** • **Your capacity for self-deception** • **How you seek to escape from from what disenchants you most**

CANCER (1901/02–1914/16) Heightens the need for emotional security; inflates the desire for strong emotional attachments; distorts sensitivity resulting in intense anxiety; dissolves emotional dependence through sacrifice to family or country.

LEO (1914/16–1928/29) Heightens the need for love, creativity and dramatic self-expression; inflates the desire for glamour, pleasure and power; distorts the self-image resulting in excessive pride, vanity and delusions of grandeur; dissolves one's sense of identity, leading to greater self-awareness.

VIRGO (1928/29–1942/43) Heightens the need for mental stimulation; inflates the desire for order and empiricism; distorts the perceptions resulting in mental confusion; dissolves reliance on analysis, opening up intuitive abilities.

LIBRA (1942/43–1955/57) Heightens the desire for peace, justice and partnership; inflates the desire to idealize relationships, and beautify the world; distorts ability to compromise, resulting in disillusionment with others' failings; dissolves reluctance to take responsibility for own shortcomings.

SCORPIO (1955/57–1970) Heightens the need for self-mastery; inflates the craving for emotionally intense experiences; distorts the emotions leading to escapist tendencies or a martyr complex; dissolves the tendency to keep feelings on a tight leash.

SAGITTARIUS (1970–1984) Heightens the need to expand consciousness through the spirit of inquiry; inflates the desire for personal freedom; distorts powerful idealistic streak, resulting in adherence to wildly unrealistic creeds; dissolves lack of discrimination, giving clear-sightedness.

CAPRICORN (1984–1998) Heightens the need for material success; inflates the desire for tradition; distorts personal integrity so that the ends justify the means; dissolves the tendency to repress emotions, allowing a sense of vision and compassion to develop.

AQUARIUS (1998–2012) Heightens the need for a vision of a better world; inflates the desire for greater freedom of information and accountability; distorts idealism resulting in unfounded hopes or fraudulent aims; dissolves narrow personal interests, opening up a more enlightened humanitarian spirit.

NEPTUNE THROUGH THE HOUSES

- **SHOWS IN WHAT AREA OF LIFE YOU SEEK TO TRANSCEND MUNDANE REALITY**
- **WHERE YOU SEEK INSPIRATION** • **WHERE YOU ARE MOST LIKELY TO EXPERIENCE DISILLUSIONMENT** • **WHERE YOUR EGO IS AT ITS MOST FRAGILE**

I FIRST Confused self-image; adapts to surroundings like a chameleon; universal appeal; often lacks motivation and consistency; highly impressionable; possible martyr complex.

II SECOND Often careless about money; strong fashion sense; susceptible to unwise investments or get-rich-quickly schemes; compulsive shopper; charitable; fund-raising abilities.

III THIRD A strong sense of imagery; a tendency to embroider the facts; difficulty in making decisions; poor concentration – a daydreamer; possible story-telling abilities.

IV FOURTH The struggle to break free from family patterns; idealized or absent parent(s); romanticized view of childhood; search for the 'ideal home'; a preference for the quiet life.

V FIFTH Highly idealistic in love and capable of great self-deception; strong powers of seduction; secret liaisons; susceptible to flattery; may make money through speculation.

VI SIXTH The search for satisfying work may be thwarted by lack of application or humility; highly attuned to environment; hard work for little reward; may be drawn to holistic therapies.

VII SEVENTH A tendency to lose sight of oneself in relationships; needs to work at establishing relationships on equal terms; may look for salvation in partner, or vice versa.

VIII EIGHTH The urge to lose oneself in emotionally intense encounters; the search for sexual bliss; giving of oneself indiscriminately; confused sexual identity; may prefer celibacy.

IX NINTH The search for 'peak' experiences; a strong herd instinct – needs to cultivate greater independence of mind; finding salvation through faith; may be drawn to mysticism.

X TENTH A flair for sensing what the public wants; lack of recognition for achievements; unclear sense of direction; may give up career for more fulfilling life; may have artistic talent.

XI ELEVENTH The desire to give oneself to a cause; vague ideals; susceptible to other people's wishes; devoting energies to the less fortunate; expects too much of friends.

XII TWELFTH Difficulty in distinguishing between fantasy and reality; needs creative outlets for vivid imagination; seeks to escape from daily concerns; drawn to spiritual path.

PLUTO

The Principle of Transformation

• ANNIHILATION • DEATH • TRANSFORMATION • REBIRTH • SUBVERSION
• MANIPULATION • COMPULSION • VIOLATION • HIDDEN POWER
• BURIED TREASURE • TABOOS • CRISIS • DECAY • CORRUPTION

The smallest, furthest and most dense planet of our solar system, Pluto also has a weight out of all proportion to its size, and heavy, too, are the matters under his domain. Brother of Jupiter and god of the underworld, Pluto – or Hades to the Greeks – was allocated responsibility for the dead, and wore a helmet of invisibility that enabled him to stalk the world of the living unseen.

In the outer world, Pluto is associated with the process of death and regeneration. In keeping with his mythology, Pluto's astro-influence is equally hard to detect, for he represents the hidden power that eats away at the fabric of society, cleansing the old order in readiness for new growth. It does not matter whether it is power for good or ill – Pluto does not make judgements – and he frequently works through the process of disintegration and decay. For this reason, we often find him working under cover as the corrupt politician, the underworld criminal, the subversive terrorist or the scheming power broker. These archetypes may seem to be furthering their own interests, but in reality they are simply operating as, often unconscious, agents of Plutonian change – destroying the old order that spawned them.

In the birth chart, Pluto's task is to strip away all the rotten, decaying, and often buried parts of ourselves; our unresolved anger, jealousy, envy, greed and loathing. He forces us to throw these things away, or he will do it for us, and not very pleasantly either. As an agent of 'transpersonal change', his function is similar to that of Uranus and Neptune, although his methods are completely different. While Uranus rudely shakes us awake and Neptune gently dissolves, Pluto brings change through elimination, breaking down those aspects of the personality we have outgrown.

When we fail to take note of his influence, his impact can be violent: he simply shoves a stick of dynamite through the letter-box and walks away, leaving us to bandage our wounds and clear up the mess. Pluto's dynamic is so threatening to the psyche that we naturally try to repress his influence, or hide from his reach. Indeed, he often 'buries' any planet that he contacts in the birth chart – as if to allow conscious expression of these energies would expose us to the fury of society. But the longer we delay in facing him, the greater the havoc he will wreak. In common with Saturn, he is the ultimate realist – 'deal with life, or life will deal with you.'

Pluto is also linked symbolically with death and sexuality. The connection between sex and death has long been understood. Indeed, the French phrase for an orgasm is *le petit mort* – the little death. But Pluto is not interested in mere physical gratification: he seeks the loss of the ego in something altogether more intense and powerful – a regeneration through the process of letting go. Ultimately, however, Pluto is a force for transformation of the kind that enables us to 'kill off' those parts of the personality that no longer serve a useful purpose.

It is worth remembering that in mythology Pluto was also given charge of hidden treasure, an indication that behind his fearful front lie great resources to be discovered within ourselves. Clearing out the basement of our psyches may be an unpleasant process, but can bring incalculable rewards in the long term by revealing what those hidden treasures are. In this sense, Pluto is the 'bringer of light', who helps us to integrate what is buried in the unconscious into our everyday lives, making us more complete individuals in the process.

In the world at large, Pluto rules any aspect of society that potentially threatens the prevailing order and is driven underground out of a collective resistance to face such issues – for instance, the criminal underworld, or social taboos. But he also presides over all activities that involve transforming hidden resources into fully harnessed power, such as mining, nuclear fuel and depth psychology.

Symbolism

The glyph often used for Pluto is ♇ – based on the initials of the planet's discover, Percival Lowell. But the version used here incorporates all three symbols of matter, soul, and spirit, representing the creative energy locked in matter that is waiting to be tapped.

PLUTO IN PERSPECTIVE

Pluto is considered to be strong or weak in:
- **Scorpio:** (Dignity). Since its discovery in 1930, Pluto has been assigned rulership of Scorpio, along with Mars. There are good grounds for this; both Scorpio and Pluto are associated with all matters dark and hidden and with the process of transformation, whereby all that is outworn is stripped away, clearing the path for regenerative growth.
- **Taurus:** (Detriment) . Although Taurus has considerable strength and determination, it is also reluctant to change, whereas Pluto forces us to acknowledge that new growth only comes through change.
- Exaltation and Fall: There is no recognized Exaltation or Fall for Pluto. Some astrologers maintain that Leo is the best candidate for Exaltation, which would make Aquarius the sign of his Fall. However this is hotly disputed.

PLUTO THROUGH THE SIGNS

- **Shows how you face the need to make fundamental changes in your life**
- **Aspects of yourself that you keep hidden from view** • **Your compulsions and obsessions** • **Your self-destructive streak**

GEMINI (1883/84–1912/14) Intensifies curiosity; offers the potential to transform this sign's obsession with novelty into constancy of effort and depth of understanding; negatively, there may be mental confusion from an inability to make sense of life's developments.

CANCER (1912/14–1937/39) Intensifies the emotions and intuition; offers the potential to transform this sign's obsession with personal security into becoming supportive of others; negatively, there can be a hardness of feeling and an inclination to cling to the past.

LEO (1937/39–1956/58) Intensifies individuality; offers the potential to transform this sign's obsession with the need for control over its destiny so that it can work positively for the benefit of others; negatively, it increases self-absorption and the craving for recognition, while undermining self-confidence.

VIRGO (1956/58–1971/72) Intensifies the need to be effective; offers the potential to transform this sign's obsession with 'getting it right' into a force for changing outmoded establishment values; negatively it increases the tendency to worry and to criticize as well as general sense of dissatisfaction with life.

LIBRA (1971/72–1983/84) Intensifies social instincts, a sense of justice and the power of appearance; offers the potential to transform this sign's obsession with not rocking the boat into real assertiveness; stresses the need to work towards establishing equality between the sexes; negatively, it can manifest as a compulsive need for relationship and a domineering attitude to partners.

SCORPIO (1983/84–1995) Intensifies passions, a sense of purpose and a love of demanding challenges; offers the potential to transform this sign's obsession with power into a positive force for social regeneration; teaches that the path to self-mastery is through self-knowledge; negatively, there is a danger of becoming extremely manipulative, or of falling prey to periodic self-destructive urges.

SAGITTARIUS (1995–2008) Intensifies impulsiveness, idealism and the quest for (higher) knowledge; offers the potential to transform this sign's obsession with personal freedom into a positive force for social reform; spiritually, it emphasizes the value of personal experience above received faith; negatively, it can register as fanatical views, bigotry and striving for unattainable goals.

PLUTO THROUGH THE HOUSES

• **SHOWS IN WHAT AREA OF LIFE YOUR COMPULSIVE SIDE MANIFESTS** • **WHERE YOU SEEK SELF-TRANSFORMATION** • **WHERE ISSUES OF POWER ARISE** • **WHERE YOU FIND YOUR SELF-DESTRUCT BUTTON** • **WHERE YOU FEEL MOST UNDERMINED**

I **FIRST** Powerful, magnetic personality, determined to have its way; highly inscrutable; thrives in a crisis; prone to outbursts of rage; may suffer from destructive subconscious urges.

II **SECOND** The ability to transform something worthless into great value; potential for great riches and losses; hidden talents that materialize later in life; can be obsessively materialistic.

III **THIRD** Mentally acute, although possibly unstable; ingenious powers of persuasion; the mind of a detective; a cutting tongue; a taste for the macabre; subversive – a natural schemer.

IV **FOURTH** Skeletons in the family cupboard; driven by unconscious patterns of behaviour; domestic life a source of transformation; may seek to dominate the home; profoundly restless.

V **FIFTH** Powerful urge to express creativity, often against all odds; explosive emotions; passionate, obsessive love affairs; sexual excess; capable of remarkable achievements.

VI **SIXTH** The urge to be of service to the community; a workaholic; may become embroiled in power struggles at work; can be fanatical about health; possible healing ability.

VII **SEVENTH** Compulsive power struggles with partners; relationships can release hidden resentments or feelings of vulnerability; may find it difficult to trust and prefer to be alone.

VIII **EIGHTH** Enormous resilience in pursuing aims; driven to impose will on others; may use sex as a way of gaining power over others; breathing new life into ailing enterprises.

IX **NINTH** An intense, penetrating mind (knowledge is power); a gift for exposing hypocrisy; the search for faith or the meaning of existence; can be extremely self-righteous.

X **TENTH** Craves influence, but without being in the limelight (a power broker); a compulsive controller; powerful will to succeed; career choice heavily influenced by parent(s).

XI **ELEVENTH** Urgent need to be accepted by others (compulsive socializing); a zealous reformer – may place aims of group above friends and family; power struggles with friends.

XII **TWELFTH** Pressing need to confront self-destructive urges; deeply buried unconscious fears; remarkable powers of regeneration; capable of profound psychological insights.

CHAPTER 4

I   II   III   IV   V   VI   VII   VIII   IX   X   XI   XII

Self   Values   Mind   Home   Creativity   Daily life   Relationships   Union   Horizons   Ambition   Groups   Transcendence

THE
HOUSES

In order to make sense of how the planets and the signs work in our daily lives, we need a frame of reference that enables us to connect the planetary movements up above with events down here on Earth. This is the function of the houses. As opposed to the planets, which represent psychological energies or modes of action, and the signs, which colour the way these energies are expressed, the houses reveal the areas of life where all this energy is most likely to find an outlet.

Establishing the Four Angles

While the planets' positions in the signs are based on their apparent movement around the Earth, the houses are derived from the rotation of the Earth on its axis. They take their starting point from the degree of the Ecliptic that is rising on the eastern horizon at the time and place of birth. This point, known as the Ascendant, or Rising degree, is the cusp that marks the beginning of the first house. The sign in which this degree falls is called the Ascendant, or Rising, sign. As the Earth is constantly rotating, the Ascendant degree changes on average every four minutes, so it is vital to have the correct time of birth.

Although the Ascendant degree is a fixed point in the birth chart, it also forms one end of an axis. Its opposite point – the degree that is setting on the western horizon – is known as the Descendant. This degree always marks the cusp of the seventh house. For instance, if the Ascendant is at 25˚ Pisces, the Descendant will be at 25˚ Virgo.

Another important area of the chart is the degree of the Ecliptic directly overhead at the time and place of birth. This is called the Midheaven or MC – short for the Latin *Medium Coeli*, or the 'middle of the heavens'. The point opposite the MC is referred to as the IC or *Imum Coeli*, meaning the 'lowest heavens'. Collectively, these four points are known as the Angles, and the signs found here reveal a great deal about how we view and experience the world, as well as how the world sees and impinges on us. Their meanings are explained later on in this chapter.

Establishing the House Divisions

Although no one disputes that the Ascendant degree marks the beginning of the first house, there is fierce controversy about how the remaining houses should be divided. In fact, there are well over twenty established ways of calculating house divisions and, to this day, astrologers cannot agree on which is the correct one. Undoubtedly the simplest and, to those who use it, the most logical method of house division is the Equal House system (supplied with *The Instant Astrologer* software), which simply divides the Ecliptic into twelve equal houses of 30˚.

Regardless of which method of house division is used, the twelve houses are counted anti-clockwise, in numerical order, starting at the Ascendant degree. In most house systems, the MC–IC axis marks the cusp of the tenth and fourth houses respectively. In the Equal House system, however, this axis can fall anywhere between the eighth–second and eleventh–fifth houses *(see box below)*.

Linking the Houses

Like the signs, the houses are not viewed in isolation but are grouped according to basic definitions. In the Equal House system, perhaps the most common way of classifying the houses is by their Qualities:

• The Cardinal houses – one, four, seven and ten – are concerned with putting energy out into the world and making an impression. Cardinal house issues tend to revolve around the need for action.

• The Fixed houses – two, five, eight and eleven – tend to consolidate the energies set in motion by the Cardinal houses. Fixed house issues tend to revolve around the need for security and control.

• The Mutable houses – three, six, nine and twelve – digest the experiences of the Fixed houses, and set the wheels in motion for further action. Mutable house issues tend to revolve around the need to learn.

It is worth noting that while tradition maintains that the Cardinal houses are the strongest placements for planets, statistical research by the French psychologist Michel Gauquelin has suggested that this seems to be a more accurate description of the Mutable houses, especially the twelfth and ninth.

Another way of linking the houses is to pair opposites – the first with the seventh, the second with the eighth, and so on. The idea behind this practice is that the more personal and subjective areas of life

HOUSE SYSTEMS

The astronomical arguments for preferring one house system to another are extremely complex, and are beyond the remit of this book.

Briefly, the crux of the problem centres on two fundamental issues. Critics of the Equal House system object that the MC–IC axis can fall anywhere between the eighth–second and eleventh–fifth houses, depending on the time of the day and year we were born. Given the significance of this axis, the MC and the IC should always coincide with the cusps of tenth and fourth houses respectively.

Alternative methods of house division, which are collectively called the Quadrant House systems, resolve this problem, but they all fail in one way or another at latitudes near the Poles. Supporters of the Equal House system argue that it is inconsistent to use a system that works for certain parts of the globe but not for others. Besides, if users of the Quadrant systems are prepared to divide the zodiac signs symbolically into twelve equal sections, why should they take issue with treating the houses in the same way?

So which system is best? Unfortunately, there are no easy answers. The Equal House system was chosen for this book because, in our opinion, it is the simplest one for beginners to use.

associated with the first six houses in the hemisphere below the horizon are to some extent the mirror opposite of the more objective and social spheres of experience symbolized by the last six houses in the upper hemisphere. For instance, the focus on the self in the first house, is counterbalanced by the need for co-operation in relationships in the seventh.

House Meanings

Most traditional meanings attributed to each house appear totally unconnected to each other. This is not really surprising, given that traditional astrology was concerned solely with predicting the outcome of external events. While these meanings are not invalid, the psychological approach to astrology is to seek out the underlying principle – the core meaning of a house – that draws us, consciously or otherwise, towards certain types of experience. The houses do not operate simply on the level of external events, they also manifest within – as processes in the psyche that are looking for some kind of release or expression in our lives.

THE NATURAL ZODIAC

The Natural Zodiac links the signs, planets and houses in a way that gives each a place in the overall scheme of the birth chart. This zodiac, which is purely symbolic, aligns Aries, the first sign of the zodiac, with the Ascendant or first house, Taurus with the second house and so on, as shown in the chart (right). Moreover, the planetary ruler of each sign is also held to be the 'essential' or natural ruler of the house associated with that sign – for instance, Mars the ruler of Aries is also the essential ruler of the first house. What this means is that when a planet occupies either its natural sign or house it is considered to gain in 'weight' or significance. The Moon in the fourth house, for example, is said to add a powerful lunar harmonic to a chart. Obviously, the effect is further strengthened when a planet occupies both its natural sign and house.

However, many astrologers reject this system of correspondences, especially the practice of assigning planetary rulerships to the houses, on the grounds that it has no basis in tradition. While they have a point, it has to be said that there are undeniable parallels between the signs, houses and planets. Jupiter, Sagittarius and the ninth house, for example, are all associated with widening our horizons in one way or another.

The point to remember is that the planets, signs and houses are not identical in meaning. While the Natural Zodiac is a useful device for seeing how these three categories interrelate, the symbolic function of each is also distinct and should not be confused with the others.

In the chart, the traditional and 'modern' planetary rulerships for Scorpio, Aquarius and Pisces have been included as many astrologers use both.

THE FIRST HOUSE

• **THE FRONT DOOR TO OUR WORLD** • **REACTION TO OUR ENVIRONMENT**
• **HOW OTHERS SEE US** • **HOW ONE INITIATES ACTIONS** • **BEGINNINGS**
• **PHYSICAL APPEARANCE AND VITALITY**

The first house, beginning at the degree of the Ascendant, is often referred to as the the 'window' or 'front door' of the personality because it holds the key to how we view life, and the way we come across to others. Different signs colour the Ascendant with different hues, which affects the view both from within looking out and from the outside looking in.

In psychological terms, the first house represents the 'persona', or mask, that we initially present to the world, for it is only as people get to know us better that we begin to drop the mask and let them see us as we really are. As a result, the first house often hides our true individuality as characterized by the other planets, especially the Sun. For example, Libra in the first house would disguise the intensity of someone born with the Sun in Scorpio, by revealing a conciliatory, equivocating face that belies the natural desire of Scorpio to get to the heart of the matter.

> **THE FIRST HOUSE AT A GLANCE**
>
> **HOUSE CLASSIFICATION:** Cardinal
> **OPPOSITE HOUSE:** Seventh
> **NATURAL RULER:** Mars
> **NATURAL SIGN:** Aries
> **CORE MEANING:** Developing the means to tackle the world
> **TRADITIONAL MEANINGS:** Beginnings, outer appearances

Physically, the first house is said to 'determine' our appearance and our vitality. It also brings a youthful enthusiasm to our instinctive self-expression. As children, we quickly learn to use our first house – as modified by the sign and any planets found here – for it is our most accessible point of entry into a large and wondrous world. Because the Ascendant marks our beginning in this life, it is also reckoned to reveal how we approach any new situation or venture.

Planets in the First House: Planets in this house tend to express their energies instinctively, demanding to have their voice heard without much awareness of or consideration for others' viewpoints. As a result, it is often difficult for an individual with first house planets to see these energies objectively, especially in terms of the effect they have on other people. A notable exception to this rule is Saturn, who is often all too concerned with what others think.

THE SECOND HOUSE

• **THE PROCESS OF VALUING** • **SELF-WORTH** • **HOW WE DEVELOP OUR NATURAL RESOURCES** • **ATTITUDES TOWARDS MONEY AND POSSESSIONS** • **EMOTIONAL ATTACHMENTS TO OBJECTS**

The second house is traditionally known as the house of money and possessions. Although this description certainly covers the 'outer' significance of this house, it does not really convey the core meaning. On a fundamental level, the second house shows how we stand in relation to the physical world and, more specifically, how we strive to make the most out of whatever resources or talents are available to us – especially those indicated by the first house.

In this respect, the second house also reveals how we value ourselves and what we hope to gain from developing our natural talents to the full. For instance, Scorpio in the second house might take the innate sense of 'taste' of Libra in the first, and find some way of turning it to its advantage in the outside world, employing the characteristic Scorpio intensity.

The second house can also pinpoint the psychological needs that shape our attitude to money and material possessions. For instance, it can show whether we want money for the freedom it buys, or to satisfy the desire for material and emotional security. It can also throw light on why money seems to slip through our fingers, or why we attach so much value to the possessions we own.

Planets in the Second House: Planets in the second house tend to hold on hard to what they value. In most cases, this translates into possessiveness, or at least a strong attachment to what is owned. But with the more freedom-loving planets such as Uranus and, to a lesser extent, Jupiter, there may be a resistance to becoming burdened by such material attachments.

In their highest expression, planets in this house describe a need to create something of lasting value, something that can be left to posterity. In their lowest form, they indicate an entirely materialistic attitude, which can lead to even people being treated as possessions.

THE SECOND HOUSE AT A GLANCE

HOUSE CLASSIFICATION: Fixed

OPPOSITE HOUSE: Eighth

NATURAL RULER: Venus

NATURAL SIGN: Taurus

CORE MEANING: Developing values and physical resources

TRADITIONAL MEANINGS: Money and possessions

THE THIRD HOUSE

- **THE IMMEDIATE ENVIRONMENT** • **HABITUAL THOUGHT PATTERNS**
- **THE 'SUBJECTIVE' MIND** • **COMMUNICATION SKILLS** • **SPEECH AND WRITING** • **RELATIONS WITH NEIGHBOURS AND RELATIVES**

Traditionally, the third house lumps together what on the surface appears to be a motley collection of unrelated activities: siblings, neighbours, short journeys and mental abilities. But there is an underlying theme to this house because it deals with all those day-to-day affairs in our lives that could be best described as familiar. In other words it represents all those areas of life with which we interact on a daily basis, and to which we give little, if any, conscious thought. In this sense, for example, 'short journeys' represent any form of travel that does not involve dealing with unfamiliar settings or schedules; while siblings and neighbours refer to relationships that are part of our daily interactions.

At a fundamental level, this house shows how we develop our mental powers, particularly our ability to reason and analyse, and how we incorporate these into our everyday lives. In our dealings with others, these skills manifest as routine communications – both oral and written. Because the ability to think and communicate develops at an early age, learning is also governed by the third house. Planets affecting this house will therefore reveal something about our early education, but, most important of all, they will show our basic 'mindset' – how our subconscious thinking shapes our experience of everyday reality.

Planets in the Third House: A concentration of planets in the third house suggests an active mind, which busily engages itself in the affairs of the immediate environment. Often, the level of engagement is not especially deep or challenging, although with the 'active' planets such as Mars and Uranus, there can be a great deal of physical and mental restlessness. However, the 'watery' planets – the Moon and Neptune – can create problems in this house as they tend to distort communications by creating confusion in the unconscious thought processes.

> **THE THIRD HOUSE AT A GLANCE**
>
> **HOUSE CLASSIFICATION:** Mutable
> **OPPOSITE HOUSE:** Ninth
> **NATURAL RULER:** Mercury
> **NATURAL SIGN:** Gemini
> **CORE MEANING:** Developing mental resources
> **TRADITIONAL MEANINGS:** Communications and day-to-day affairs

THE FOURTH HOUSE

• **OUR PSYCHOLOGICAL FOUNDATIONS** • **OUR SENSE OF BELONGING** • **HOME AND FAMILY ISSUES** • **HOW WE ARE IN PRIVATE** • **CHILDHOOD CONDITIONING** • **THE 'NURTURING' OR 'HIDDEN' PARENT** • **LATER YEARS IN LIFE**

Lying at the base of the birth chart, the fourth house underpins our very existence, for it is here that we gain access to the most profound influences that shape us. At the deepest level, this house reflects our psychological foundations not just in a personal sense, but in a way that connects us to our ancestral, national and even our racial origins. Although much of this is likely to be unconscious, it nevertheless provides us with our sense of belonging – of where we fit into the world.

On a personal level, the fourth house represents the place we return to when we withdraw from the world 'out there'. In a literal sense, it symbolizes our physical home, and it shows what we are like behind closed doors. But it also shows how and where we look for emotional support and sustenance.

As far as childhood is concerned, this house has a great deal to say about our early conditioning and the kind of parenting we received, or at least felt we received. Confusingly, there are convincing arguments for attributing this house to the mother and the father – the debate focusing on whether it represents the 'nurturing' (mother) or 'hidden' (father) parent. In practice, though, the overall balance of the chart needs to be assessed before deciding which parent is represented here.

Traditionally, the fourth house is also associated with 'endings'. On one level, this corresponds to our later years in life when we retire from the world, while on another level it shows how we bring matters to a conclusion.

Planets in the Fourth House: A focus of planets in the fourth house suggests a highly personal approach to life, together with a strong need for privacy. Not all the planets find this house an easy place to be. Saturn and Uranus, for example, are inclined to feel awkward or out of place, and often view the whole issue of the home with an air of detachment and coldness.

THE FOURTH HOUSE AT A GLANCE

HOUSE CLASSIFICATION: Cardinal

OPPOSITE HOUSE: Tenth

NATURAL RULER: The Moon

NATURAL SIGN: Cancer

CORE MEANING: Developing psychological foundations

TRADITIONAL MEANINGS: The home, family background, end of life

---

THE FIFTH HOUSE

- **CREATIVE INSTINCTS** • **THE URGE TO EXPRESS OURSELVES SPONTANEOUSLY**
- **AFFAIRS OF THE HEART** • **SPECULATIVE VENTURES** • **CHILDREN**
- **LEISURE ACTIVITIES** • **PLAY AND GAMES**

Emerging from the fetid darkness of the fourth house, we enter the imaginative realm of the fifth. Traditionally, this house includes such disparate activities as creativity, games, gambling, pleasures, children and love. However, none of these descriptions really touches the essence of this house's meaning, which is to play. This is not play in the sense that we commonly understand it – an escape from the responsibilities of the outside world. It is the productive play of free association, of active imagination, that enables us to express the core of our being and discover who we truly are.

In many ways, the fifth house corresponds to the child within us daring to venture, win or fail, in order to discover what life throws back – hence this house's association with gambling. This house therefore holds the key to our self-development in childhood, our ability to build bridges between our inner universe and the outer world and the pleasure we derive from creative self-expression by engaging ourselves in what we are doing with our total being – simply for the love of it.

As adults, perhaps the most natural form of self-expression is love – another fifth house affair – for whereas children love to play, adults love to love. And it is when we are in love that we feel most complete, most in touch with ourselves – often with a childlike sense of wonderment. Finally, the drive to play finds it release through the adult's love of children, and the fifth house has much to say about how we relate to children in general, but especially our own.

Planets in the Fifth House: Planets in this house describe how creative energy is released. With most planets, the emphasis will tend to be on a wealth of ideas, as well as a strong 'pleasure principle', but with the heavyweight planets such as Saturn and Pluto, there can be intensity of expression that is ill at ease with the symbolism of this house.

THE FIFTH HOUSE AT A GLANCE

HOUSE CLASSIFICATION: Fixed
OPPOSITE HOUSE: Eleventh
NATURAL RULER: The Sun
NATURAL SIGN: Leo
CORE MEANING: Developing creative self-expression
OUTER MEANINGS: Love affairs, leisure activities, children

THE SIXTH HOUSE

• DAILY ROUTINES AND OBLIGATIONS • WORK AND RELATIONS IN THE
WORKPLACE • PRACTICAL SKILLS • HEALTH ISSUES • LIFESTYLE
• THE BALANCE BETWEEN MIND AND BODY

Traditionally associated with work and health, the sixth house is a watershed between the upper and lower hemispheres of the birth chart. As the last house below the horizon, preceding the house of personal relationships, it prepares us for our first encounters with the external world – and the notion of co-operating with others. But it also follows on from the fifth where, as we have seen, the creative principle prevails. No matter how good our creative ideas may be, they require hard work and skill to bring them into being. The focus of this house, therefore, is on necessity – the need to adjust to the mundane realities of life.

This can be an extremely testing house for planets to handle. On the one hand, it demands that we attend to the endless number of practicalities, in particular our work and our relations with work colleagues, that we ignore at our peril, a fact that is made clear by this house's position opposite the twelfth – the so-called house of 'self-undoing'. On the other hand, too much time devoted to our daily obligations and not enough on pleasurable pursuits can erode our physical and mental wellbeing, especially if our work holds little meaning for us. This is why this house is concerned with health; at a fundamental level, it directs us to find a balance between the demands of external reality and our 'me' time. If it is ignored the finely tuned balance between the mind and body will suffer.

Planets in the Sixth House:
Planets in the sixth house can indicate healing abilities or an interest in health and fitness issues. They can also reveal how well we work with others, as well as the kind of work to which we may be suited. Uranus and Neptune here may find it particularly hard to find fulfilling employment, due to a restlessness of spirit and frustration with routine working practices.

THE SIXTH HOUSE AT A GLANCE

HOUSE CLASSIFICATION: Mutable

OPPOSITE HOUSE: Twelfth

NATURAL RULER: Mercury

NATURAL SIGN: Virgo

CORE MEANING: Developing the skills to deal with external necessity

OUTER MEANINGS: Work, service, health issues

THE SEVENTH HOUSE

• **ONE-TO-ONE RELATIONSHIPS** • **OPEN ENEMIES** • **HOW WE CO-OPERATE OR COMPETE WITH OTHERS** • **PARTNERSHIPS OF ALL KINDS** • **LAWSUITS** • **QUALITIES WE FEEL WE LACK** • **WHAT WE PROJECT ONTO OTHERS**

Opposing the first house of the 'self', the seventh takes us into the realm of the 'not-self', traditionally defined as the house of partnerships, marriage and open enemies. While it is certainly true that the sign on the seventh house cusp can describe what we look for in a partner, this is not the core meaning of this house.

At the heart of seventh house experiences is the mirror that life holds up to us. Where the first house says, 'Look at me, this is who I am,' the seventh says, 'Let me look at you, who are you?' In other words, this house describes what we least recognize in ourselves and therefore unconsciously seek in our most intimate relationships.

Through our seventh house we often project qualities we feel we lack, or subconsciously dislike in ourselves, on to those with whom we become closely involved. Ideally, with experience, we can learn to 'own' these qualities for ourselves. But if we continually give our power away by depending on others to compensate for us, the build up of resentment can lead to open hostility and even the law courts – hence the litigious side of the seventh house.

Ultimately, this house teaches us that the path to greater self-awareness is through understanding others' viewpoints. Repeated lack of success in our close relationships, for instance, tells us more about ourselves than it does about our partners – as do conflicts with our enemies. The lessons of the seventh may be tough, but they are fair, for we only get back what we put out.

THE SEVENTH HOUSE AT A GLANCE

HOUSE CLASSIFICATION: Cardinal
OPPOSITE HOUSE: First
NATURAL RULER: Venus
NATURAL SIGN: Libra
CORE MEANING: Expanding self-awareness through one-to-one relationships
OUTER MEANINGS: Marriage, partnerships, open enmity

Planets in the Seventh House: Planets in the seventh indicate a strong need for relationship, and describe qualities we bring into and receive from our close encounters. Mars and Uranus, for instance, may find it hard to give up their individuality, a resistance that, through the mechanism of projection, can be acted out by either party in a relationship.

THE EIGHTH HOUSE

• DEATH AND REBIRTH • THE FRUITS OF WHAT WE SHARE WITH OTHERS • SEXUAL ENERGY • OTHER PEOPLE'S MONEY AND POSSESSIONS • EMOTIONAL UNION • LEGACIES • LOSSES • CRISES • THE 'OCCULT'

The eighth house is ominously referred to as the house of death and legacies – a relic from the days of predictive astrology. Although the link remains, the kind of death involved is no longer seen as physical, but transformational, for the issues at stake in the eighth are concerned more with psychological death and resurrection.

On the emotional level, this house signifies our search for security, particularly in our close relationships. In part, this is an inheritance from the seventh house, where the seeds of relationship are sown. But the eighth, as the house of other people's values and resources, opposes the second, the house of our own values and resources. Consequently, the eighth describes how we merge with others both on the practical front – for instance, through joint finances – and on the emotional plane, especially through sex.

Any true merger must involve a loss of individuality for the union to transform into something more than its separate parts – witness the temporary loss of ego consciousness experienced during orgasm, which is frequently described as a symbolic death. (The same is true of the 'enlightenment experience' of mysticism, which is why this house is linked with the 'occult'.)

The transformation entailed in eighth house experiences can be a source of renewed vigour and security. But if we resist making the adjustments required of this house, our dealings with others can become a battleground of warring passions, power struggles and emotional crises.

Planets in the Eighth House: Planets in this house show how we look for emotional security through merging with others. Jupiter in the eighth, for example, may seek security through a shared interest in religion, metaphysics or mysticism, wealthy partners or, at its most dissolute, through endless sexual encounters.

THE EIGHTH HOUSE AT A GLANCE

HOUSE CLASSIFICATION: Fixed

OPPOSITE HOUSE: Second

NATURAL RULER: Pluto/Mars

NATURAL SIGN: Scorpio

CORE MEANING: Expanding self-awareness through merging with others

OUTER MEANINGS: Other peoples resources, legacies, sex, death

---

THE NINTH HOUSE

- **BELIEF SYSTEMS** • **THE 'OBJECTIVE' MIND** • **FOREIGN TRAVEL AND CULTURES**
- **THE SEARCH FOR MEANING** • **CONSCIOUSNESS EXPANSION**
- **HIGHER EDUCATION** • **RELIGION** • **LAW**

The ninth house endeavours to give meaning to all the seemingly random experiences of life by incorporating them into a coherent set of beliefs or universal truths. In many ways, this house develops the themes of the eighth house by synthesizing our experience of others, and what these encounters teach us about ourselves, into ideas about the nature of existence. This explains the ninth's traditional link with religion, philosophy and the law, as all these disciplines address the question of where we as individuals fit into the greater scheme of things.

In a sense, the ninth house is the polar opposite of the third. Whereas the third deals with our instinctive mental programming, the ninth ventures into unfamiliar territory, broadening the mind through 'journeys' that increase our awareness of the universe and, hopefully, our place in it. These unfamiliar journeys can be literal, taking us to foreign lands, but more often than not they symbolize consciousness-expanding pursuits: further education, spiritual enlightenment, hallucinogenic trips – in fact, anything that gives us fresh insight into the nature of existence.

It is this ability to give meaning, to conceptualize, that distinguishes the mental activities of the ninth house from the third. In the ninth we enter the realm of the 'objective' mind – which deals with where we stand in relation to the whole – as opposed to the 'subjective' mind of the third, which simply defines our relationship to our immediate surroundings.

Planets in the Ninth House: Planets in the ninth are often 'systems orientated', in the sense that they look for basic patterns or laws that underpin existence. For example Saturn might want to investigate the physical laws of the universe, while Neptune may be drawn to look for spiritual truths. On the other hand, planets here may simply denote a love of travel and foreign cultures.

THE NINTH HOUSE AT A GLANCE

HOUSE CLASSIFICATION: Mutable

OPPOSITE HOUSE: Third

NATURAL RULER: Jupiter

NATURAL SIGN: Sagittarius

CORE MEANING: Expanding self-awareness through broadening horizons

OUTER MEANINGS: Philosophy of life, travel, higher education

THE TENTH HOUSE

• **OUR PUBLIC ROLE** • **HOW WE STRIVE FOR RECOGNITION** • **CAREER AND AMBITION** • **RELATIONS WITH AUTHORITY** • **THE IMPORTANCE OF STATUS** • **THE 'DISCIPLINARIAN' OR 'TEACHING' PARENT**

Perched at the top of the chart, the tenth house takes the insights gained from the ninth and applies them to the 'real' world of action. As it also opposes our most private world, in the shape of the fourth house, the tenth is where we present our most public face. Commonly known as the house of attainment, reputation and authority, the tenth house describes our standing in the world in terms of how we would most like to be seen and the contribution we would like to make to society.

Traditionally, the tenth is also often referred to as the house of career, but this is only really true insofar as our career is an expression of our worldly ambition – that is, if we identify with what we do and are identified by it. If this is not the case, and it is just a means of earning a living, then it corresponds more to sixth house type of work.

Tenth house functions are strongly shaped during childhood by our parents, or at least by the one who most represents authority and discipline. Again, as with the fourth house, there are no fixed rules for determining which parent plays the dominant tenth house role – the consensus is that it is the parent whom we perceive to have taught us the ways of the world. Later in life, this house shows our response to authority figures in general and, if we make it to the top, how we handle authority ourselves.

One point worth bearing in mind is that tenth house energies can reveal how our career expectations may be influenced by our parents, and how we can burden our children with our own unfulfilled ambitions.

Planets in the Tenth House: Tenth house planets tend to stress a need for worldly achievement and recognition and a desire to be in control of our lives. But they are no guarantee of fame and fortune. With the Sun in the tenth, our sense of identity can become inextricably bound up with our public image, although success and social standing can just as easily be sought through a partner as through our own achievements.

THE TENTH HOUSE AT A GLANCE

HOUSE CLASSIFICATION: Cardinal

OPPOSITE HOUSE: Fourth

NATURAL RULER: Saturn

NATURAL SIGN: Capricorn

CORE MEANING: Expanding self-awareness through public role

OUTER MEANINGS: Status, reputation, vocation, authority

THE ELEVENTH HOUSE

• **The need for friendship** • **Social life and circle** • **Shared interests and ideals** • **Group activities** • **Social causes** • **How we blend with the needs of the group**

Where the tenth house describes our standing in society as an individual, the eleventh defines our relationship to society on the collective level. This is the house of groups and friends, where we seek to identify with something greater than ourselves – as opposed to the fifth, where the focus is on exploring our self-identity for own pleasure. Although both houses are concerned with self-expression, the eleventh is not really self-oriented, for it operates in a social setting that requires us to temper the desire to express ourselves with the need to get along with others.

On a day-to-day basis, the eleventh house concerns what are loosely called 'friends'. These are not intimate friendships, which properly belong to the seventh house, but acquaintances from our wider social circle – people we meet regularly, perhaps at the local pub or health club, or at parties. On a broader scale, this house denotes the kind of organizations that we might be tempted to join, because they embody the same interests or social ideals as our own.

This house is also referred to as a house of ambition, and it is common to find people with an eleventh house emphasis actively involved in public life, having climbed their way up the organization hierarchy. But, whatever the goals, eleventh house ambitions, unlike the tenth, cannot be achieved purely through individual effort – they need the support of the group.

Planets in the Eleventh House: Apart from revealing the kind of social life and friends that attract us, planets in this house show our need to identify with a social cause or group. The Sun in the eleventh, for instance, has a strong need for a group identity, as does the Moon. However, Saturn, Uranus and Pluto may find the group ethos too restrictive, although Pluto can just as readily aim for a position of influence within a group.

THE ELEVENTH HOUSE AT A GLANCE

HOUSE CLASSIFICATION: Fixed

OPPOSITE HOUSE: Fifth

NATURAL RULER: Uranus/Saturn

NATURAL SIGN: Aquarius

CORE MEANING: Expanding self-awareness through wider social issues

OUTER MEANINGS: Friends, groups, hopes and wishes

THE TWELFTH HOUSE

• SACRIFICE AND SERVICE TO A GREATER CAUSE • FEARS THAT WE PROJECT ON TO OTHERS • THE UNINTEGRATED, UNCONSCIOUS SELF • HOSPITALS AND PRISONS • ESCAPISM

As the rhythm of the houses unfolds, we finally reach the twelfth, the most puzzling of all the houses to unravel. On the one hand, it is the last in the cycle, and therefore symbolizes completion; on the other, as it lies just above the horizon, it is the first to receive the light of dawn, and so stands at the beginning of a cycle. Both these standpoints have a bearing on this house's meaning.

Traditionally, the twelfth holds a grim portfolio, which includes secret enemies, acts of 'self-undoing' and institutions such as hospitals and prisons. These descriptions become clearer if we understand the polarity between the sixth and twelfth houses: the sixth represents the need to incorporate external reality into our psyches, whereas the twelfth symbolizes the need for the complete integration of our psyches with life.

Because of their position in the birth chart, twelfth house energies are extremely susceptible to early conditioning. If these energies are perceived

---

THE TWELFTH HOUSE AT A GLANCE

HOUSE CLASSIFICATION: Mutable
OPPOSITE HOUSE: Sixth
NATURAL RULER: Neptune /Jupiter
NATURAL SIGN: Pisces
CORE MEANING: Expanding self-awareness through self-integration
OUTER MEANINGS: Self-undoing, sacrifice, confinement, secret enemies

---

to be threatening in any way, the ego – adapting as it does to the demands of the external world – will bury them in the unconscious. But these hidden fears will eventually re-emerge as neuroses, people or events that appear to subvert our intentions. This accounts for the twelfth house's association with ill-health and secret enemies.

Alternatively, suppression can result in escapist and destructive behaviour. However, through transcending the ego, sacrificing some of its most cherished preconceptions, we can assimilate twelfth house energies into our lives, and find a renewed sense of purpose in the process.

Planets in the Twelfth House: For people who have undertaken a journey of self-discovery, or for whom twelfth house planets do not present a particular threat, planets in this house, especially the Sun, can be one of the most powerful indicators of achievement and fulfilment in life.

THE ANGLES

THE ASCENDANT-DESCENDANT AND
THE MC-IC AXES IN THE BIRTH CHART

We share our birthdays with countless other people around the world, but our chart is unique to us because our time and place of birth determines the most personal points in the chart. These are the Ascendant and the MC (Midheaven) and their opposite points, the Descendant and the IC.

The Ascendant: shows what energies were being pulled out of the darkness of our inner world below the horizon into the light above at the moment of birth. This is the point at which the self becomes visible to the world. The sign on the Ascendant describes how we approach and view life, and how we come across to others.

The Descendant: is the point where external reality impacts on our inner world, as the light dips beneath the horizon. Whereas the Ascendant is concerned with the instinctive self stamping itself on the world, the Descendant shows the self in relation to others – what we seek, consciously or otherwise, from relationships. It also symbolizes aspects of ourselves that we may look for others to provide.

The MC (Midheaven): reveals our energies at their most elevated, and therefore signifies our aspirations; qualities we strive to develop in order to impress; the direction we wish to take; our conscious goals; our need for public recognition and social position; our ambition and our career or vocation.

The IC: signifies the exact opposite to the MC: our least consciously acknowledged self; the roots of our being; our deepest motivations; our past and family conditioning. Whereas the MC generally describes the direction in which we are heading, the IC shows us the direction from which we are coming.

Floating MC–IC: Whenever the MC–IC axis falls in different houses to the tenth and fourth, it offers further insight into our conscious and unconscious motives. Many astrologers believe that this axis also symbolizes our idealized view of ourselves. So, if the MC–IC represents our most personal dreams of what we would like to become, the tenth and fourth houses show what in reality – given practical considerations, such as our family background – we are most likely to achieve.

THE ANGLES

THE ASCENDANT-DESCENDANT AXIS THROUGH THE SIGNS
ARIES–VIRGO

ARIES ASCENDANT

Typical strengths: enthusiastic, assertive, direct, honest. Needs to channel dynamic energies into enterprising ventures; actions can be fearless and often inspired.
Typical weaknesses: over-aggressive, abrasive, impatient; lack of progress generates great frustration.
Libra Descendant: shows a need to take account of other people's feelings and opinions.

TAURUS ASCENDANT

Typical strengths: methodical, steady, sensual, self-reliant. Needs a stable environment within which to function. Derives huge enjoyment from physical pleasures, refusing to be rushed.
Typical weaknesses: lazy, stubborn, over-indulgent, uncommunicative; becomes easily habit-bound.
Scorpio Descendant: calls for outmoded patterns of behaviour to be transformed.

GEMINI ASCENDANT

Typical strengths: inquisitive, versatile, lively, mobile. Needs constant and varied stimulation to occupy the mind. Enjoys communicating, exchanging views and dealing with people.
Typical weaknesses: talking too much, changeability, easily distracted; scatters energies too thinly.
Sagittarius Descendant: teaches the value of finding a mental framework to gain depth of understanding.

CANCER ASCENDANT

Typical strengths: intuitive, tenacious, shrewd, gentle. Needs to use acute sensitivity in a nurturing rather than a defensive way, although can be immensely protective and supportive of loved ones.
Typical weaknesses: moody, easily slighted, subjective; can be far too dependent emotionally.
Capricorn Descendant: provides the strength and detachment to stabilize fluctuating emotions.

LEO ASCENDANT

Typical strengths: dignified, authoritative, big-hearted, courageous. Needs to feel appreciated to make the most of creative talents. Enjoys splendour and good living.
Typical weaknesses: self-important, arrogant, bossy, pretentious; expects respect as a matter of right.
Aquarius Descendant: encourages a social sense of awareness, beyond the needs of the self.

VIRGO ASCENDANT

Typical strengths: discriminating, modest, conscientious, observant. Needs to acquire practical, detailed information about how things work; dislikes being kept in the dark.
Typical weaknesses: fussy, over-critical, pedantic; can be obsessed with correctness.
Pisces Descendant: indicates a need to become more 'fluid' by dismantling over-rigid boundaries.

THE ANGLES

THE ASCENDANT-DESCENDANT AXIS THROUGH THE SIGNS
LIBRA–PISCES

LIBRA ASCENDANT

Typical strengths: charming, placid, sociable, considerate, romantic. Needs a partner to provide balance and purpose in life; usually has a fine aesthetic sense and an awareness of how to please.
Typical weaknesses: narcissistic, frivolous, precious, indecisive; often craves approval.
Aries Descendant: encourages the need to take a firm stand and fight for what one wants.

SCORPIO ASCENDANT

Typical strengths: resourceful, dedicated, passionate. Needs to channel intense emotions positively; enjoys exploring what makes other people tick, but does not always know when to pull back.
Typical weaknesses: secretive, wilful, ruthless, jealous, vindictive, fanatical; often fears letting go of control.
Taurus Descendant: suggests a need to temper extreme reactions and create a more harmonious environment.

SAGITTARIUS ASCENDANT

Typical strengths: optimistic, open-minded, cheerful, active. Needs to direct energy and enthusiasm towards far-reaching aims, usually with some ideal in mind; enjoys preaching to the unconverted.
Typical weaknesses: irresponsible, hypocritical disorganized, self-pitying; can take others for granted.
Gemini Descendant: suggests accepting the world for what it is rather than wanting constantly to change it.

CAPRICORN ASCENDANT

Typical strengths: self-disciplined, logical, industrious, purposeful. Needs to be self-sufficient and in control; has the ability to find the right means to achieve the desired end.
Typical weaknesses: cynical, impersonal, inhibited, shy; overly concerned with reputation and position.
Cancer Descendant: stresses the need for greater sensitivity and an emotionally supportive environment.

AQUARIUS ASCENDANT

Typical strengths: independent, rational, quirky, constructive, unpredictable. Needs to have wide-ranging interests to keep active mind occupied; often displays an intuitive grasp of a situation.
Typical weaknesses: dogmatic, distant, naive; can be unthinkingly dismissive of personal emotions.
Leo Descendant: calls for greater emotional warmth and respect for others' needs.

PISCES ASCENDANT

Typical strengths: imaginative, receptive, sensitive, often immensely creative. Needs to find an outlet for compassionate nature through some kind of service to others.
Typical weaknesses: vague, gullible, manipulative, invasive; can become a victim of own good intentions.
Virgo Descendant: calls for the ability to discriminate and to understand the meaning of personal boundaries.

THE ANGLES

THE MC–IC AXIS THROUGH THE SIGNS
ARIES–VIRGO

ARIES MIDHEAVEN

Typical strengths: comes across as positive, determined and fiercely ambitious. Looks to take the initiative and to set clearly focused objectives; can indicate a physical occupation or flair for business. **Typical weaknesses:** over-hasty, intolerant; makes enemies easily through ruthless pursuit of aims. **Libra IC:** suggests the need for an inner sense of equilibrium for one's individuality to flower.

TAURUS MIDHEAVEN

Typical strengths: comes across as persistent, conscientious, stable. Looks for job security and to improve social standing by cultivating the right contacts; can indicate artistic talent in the widest sense. **Typical weaknesses:** slow, inflexible, narrow-minded, hard to satisfy; can be obsessed with material needs. **Scorpio IC:** suggests that ambitions may stem from deep-rooted emotional insecurities.

GEMINI MIDHEAVEN

Typical strengths: comes across as alert, bright, often articulate. Sees knowledge as a means to self-advancement; likes to explore as many outlets as possible; can indicate more than one profession. **Typical weaknesses:** unstable, cynical, lack of concentration; often guilty of a butterfly mentality. **Sagittarius IC:** suggests a need to invest one's ambitions with a sense of vision.

CANCER MIDHEAVEN

Typical strengths: comes across as dedicated, shrewd, insistent. Looks for success to feed security needs; mild manner often hides fierce ambition; can indicate career in business or public service. **Typical weaknesses:** resentful, grasping, defensive; devious methods can cause an atmosphere of distrust. **Capricorn IC:** suggests that the desire for fame and fortune is fuelled by a need for public recognition.

LEO MIDHEAVEN

Typical strengths: comes across as genial, self-confident, imposing. Holds high ambitions and looks to be in charge and organize affairs; strong powers of persuasion; can indicate managerial abilities. **Typical weaknesses:** selfish, pompous, huffy; can try to assert authority by playing high and mighty. **Aquarius IC:** suggests a need to incorporate wider social issues in one's personal ambitions.

VIRGO MIDHEAVEN

Typical strengths: comes across as organized, discerning, well-informed. Looks to establish a secure career; lays careful plans; can indicate a career involving precision work or craftsmanship. **Typical weaknesses:** over-cautious; hypersensitive, can become obsessed with particulars. **Pisces IC:** suggests a need to be less rational and open oneself up to the intuitive side of the mind.

T H E   A N G L E S

THE MC–IC AXIS THROUGH THE SIGNS
LIBRA–PISCES

LIBRA MIDHEAVEN

Typical strengths: comes across as tactful, co-operative, adaptable. Looks to canvass support from people offering professional advancement; can indicate natural negotiating skills.

Typical weaknesses: unctuous, exploitative; pleasant manner can mask a mercilessly calculating mind.

Aries Descendant: suggests a need to be more forthright about one's motives.

SCORPIO MIDHEAVEN

Typical strengths: comes across as highly focused, persevering, industrious. Likes to be in control; has the courage to dismantle in order to rebuild; can indicate the need for a 'mission'.

Typical weaknesses: excessive, defensive, over-powering; can overestimate own abilities and stamina.

Taurus IC: suggests the need to adopt a more relaxed approach to life and to enjoy what one does.

SAGITTARIUS MIDHEAVEN

Typical strengths: comes across as up-beat, high-minded, far-sighted. Looks for inner or spiritual fulfilment as much as material success; can indicate managerial abilities or business acumen.

Typical weaknesses: unreliable, impractical, inconstant; can suffer from inflated self-importance.

Gemini IC: suggests the need to take a more light-hearted attitude to personal beliefs.

CAPRICORN MIDHEAVEN

Typical strengths: comes across as reliable, self-contained, capable. Driven by worldly ambition, but often ploughs a solitary, cautious furrow; can indicate delayed success, finding a vocation later in life.

Typical weaknesses: pessimistic, unimaginative; reserved exterior often masks considerable self-doubt.

Cancer IC: suggests that ambitions are nurtured by an emotional need to be accepted by one's public.

AQUARIUS MIDHEAVEN

Typical strengths: comes across as gregarious, perceptive, fair-minded. Looks for freedom of movement and expression; can indicate interest in ground-breaking ideas or technologies.

Typical weaknesses: undisciplined, rebellious, intolerant, unrealistic; likes to dominate in a group.

Leo IC: suggests a need for a more personal approach in dealings with others.

PISCES MIDHEAVEN

Typical strengths: comes across as easy-going, imaginative. Takes a wait-and-see approach to career, often relying on lucky breaks; can indicate creative flair or concern for the welfare of others.

Typical weaknesses: indecisive, manipulative, chaotic; tries to be all things to all people.

Virgo IC: suggests a need to make a clearer distinction between real and imagined ambitions.

PLANETS IN THE
HOUSES

The traditional guidelines for interpreting how the planets and signs interact with the houses are as follows:

1. One or more planets occupies a house

This is most immediate and powerful way that a planet manifests its energies through a house. The more planets that occupy a house, the more outlets that house will have in daily life.

2. A planet in one house aspects a planet in another

This is a development of (1). Although we shall be looking at the aspects in the next two chapters, it is important to raise the point here that aspects between planets also implicate the relevant houses.

3. A planet aspects a house cusp

This is particularly important when the cusp in question is the Ascendant and, by association, the Descendant. In the Equal House system, this rule seldom applies to the MC–IC axis, as it rarely coincides with the cusps of the tenth and fourth houses. Aspects to the other house cusps are widely believed to be much less significant, although some astrologers use them.

4. A planet rules the sign on a house cusp

Regardless of how many planets occupy a house, the position of the ruler of the sign on a house cusp – referred to as the 'accidental' ruler – must also be taken into account. So, if the cusp of the second house is in Taurus, the accidental ruler is Venus, and her sign and house position in the chart, together with any aspects she makes to other planets, will have a bearing on second house matters. For a full chart interpretation, this process should be applied to each sign ruler on the cusp of all twelve houses *(see 6)*.

5. A house is occupied by its essential ruler

As mentioned in the description of the Natural Zodiac *(see page 88)*, if the essential ruler of a house occupies its own house, its position in the birth chart is strengthened.

6. Chart ruler

The planet ruling the sign on the Ascendant is called the chart ruler. It is an important factor in the chart, because its position and aspects to other points in the chart modify the way the all-important Ascendant is expressed. A Leo Ascendant, for example, would make the Sun the chart ruler and give the chart an overall 'solar' flavour.

7. Empty houses

As there are twelve houses and only ten planets, at least two houses in a chart will be untenanted. This does not mean that an empty house plays no role in a chart, just that there is no planetary focus in that area. To discover how such a house is 'activated', follow the procedure set out in (4) – look at the sign and house positions and the aspects of the planet ruling the sign on the cusp of an empty house.

| Conjunction | Semisextile | Semisquare | Sextile | Square | Trine | Sesquiquadrate | Quincunx | Opposition |

THE
ASPECTS

As the planets move along their orbits at widely differing speeds, they appear from our standpoint on Earth to engage in a cosmic dialogue with one another. This imaginary exchange of views takes the form of a constantly changing pattern of angular relationships, or distances, between the planets, which are measured in degrees and minutes of longitude (there are sixty minutes to a degree).

When a chart is drawn up for a certain time and place, these relationships between the planets are 'freeze-framed', giving us a snapshot of the planetary 'cross-talk' for that particular moment. However, astrology is only interested in certain types of angular relationships, because they are considered to stand out above the general hubbub of planetary chatter going on in a chart. These particular angular relationships form the basis of the planetary aspects in the birth chart.

The aspects, which are always measured by the shortest distance between the planets concerned, are assumed to correspond to prominent character traits in our psychological make-up that are in a more-or-less permanent state of interaction.

Major and Minor Aspects

Traditionally, astrology classifies these aspects as 'major' and 'minor'. The major aspects are derived by dividing the 360° circle of the Ecliptic by one, two, three, four and six.

Aspect Angle	Aspect Name	Aspect Symbol	Division of Circle by
0°	conjunction	☌	1
60°	sextile	⚹	6
90°	square	□	4
120°	trine	△	3
180°	opposition	☍	2

Over the centuries astrologers have found that divisions of the Ecliptic by other whole numbers, such as five (the quintile), seven (the septile), nine (the novile) and so on, also yield telling insights into our character. However, because they take us into the realm of advanced astrology, these aspect types have not been included in *The Instant Astrologer* software. As they will not appear on the birth chart you produce, they are not considered here.

The minor aspects are simply multiple subdivisions of the numbers two and three. For instance, the semisquare divides the circle by eight, or 2 X 2 X 2, whereas with the semisextile the circle is divided by twelve, or 3 X 2 X 2.

Aspect Angle	Aspect Name	Aspect Symbol	Division of Circle by
30⁰	semisextile	⊻	1/12
45⁰	semisquare	∠	1/8
135⁰	sesquiquadrate	⍁	3/8
150⁰	quincunx	⊼	5/12

Before looking at what the individual aspects mean, various factors need to be taken into account.

• **Orbs:** Aspects in a chart are rarely exact, and their effects are considered to operate within a margin of several degrees either side of exactitude. This sphere of influence is known as an orb (*see box below*).

• **Applying and separating aspects:** When an aspect is not exact it is either 'applying' – yet to reach exactitude – or 'separating', that is, past its point of greatest intensity. Some astrologers believe that applying aspects are stronger than separating ones, and give them a correspondingly larger orb; others see little or no difference between them. This is yet another example of how widely people's experience of astrology differs.

There is universal agreement, however, that the closer an aspect is to being exact, the more potent its effects will be.

• **Planetary protocol:** When interpreting aspects, the traditional approach is to follow a planetary pecking order whereby the further a planet is from the Sun the more weight it is given. (In this hierarchy, the Moon always follows the Sun.) For example, when the Moon is in aspect to Pluto, it is Pluto's 'influence' that is believed to dominate. While this is a helpful way of learning the relative 'weight' of each planet –

ASPECT ORBS

The question of what orb to allow aspects is one of the thorniest issues in astrology. The problem lies in establishing at what point the effects of an aspect start and stop. It is rather like trying to determine when the sound of a passing car comes into and fades out of earshot. It depends on many factors, not least the level of background noise. Aspects work in an equally subtle way, gradually increasing in intensity as they approach exactitude, and slowly merging into the background as the planets separate.

Some astrologers use extremely wide orbs – up to 15⁰ for a conjunction – whereas others use orbs of no more than 5⁰. The trouble with wide orbs is that they can be indiscriminate – the more planets that end up

in aspect, the more the significance of close aspects is lost. With tight orbs, the opposite is true – a situation can arise in which there are very few aspects in a chart.

The conventional practice, which is used in *The Instant Astrologer* software, is to give the conjunction, square, trine and opposition orbs of 8⁰ either side of exactitude, the sextile 6⁰ and the remainder 2⁰. There are, however, exceptions to these conventions:
• Aspects to the Sun and Moon – some astrologers also include the chart ruler – are traditionally given orbs of 2⁰ more than the other planets.
• Planets involved in aspect patterns – a series of interconnected aspects involving three or more planets (*see Chapter 6*) – are also given wider orbs.

and a method adopted in this chapter – it is essential to look at the overall strength of each planet in the chart. For example, the Moon or its sign Cancer may be prominent in the chart, in which case the Moon's qualities could easily hold sway over Pluto. By the same token, if Scorpio or Pluto are strong, then Pluto's energies are likely to prevail.

• **Planets in aspect:** Aspects used to be classified as 'benefic' or 'malefic'. Modern astrology no longer takes this decidedly deterministic, line but sees them as either 'hard' or 'challenging', or 'soft' or 'flowing'. Hard aspects indicate areas of potential tension and instability in the personality, whereas soft aspects represent areas of potential ease and stability. As both categories can have positive or negative effects, neither is inherently good nor bad. For this reason, it is more important to look at the nature of the planets in an aspect than to focus too much on whether the aspect itself is, say, a square (hard) or a trine (soft).

As shown in the table *(below)*, some planetary pairings are held to be more compatible than others, while some are 'neutral' – they may get along or they may not. However, these pairings are by no means written in stone. It is perfectly possible to make a hash out of favourable planetary pairings as it is to benefit from ostensibly challenging ones.

Table of Planetary Pairings

	☉	☽	☿	♀	♂	♃	♄	♅	♆	
☽	N									☽
☿	N	N								☿
♀	S	S	S							♀
♂	N	H	N	N						♂
♃	S	S	S	S	N					♃
♄	N	H	N	H	N	N				♄
♅	N	H	S	N	H	N	N			♅
♆	H	N	H	N	N	H	N	N		♆
♇	H	H	N	H	N	N	H	N	N	

H= normally hard; S= normally soft; N= neutral; the pairing can be hard or soft.

UNASPECTED PLANETS

Occasionally, a planet in a chart forms no aspects at all. Far from being irrelevant, such a planet can acquire a magnified role as its energies seek to become integrated in the psyche. An unaspected planet usually behaves unpredictably, its energy suddenly bursting into life, for no obvious reason, and then equally inexplicably disappearing from view.

People with an unaspected Sun, for instance, can veer from a lack of any sense of purpose in life to suddenly being fired up with a mission. Those with unaspected Moon can at times be highly emotional and, at others, totally disconnected from their feelings. Mercury unaspected can have moments of great perspicacity, followed by periods when it appears to lose control of its mental powers. With an unaspected Venus, there is a tendency to swing from being very loving and considerate to acting out of pure self-interest. A Mars with no aspects can suffer from bouts of indolence and lack of drive interspersed with outbursts of feverish activity. An unaspected Jupiter is inclined to fluctuate between expressing his optimistic, generous and life-affirming side and playing the heavy handed moralist, while Saturn can alternate between being the cold, harsh disciplinarian and the unfettered opportunist.

No aspects to the outer planets – Uranus, Neptune and Pluto – often means that their 'effects' are only felt through circumstances that affect a generation.

THE MAJOR ASPECTS
The Conjunction (☌)

Angle: 0° (Neutral) Orb 8°
Keyword: Union.

The conjunction combines the energies of adjoining planets (*figure 5.1*). This is an extremely powerful aspect as the energies function in tandem, although, as with all aspects, how they combine depends largely on the nature of the planets concerned (*see table on page 109*).

The proximity of planets in conjunction can generate an immensely

Fig 5.1

productive, high-intensity energy. But because both planets are jostling for the same position, it is often difficult to distinguish which one is doing what and when. This often results in a lack of perspective, a blind spot that prevents us from seeing ourselves as other people do. The conjunction works most effectively, therefore, when we learn to separate ourselves from our thoughts and actions and see ourselves more objectively.

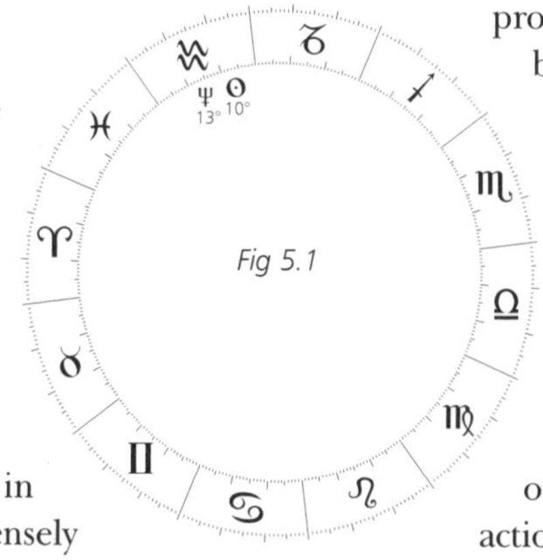

The Opposition (☍)

Angle: 180° (Soft) Orb 8°
Keyword: Duality.

The opposition usually links planets in signs of the same Quality and Polarity, but different, though compatible, Elements (*figure 5.2*). This aspect signifies conflict, which results from a feeling of being pulled apart by opposite tendencies, although each end of the opposition also has something to offer that the other lacks.

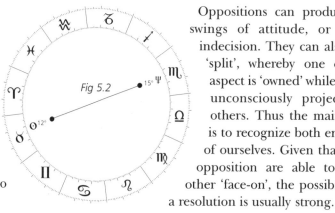

Fig 5.2

Oppositions can produce extreme swings of attitude, or paralyzing indecision. They can also lead to a 'split', whereby one end of the aspect is 'owned' while the other is unconsciously projected on to others. Thus the main challenge is to recognize both ends as facets of ourselves. Given that planets in opposition are able to 'see' each other 'face-on', the possibility of such a resolution is usually strong.

THE MAJOR ASPECTS
The Square (□)

Angle: 90° (Hard) Orb 8°
Keyword: Challenge.

In principle, the square links planets in signs of the same Quality, but conflicting Elements and Polarities *(figure 5.3)*. As a result, the energies of planets in square are at odds, so that a constant tension ensues. Often, this tension manifests itself through people and events that appear to thwart our actions. But this is only a symptom of a deeper conflict,

Fig 5.3

because, at root, this aspect shows our innermost fears and anxieties.

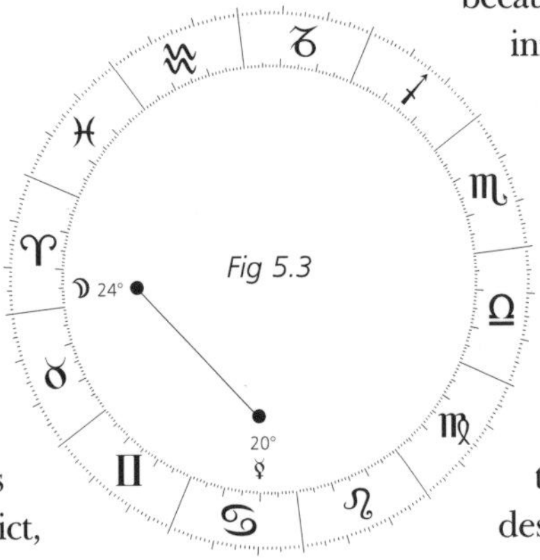

Negative though this sounds, squares are, in fact, essential to psychological growth. By throwing obstacles in our path, squares can give us the dynamism to overcome self-doubt and prove ourselves in the world. It is only when we avoid the issues raised by this aspect that the build-up of tension can reach self-destructive levels.

The Trine (△)

Angle: 120° (Soft) Orb 8°
Keyword: Ease.

The trine commonly connects planets in signs of the same Element *(figure 5.4)*. In stark contrast to the hard aspects, this aspect is a haven of calm, as the energies of the planets flow freely in a state of ease. Consequently, planets in trine reveal aptitudes that find their expression through little conscious effort – the energies are so well

Fig 5.4

integrated that the individual is instinctively attuned to them.

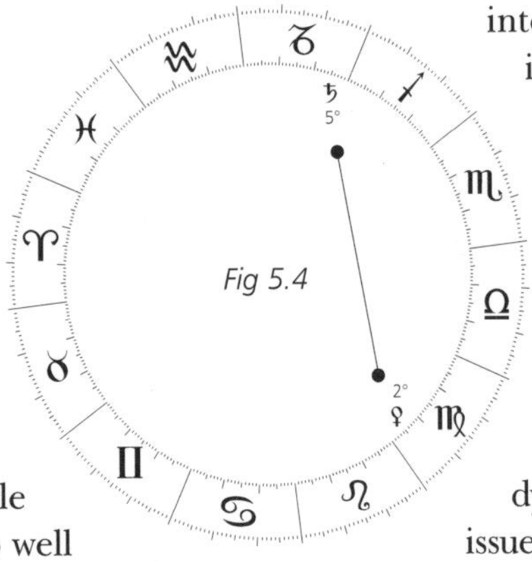

Because it is fundamentally stable, the trine points to interests and abilities where we can find a sense of enjoyment, relaxation and acceptance. However, the ease with which the energies between the planets flow causes its own problems – notably complacency, a lack of dynamism and a reluctance to bring issues out into the open.

THE MAJOR ASPECTS
The Sextile (✳)

Angle: 60° (Soft) Orb 6°
Keyword: Opportunity

Sextiles normally connect planets in signs of different but compatible Elements and opposite Polarities (*figure 5.5*). The flow of energy combines the ease of the trine with the conflict of the opposition. As a result, planets in sextile tend to generate a stimulating blend of fluency and contrast.

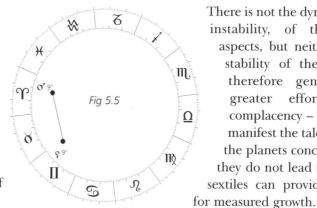

Fig 5.5

There is not the dynamic tension, or instability, of the challenging aspects, but neither is there the stability of the trine. Sextiles therefore generally demand greater effort – or less complacency – than the trine to manifest the talents indicated by the planets concerned. Although they do not lead to rapid change, sextiles can provide opportunities for measured growth.

The Quincunx (⊼)

Angle: 150° (Hard) Orb 2
Keyword: Frustration

The quincunx links planets in signs that have little in common (*figure 5.6*). In fact, this aspect combines the stability of the trine with the stress of the square in a way that seems to trigger frustration and friction – albeit not on the scale of the square or opposition. But then, this aspect does not hold the same

Fig 5.6

potential for resolution either. What often happens with the quincunx is that circumstances in life seemingly conspire to pull the individual in two unrelated directions, neither of which can be ignored. Often, the only way to resolve this niggling stalemate is to negotiate a truce, whereby both sides of the dilemma are somehow accommodated in an uneasy equilibrium.

THE MINOR ASPECTS

The Semisextile (⊻)

Angle: 30° (Hard) Orb 2° Keyword: Accommodation

The semisextile is similar to the quincunx, but less stressful. Like neighbours, planets in semisextile have to learn to get along, which is not always easy (*figure 5.7*). The semisextile gains in significance when it acts as a bridge between what would otherwise be unconnected areas of a chart.

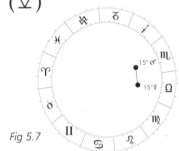

Fig 5.7

The Sesquiquadrate (⊡)

Fig 5.8

Angle: 135° (Hard) Orb 2° Keyword: Tension

Related to the square, the sesquiquadrate indicates dynamic tension between two or more planets (*figure 5.8*). This aspect symbolizes crisis of a sudden and unexpected nature. This may be because the conflicts that the planets involved symbolize are less conscious in the psyche of the individual.

The Semisquare (∠)

Angle: 45° (Hard) Orb 2° Keyword: Tension

The semisquare (*figure 5.9*) is very similar to the sesquiquadrate – in fact, the two are often lumped together. Both are classed as minor aspects, but their effects should never be underestimated. Indeed, a close-orbed sesquiquadrate or semisextile is considered more powerful than a wide-orbed square.

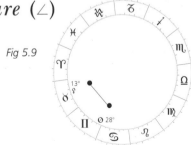

Fig 5.9

MAJOR AND MINOR ASPECTS
Dissociate Aspects

One area concerning the aspects that is a constant source of controversy, is the so-called dissociate aspect. A square, for instance, is usually formed between planets in signs of the same Quality, but incompatible Elements. As explained in Chapter 2, the Qualities group together signs with similar tendencies but very different energies, which makes them mutually 'unsympathetic', hence the tension of the square.

A problem arises, however, when one planet at the end of a sign forms a square with a planet at the beginning of another in signs of the same Element. These signs are supposed to get along, so it is hard to justify how planets that fall in compatible signs could be simultaneously forming a challenging aspect. Exactly the same kind of dilemma can arise with all the other major aspects.

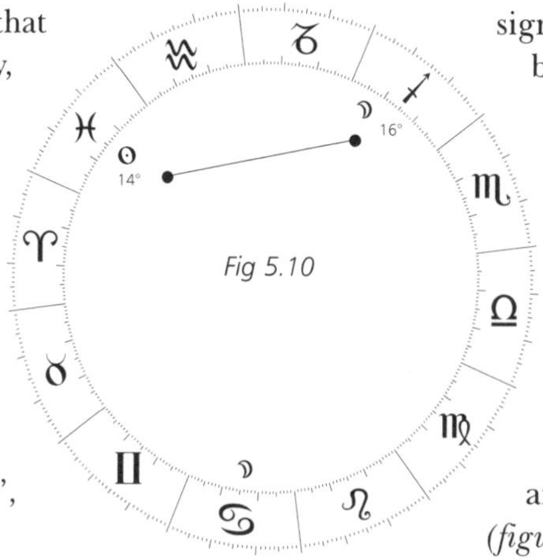

Astrologers disagree about the

Fig 5.10

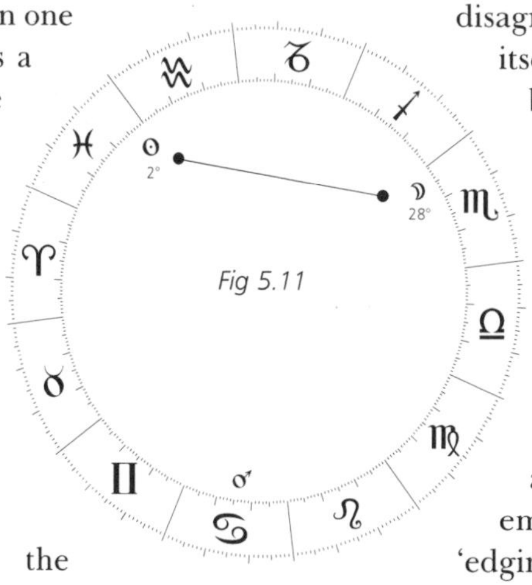

Fig 5.11

significance of dissociate aspects. One body of opinion maintains that the nature of the signs involved must have a bearing on the way a dissociate aspect will function. According to this viewpoint, a square between the Sun in Pisces and the Moon in Sagittarius (*figure 5.10*) is subtly different from a square between the Sun at the beginning of Pisces and the Moon at the end of Scorpio (*figure 5.11*). Other astrologers disagree, insisting that it is the aspect itself rather than the relationship between the signs that defines the nature of the aspect's meaning.

For the beginner, perhaps the best advice is to think of a dissociate challenging aspect as being more flowing than it might otherwise be; a dissociate flowing aspect as being slightly more challenging; and a dissociate conjunction as embracing something of the 'edginess' of a semisextile.

SUN – MOON

The Will to Integrate

• How your needs shape your goals • The child within the adult
• The quest for inner peace • The balance between home and public life
• Your experience of father and mother • Illuminating the past

PLANETARY PRINCIPLE

The character is essentially self-contained with the emotions and the will in balance; at best this creates an aura of self-assurance that others can respond to positively.

This pairing denotes the 'loner', the person who feels that they have everything necessary for life contained within themselves and need minimum feedback from the outside world.

IN RELATIONSHIPS

The ability to give of oneself without feeling vulnerable or threatened; the desire to throw heart and soul into a relationship; expresses sensitivity through protecting and nurturing.

Overly self-contained through a fear of opening up to others; drawn to 'clingy' relationships out of a need for dependency; shows insecurities through smothering love.

PSYCHOLOGICAL TRAITS

A secure self-image with the balance between 'male' and 'female' energies producing an even temperament that is both dynamic and adaptable; the desire to be at ease with oneself.

The emotions and the will pull in opposite directions, creating inner conflict between conscious goals and unconscious needs; may be too deeply attached to the past.

IN DAILY LIFE

Favours: any work which provides a high degree of personal motivation, or an inner sense of fulfilment; positions of influence; pioneering work; working with children.

Dangers: conflict between home and work; an inability to take criticism; overreacting to minor slights; false sense of pride; lack of perspective; taking success for granted.

Over the following pages, in this chapter and the next, the light symbols correspond to positive traits and the dark symbols to negative ones.

SUN – MERCURY

The Will to Communicate

• CREATIVE IDEAS • FORCEFUL VIEWS • THE IMPORTANCE OF KNOWLEDGE • THE AUTHORITATIVE THINKER • THE POWER OF SPEECH • A BLINKERED MIND • CONCEITED OPINIONS • THE URGE TO COMMUNICATE

PLANETARY PRINCIPLE

 Mercury benefits from the Sun's vigour in the form of a balanced mind and strong powers of expression; at best, it confers the strength to know one's mind and the courage to speak it.

 Mercury can be completely over-powered by the Sun making the mind 'feverish' and lacking in concentration; at worst this can result in nervous restlessness and impatience.

PSYCHOLOGICAL TRAITS

 Wit, lucidity and the pursuit of knowledge play an important part in the overall make-up; a spirit of inquiry is matched by a powerful need and ability to communicate.

 Unreceptive to the ideas or advice of others; a tendency to claim others' ideas as one's own; dogma and subjectivity take the place of reasoned thought; a one-track mind.

IN RELATIONSHIPS

 A passionate heart with a silvery tongue; the ability to communicate desires and needs clearly and directly; the ability to take others' plans on board.

 Misunderstandings can easily arise through misinterpreting others' needs; a tendency towards being mentally overbearing; over-sensitive to criticism.

IN DAILY LIFE

 Favours: any profession where the mind is actively stretched, hence teaching or writing; commercial enterprise, in particular 'sales'; being in charge of one's own projects.

 Dangers; talking out of turn; talking at people; vacuous chatter; indulging in back-biting gossip; inattention to detail; a belief in the infallibility of one's mind.

Only aspects within 28° are possible as the Sun and Mercury are never more than this distance apart.

SUN – VENUS

The Will to Love

• **The power of attraction** • **A malleable sense of identity** • **Pride in appearance** • **The desire to please** • **Love rivalries** • **Personal charm** • **A love of pleasure** • **The need to find self-love**

PLANETARY PRINCIPLE

 Venus increases the Sun's desire to love and be loved; at best it gives an understanding of the need to give and to receive, both of which are accomplished with grace and subtlety.

 Venus raises the Sun's expectations of love to an inordinate degree; at worst, it can demand too much from partners and behave in a self-serving manner when hopes are not fulfilled.

PSYCHOLOGICAL TRAITS

 An optimistic outlook born of high self-esteem; the desire to be at peace with oneself; a friendly, out-going nature that always looks for the best in a situation; inspired by beauty.

 Over-concerned with creating the right impression; craving for popularity leads to damaging levels of compromise; seeks the easy way out rather than fighting for values.

IN RELATIONSHIPS

 A romantic, affectionate nature; the ability to bring tact and harmony into all personal dealings; treats partners' interests and needs with the utmost respect.

 Resentments through continuously placing the needs of others first; an indiscriminate need for affection; self-indulgent, using charms to manipulate ever-increasing levels of attention.

IN DAILY LIFE

 Favours: traditionally linked with artistic talent, especially music and dance; all forms of creative expression; sophisticated presentation skills; any work needing a good aesthetic sense.

 Dangers: allowing oneself to be a soft touch; a foppish manner; low self-worth; extravagant tastes; a talent for prevaricating; dilettante pursuits; adopting too many airs and graces.

Only aspects within 48⁰ are possible as the Sun and Venus are never more than this distance apart.

SUN – MARS

The Will to Act

- **HEROIC DEEDS** • **A FORCEFUL SENSE OF IDENTITY** • **FINDING THE WILL TO FIGHT**
- **THE IMPORTANCE OF COURAGE** • **PRIDE IN WINNING** • **THE MILITANT PACIFIST**
- **LEADING FROM THE FRONT** • **FIGHTING FOR CAUSES** • **AT WAR WITH ONESELF**

PLANETARY PRINCIPLE

 Mars boosts the Sun's will and vitality to produce a powerhouse of fiery energy; at best, it confers considerable authority, together with the ability to get what one wants.

 Together, Mars and the Sun can become over-energized to produce an extremely aggressive and competitive nature, which, at worst can degenerate into extreme, antisocial behaviour.

IN RELATIONSHIPS

 Brings spontaneity and directness of approach to all close contacts; the ability to instill new life into relationships; a powerful sexuality marked by physical intensity; pride in partner.

 Tends to run out of steam once the initial enthusiasm wears off; takes out pent-up anger or frustration on partners; self-gratification takes precedence over others' needs.

PSYCHOLOGICAL TRAITS

 A strong sense of personal power, which is exercised judiciously; the ability to command respect through actions; the drive to maximize any opportunity that presents itself.

 Hot-blooded nature results in a tendency to overreact; a 'force or be forced' attitude; an uncompromising insistence on freedom of action; an extreme dislike of losing.

IN DAILY LIFE

 Favours: activities demanding stamina and hard work; any opportunity to excel through personal effort; the ability to initiate new enterprises; championing the underdog.

 Dangers: forcing the issue; inconsistent energy levels; rash decisions; a fear of one's own strength; being pushed around; lack of tact; underestimating the virtue of patience.

SUN – JUPITER

The Will to Expand

• THE SPIRIT OF ADVENTURE • THE QUEST FOR MEANING • EXPANSIVE BELIEFS
• AN INFLATED SENSE OF IDENTITY • EXAGGERATED PRIDE • GREAT EXPECTATIONS
• THE SEARCH FOR POWER AND GLORY • THE GETTING OF WISDOM

PLANETARY PRINCIPLE

 Jupiter expands the Sun's enthusiasm for adventure, bestowing a limitless appetite for life; at best there is an innate faith that the universe will provide – which it often does.

 Jupiter over-inflates the Sun's quest for a sense of identity and purpose; at worst, there is a tendency to assume a position of moral superiority founded on no real grounds.

IN RELATIONSHIPS

 Believes in fidelity and honesty as the cornerstones of close involvements; the ability to enliven every aspect of a relationship with an infectious optimism and buoyancy.

 A restlessness of spirit that finds close ties too confining; neglectful of others' needs; fails to live up to initial promise; patronizing towards others' imperfections; extremely overbearing.

PSYCHOLOGICAL TRAITS

 A cheerful, benevolent temperament, even in the difficult times; abundant mental energy; the ability to create one's own good fortune and share it with all and sundry.

 An arrogant belief in one's own importance; a tendency to take luck for granted; talents wasted through carelessness and laziness; lacks any sense of moderation; hugely self-centred.

IN DAILY LIFE

 Favours: mentally challenging occupations such as philosophy, the law or publishing; knowing what the public wants, hence selling and advertising; work connected with travel.

 Dangers: indulging gluttonous appetites; blind optimism; running out of control; brittle self-confidence; being satisfied with second best; not knowing when to apply the brakes.

☉ ♄

SUN – SATURN

The Will to Structure

• **RECOGNITION THROUGH EFFORT** • **PRIDE IN DUTY** • **ILLUMINATING FEARS**
• **A REALISTIC SENSE OF IDENTITY** • **IMPORTANCE OF RESPONSIBILITY** • **BECOMING
ONE'S OWN AUTHORITY** • **CONTROLLED ENERGY** • **INHIBITED WILL**

PLANETARY PRINCIPLE

Saturn gives the Sun the power of endurance and thus the ability to conserve anything that is felt to be of value; at best, it can build lasting achievements based on hard experience.

Saturn can chill the Sun's rays so that inner fears create an inferiority complex; at worst, a meanness of spirit and feelings of emptiness and inhibition can destroy self-confidence.

IN RELATIONSHIPS

Seeks to build lasting relationships on strong and stable foundations; the ability to hold things together in the face of adversity; capable of being immensely thoughtful and trustworthy.

Cold and defensive, lives in fear of rejection; compensates for negative feelings by controlling or criticizing others; may choose partners for their usefulness rather than for love.

PSYCHOLOGICAL TRAITS

A sure-footed approach to life based on a profound awareness of one's own limitations; the ability to overcome feelings of inadequacy; the desire to build a 'true' sense of identity.

A deep lack of self-respect resulting from one's sense of identity being crushed in childhood; secretly craves recognition, but a fear of failure means that ambitions are inhibited.

IN DAILY LIFE

Favours: any activity in which hard work, long-term planning and responsibility are prerequisites; achievements through steady application; working in seclusion.

Dangers: taking life too seriously; 'copping out' under pressure; putting up too many barriers; pushing oneself too hard; bitterness at lack of recognition; hiding one's light under a bushel.

SUN – URANUS

The Will to Liberate

• SPIRIT OF REBELLION • AN IDEALIZED SENSE OF IDENTITY • PRIDE IN INDEPENDENCE • THE URGE TO STAND OUT FROM THE CROWD • RADICAL AIMS • THE DESIRE TO SHOCK • THE WILL TO OVERCOME RESISTANCE

PLANETARY PRINCIPLE

 Uranus fortifies the Sun emphasizing strength of will and the desire for independence; at best, this combination gives the determination to work for progress and freedom for all.

 Uranus can make the Sun perversely rebellious and erratic; at worst this produces an arrogant belief in one's own authority and a cussed refusal to recognize established conventions.

IN RELATIONSHIPS

 Seeks to sweep away the fetters of traditional role play in close involvements; brings an edge of unpredictability and freedom to all relationships; responds best to honesty.

 The desire for independence means that commitment is low on the agenda; extremely inconsistent; seeks to satisfy need for novelty and excitement through many relationships.

PSYCHOLOGICAL TRAITS

 An independent spirit; the ability to use one's position as an 'outsider' to push for change in the world; immense breadth of vision and depth of insight; a genuine humanitarian.

 Intolerant of those who do not share the same outlook; insists on the right to do things own way for fear that individuality will be crushed; a stubborn resistance to personal change.

IN DAILY LIFE

 Favours: any work demanding an innovative approach and lateral thinking; freedom of thought and expression; campaigning for civil rights; new technologies; positions of power.

 Dangers: throwing the baby out with the bathwater; sudden rushes of blood to the head; constant contrariness; refusing to be told what to do; lack of application.

SUN – NEPTUNE

The Will to Transcend

• CRAVING TO BE SPECIAL • SELF-DELUSION • A CONFUSED SENSE OF IDENTITY
• THE PURSUIT OF A VISION • INFLATED VANITY • POWERS OF PERCEPTION
• SHIFTING AIMS • SPIRITUAL PRIDE • THE SEARCH FOR PERFECTION

PLANETARY PRINCIPLE

 Neptune refines the Sun permeating conscious aims with a sense of vision; at best, there is an intuitive awareness of how to make innermost dreams, whether material or spiritual, a reality.

 Neptune mystifies the Sun so that simple 'head in the clouds' dreaming is confused with idealism; at worst, fantasy becomes a means of finding a way out of the 'ordinary'.

IN RELATIONSHIPS

 Gentleness and empathy bring sensitivity and harmony to all personal relationships; adept at fathoming partners' needs; the ability to transcend self-interest and help others.

 Disappointments through a tendency to over-idealize partners; leaves a trail of confusion through the desire to 'have one's cake and eat it'; extremely unreliable; a subtle manipulator.

PSYCHOLOGICAL TRAITS

 The capacity to find one's identity through devotion to a cause or an ideal; a perfectionist who seeks to act out of the highest motives; the ability to accept life for what it is.

 A dreamy facade camouflages a slippery nature; a propensity to feel victimized by life; an inability to face the truth; discontentment resulting from self-doubt; inflated self-image.

IN DAILY LIFE

 Favours: creative imagination, especially in drama, music, writing and art; philanthropy; financial investments; healing professions; interest in psychic phenomena or spiritualism.

 Dangers: wishful thinking; wallowing in self-pity; chasing after glamour; giving power away to 'guru' figures; addictive habits; giving up the ghost; duplicitous dealings; a saviour complex.

SUN – PLUTO

The Will to Transform

• **HIDDEN POWER** • **STRIVING FOR AUTHORITY** • **SELF-OBSESSION** • **FEAR OF FAILURE** • **INTENSE POWER STRUGGLES** • **ILLUMINATING THE DARK SIDE OF HUMAN NATURE** • **TRANSFORMING ONE'S SENSE OF IDENTITY** • **THE WILL TO SURVIVE**

PLANETARY PRINCIPLE

 Pluto intensifies the Sun's quest for a sense of empowerment; at best this combination signifies the courage to implement the kind of change that leads to self-regeneration.

 Pluto in combination with the Sun can become power hungry; at worst, it can be brutal and domineering, and the desire for recognition will override any moral considerations.

IN RELATIONSHIPS

 A profound sensitivity, coupled with a need to live life to the full means that relationships can be both intense and rewarding; demands, and is capable of, undying loyalty.

 Loves lust but also lusts for love; debases sex by using it as a means of exerting power and control; magnetic charms are turned to Machiavellian intent; obsessively possessive.

PSYCHOLOGICAL TRAITS

 The urge to become master of one's destiny; strength of purpose; the capacity to discover underlying motives through rigorous self-analysis; the ability to grow through hardship.

 Compulsive or obsessive behaviour resulting from lack of self-respect; highly self-centred and manipulative; tends to deny unacceptable aspects of the personality and resist change.

IN DAILY LIFE

 Favours: positions of authority; working in life-or-death situations; helping others transform their lives; pushing abilities to the limit; developing healing powers.

 Dangers: fiercely competitive rivalries; excessive pride; ruthless pursuit of goals; intolerance of others' weaknesses; always trying to be the best; the power of hate.

MOON – MERCURY

The Instinct to Communicate Feelings

• **FLEETING MOODS** • **CHANGEABLE OPINIONS** • **MENTAL TENACITY** • **PERCEPTIONS**
AFFECTED BY FEELINGS • **SUBJECTIVE THINKING** • **SUPERFICIAL CHAT**
• **AN EMPATHY FOR WORDS** • **SECURITY IN TALKING**

PLANETARY PRINCIPLE

 The Moon softens Mercury's analytical powers resulting in a richly imaginative mind; at best it produces a good balance between head and heart resulting in much common sense.

 The Moon can colour Mercury's 'detachment' producing a highly subjective mind; at worst it creates self-doubt together with a tendency to overlook key facts and let prejudices prevail.

IN RELATIONSHIPS

 An intuitive understanding of others' thoughts and emotional states; highly sympathetic to partners' needs; the ability to communicate feelings and to listen to others.

 Tends to rationalize the emotions, giving off a feeling of coolness; a refusal to take partner's views on board; a stubbornness of attitude that precludes honest debate; prone to moodiness.

PSYCHOLOGICAL TRAITS

 Great mental creativity, with a constant stream of inventive ideas; a powerful capacity to sway the opinions of others; the ability to convey feelings through the spoken and written word.

 Mental restlessness arising from over-sensitivity to surroundings; a tendency to overreact to people's opinions; a habit of holding on to painful memories; quick to take offence.

IN DAILY LIFE

 Favours: any work involving attention to detail or the need for sharp perceptions; strong sales skills; 'bookish' interests; writing and public speaking; the ability to imitate; humour.

 Dangers: unfocused thinking; frequent changes in career path; the tendency to gossip; being over-opinionated; holding on to old attitudes; taking slights too personally.

MOON – VENUS

The Instinct to Feel Love

- THE NEED FOR SECURITY IN RELATIONSHIPS • ROMANTIC INSTINCTS
- SECURITY IN LOVING • THE SEARCH FOR PEACE • BALANCED EMOTIONS
- A LOVE OF BEAUTIFUL SURROUNDINGS

PLANETARY PRINCIPLE

 Venus blends harmoniously with the Moon to produce an openness of heart and warmth of feeling; at best it is a sign of the true 'party animal' with a limitless capacity for enjoyment.

 Venus can over-indulge the Moon's need for security leading to excessively ingratiating behaviour; at worst, the nature can be too pliable resulting in loss of self-respect.

IN RELATIONSHIPS

 Seeks involvements based on real intimacy; the desire to love through nurturing; displays affections openly and sincerely; sensitive to the needs of others; a sensual approach to love.

 Changeable attitude to giving and receiving love; forms relationships indiscriminately out of a need to be needed; a tendency to be over-trusting in affections; emotionally oversensitive.

PSYCHOLOGICAL TRAITS

 A cheerful outlook; the desire to settle differences through diplomacy; a strong concern for personal comfort and security; a keen sense of justice and fairness for all.

 An over-indulgent nature with a particular fondness for all things physical; a reluctance to face up to life's realities; the ability to elevate indecision to an art form; excessive vanity.

IN DAILY LIFE

 Favours: any work requiring artistic taste and sensitivity, hence interior design, catering, fine art or fashion; occupations that demand tact; conservation and ecology.

 Dangers: caving in under pressure; excessive indolence; taxing health through rich living; get-rich-quick schemes; financial difficulties through overspending; being taken for granted.

MOON – MARS

The Instinct to Act on Feelings

• **EXCITABLE FEELINGS** • **ACTIONS GOVERNED BY EMOTIONS** • **LIFE IS A BATTLE**
• **SENSITIVE TO CONFLICT** • **IMPULSIVE NURTURING** • **POWERFUL REACTIONS**
• **SECURITY THROUGH SELF-ASSERTION** • **DEFENSIVE FEELINGS**

PLANETARY PRINCIPLE

 Mars energizes the Moon, giving a rare mixture of inner strength and sensitivity; at its best this combination has the ability to be emotionally very honest and passionate.

 Mars can aggravate the Moon so that emotions become volatile and actions are driven by blind impulse; at worst this pair can produce selfishness masquerading as independence.

PSYCHOLOGICAL TRAITS

 The ability to channel considerable physical and emotional energy towards constructive ends; actions guided by a strong sense of inner security; the courageous crusader.

 Emotionally highly vulnerable, tending to see slights on all sides; overreacts to the slightest stimuli; lacks self-control, or tends to suppress anger for fear of own strength.

IN RELATIONSHIPS

 Seeks intimacy through spontaneous show of emotions; the ability to still others' fears and doubts; fiercely protective of loved ones; a marked and often exciting sexual energy.

 Emotional security undermined by irrational fears, hence jealousy can be a big issue; may take out unresolved anger on partners; lack of sympathy to others; over-defensive in love.

IN DAILY LIFE

 Favours: self-employment; all activities that involve the physical release of energy, especially sports; business enterprise; manual (DIY) skills; property or building trades.

 Dangers: routine work; being on constant 'red alert'; lack of caution; bolting down food; digestive upsets; the need for reckless excitement; quarrelsome attitudes.

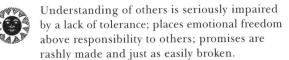

MOON – JUPITER

The Instinct to Expand Feelings

• GENEROUS FEELINGS • THE MILK OF HUMAN KINDNESS • EMOTIONAL EXCESS
• NOURISHED THROUGH FAITH • EXAGGERATED RESPONSES • GREEDY FOR
NURTURE • GAMBLING INSTINCTS • SECURITY IN POPULARITY

PLANETARY PRINCIPLE

 Jupiter expands the Moon's energy creating optimism and emotional warmth in every aspect of life; at best it gives a benevolent and sympathetic disposition.

 Jupiter can drive the Moon to excess in all things so that judgment is coloured by the emotions; at worst it produces extravagance, self-indulgence and a lack of humility.

IN RELATIONSHIPS

 Considerate and protective; highly supportive of the needs and wants of partners; forms strong attachments to family and friends; fidelity and honesty come entirely naturally.

 Understanding of others is seriously impaired by a lack of tolerance; places emotional freedom above responsibility to others; promises are rashly made and just as easily broken.

PSYCHOLOGICAL TRAITS

 The ability to develop a philosophical approach to life; good fortune through an innate faith in Providence; capable of deep emotional insights; generosity of spirit.

 Emotions run out of control, resulting in inappropriate responses and misplaced generosity; indolence through an arrogant assumption that life will somehow deliver.

IN DAILY LIFE

Favours: the caring professions; social welfare or charitable work; shrewdness in business; interest in foreign cultures; living abroad; religious or educational causes; journalism.

Dangers: believing one is always right; being judgmental; inappropriate gestures of largesse; optimism run riot; gambling assets away; extravagant mood swings; king-size appetites.

MOON – SATURN

The Instinct to Structure Feelings

• RESTRAINED FEELINGS • PRACTICAL NURTURING • SECURITY IN ORDER • AUSTERE EMOTIONS • REPRESSED NEEDS • EMOTIONAL ISOLATION • SINCERITY OF AFFECTIONS • MATERIAL SECURITY • THE DUTIFUL CARER

PLANETARY PRINCIPLE

 Saturn stabilizes the Moon, producing realism and inner strength on the emotional level; at best, situations that might break others are taken in their stride with calm composure.

 Saturn can torment the Moon with insecurities about being unlovable and unwanted – fears that often have their roots in childhood; at worst, these feelings can stunt emotional development.

IN RELATIONSHIPS

 Makes up for lack of spontaneity by being extremely dependable; highly sensitive, taking commitment in great earnest; hard times and emotional setbacks are handled with equanimity.

 Can be emotionally cold for fear of being scorned or misunderstood; an inability to face up to or express feelings; a lack of empathy; difficulty in letting go of past relationships.

PSYCHOLOGICAL TRAITS

 The ability to give structure to feelings; a powerful sense of duty, hence takes responsibilities seriously; a strong sense of tradition; patient in the face of adversity.

 Behaviour dominated by fear of rejection; bears responsibilities heavily, often feeling unsupported; takes self-containment to extremes; a tendency to depression.

IN DAILY LIFE

 Favours: any activity requiring endurance, patience and objectivity; organizational abilities; shrewd business acumen; positions of responsibility; a sharp sense of timing.

 Dangers: being over-critical; treating others harshly; narrow-mindedness; rigid attitudes; prone to meanness; being excessively self-preoccupied; lack of motivation.

MOON – URANUS

The Instinct to Liberate Feelings

• **LIGHTNING-SPEED REACTIONS** • **INSTINCTIVE INSIGHTS** • **ERRATIC FEELINGS**
• **EMOTIONAL OVERLOAD** • **SECURITY IN INDEPENDENCE** • **UNSTABLE FAMILY**
BACKGROUND • **BREAKING FREE FROM EMOTIONAL CONDITIONING**

PLANETARY PRINCIPLE

 Uranus excites the Moon to seek emotional independence and freedom of expression; at best, it gives a highly idealistic streak and a willingness to fight for the underprivileged.

 Uranus agitates the Moon creating emotional tension and instability; at worst, this can cause an uncompromising spirit of non-conformity and a refusal to accept responsibilities.

IN RELATIONSHIPS

 Seeks unorthodox emotional attachments; gives great freedom to partners and is largely free from possessiveness and jealousy; injects excitement and novelty into all relationships.

 A highly erratic temperament part needy, part craving personal liberty; finds close ties stifling; prone to violent emotional outbursts; tends to blame partners for problems in relationships.

PSYCHOLOGICAL TRAITS

 An intuitive understanding of human nature; the energy and determination to achieve; a willingness to sacrifice personal needs to an ideal; the urge to seek out unusual experiences.

 Feels in some way detached from life with no sense of belonging or fitting in; frequent and sudden changes of mood; takes individualism to extremes, hence the urge to be disruptive.

IN DAILY LIFE

 Favours: working on behalf of the underclass; social reform in areas such as housing, family life, parenting; unusual forms of expression; a flair for business in new technologies.

 Dangers: easily bored; unable to accept instructions from others; frequent changes in direction; lack of consideration; an off-hand manner; refusing to abide by regulations.

MOON – NEPTUNE

The Instinct to Refine Feelings

- **RARIFIED FEELINGS** • **EMOTIONALLY IMPRESSIONABLE** • **SECURITY IN MERGING**
- **CRAVING PROTECTION** • **FANTASIZED NEEDS** • **ADDICTED TO HOME COMFORTS**
- **SACRIFICING PERSONAL NEEDS** • **FLIGHT FROM OUTER REALITY**

PLANETARY PRINCIPLE

 Neptune sensitizes the Moon intensifying the emotions and the imagination; at best, this results in a compassionate nature and a desire to live by the highest moral or spiritual code.

 Neptune can make the Moon too idealistic so that disappointment and disillusionment inevitably follow; at worst, this can produce a self-pitying duplicitous nature.

IN RELATIONSHIPS

 Altruistic and sympathetic to others' needs; sensuous and subtle, capable of reaching great heights of tenderness and devotion; highly receptive to every emotional nuance.

 Lacks clear emotional boundaries and can thus be extremely manipulative, sending confused signals to partners; prone to infidelity; drawn to relationships in which neediness is an issue.

PSYCHOLOGICAL TRAITS

 Seeks to experience life as out of the ordinary; the desire to work for a vision of a better life for all; an open approach to life; lives for beauty, art and romance; highly sensitive.

 Lives in a fantasy world, longing for the impossible; an addictive personality prone to escapism; a lack of moral substance; takes advantage of others weaknesses; easily hurt.

IN DAILY LIFE

 Favours: any activity involving the use of imagination, such as poetry, photography, film, music and acting; working to alleviate suffering; interest in mysticism and the occult.

 Dangers: ignoring mundane responsibilities; ending up the 'victim' in playing 'saviour' to others; lack of discrimination; alcohol and drug abuse; morbid fears; laziness.

MOON – PLUTO

The Instinct to Control Feelings

• PROFOUND INSIGHTS • EMOTIONAL POWER • SECURITY IN SELF-PRESERVATION
• BURIED EMOTIONS • SKELETONS IN THE CUPBOARD • BREAKING AWAY FROM
EMOTIONAL CONDITIONING • VIOLENT FEELINGS • INNER TURMOIL

PLANETARY PRINCIPLE

 Pluto heightens the Moon so that feelings are underpinned by an incredible intensity and insight; at best, it gives the resilience to admit to and purge destructive emotions.

 Pluto can terrorize the Moon into becoming over-sensitive, fearful and thus secretive and tyrannical; at worst, passions run out of control and personal needs are gratified at all costs.

IN RELATIONSHIPS

 Brings emotional strength and security to all personal relationships; feelings are expressed with great depth and passion; has a natural ability to unlock buried feelings in partners.

 Uses emotional blackmail as a method of controlling others and disguising personal shortcomings; given to extreme jealousy; fears the emotional exposure that intimacy demands.

PSYCHOLOGICAL TRAITS

 Intuitively knows how to touch the emotions of others and use this power productively; enormous emotional stamina; the capacity for self-improvement through inner change.

 Highly vulnerable, tormented by feelings of betrayal and abandonment; puts up emotional barriers for protection and then feels isolated as a result; takes criticism very personally.

IN DAILY LIFE

 Favours: working to tight deadlines; any work involving the controlled exercise of power; unravelling mysteries, especially the complexities of the psyche; counselling.

 Dangers: suppressing emotional power; the seamy side of life; festering resentments; emotional bullying; refusing to forgive; dragging others down to one's level.

131

MERCURY – VENUS

The Fair Mind

• **THE VOICE OF REASON** • **TURNED ON BY HUMOUR** • **SHARING ONE'S THOUGHTS**
• **LOVING EXCHANGES** • **HARMONIOUS EXPRESSION** • **ARTISTIC FLAIR**
• **THINKING ABOUT APPEARANCES** • **THE IMPORTANCE OF STYLE**

PLANETARY PRINCIPLE

 Venus refines Mercury, creating a finely balanced mind with the ability to weigh all the facts before reaching a decision; at best, this is a soothing influence emphasizing fair play.

 Venus can trivialize Mercury resulting in a lightweight intellect that prefers to function on a superficial level; at worst, there is a tendency to seek approval rather than speak one's mind.

IN RELATIONSHIPS

 Seeks a meeting of minds; motivated by the desire to find the common ground; an ability to communicate feelings objectively; sexually, is likely to be curious rather than passionate.

 Prefers to avoid intense emotional showdowns; often caves in simply to keep the peace; can be cool or inconstant in affections; turned on more by the thought of love than the reality.

PSYCHOLOGICAL TRAITS

 An elegant mind with a strong aesthetic sense; often has great charm, tact and a graceful way with words; highly observant about people, which can confer a talent for mimicry.

 A frivolous mind that prizes style above content; a smooth talker, tending to say what others want to hear; likes the sound of its own voice; can be extremely vain.

IN DAILY LIFE

 Favours: styling; design; the beauty and fashion industries; public relations; agents for artists; creative writing; any activity involving use of the voice – especially singing

 Dangers: taking on heavy responsibilities; vulgar company; hostile competition; working on one's own; discordant surroundings; towing the company line; joining the rat race.

Only aspects within 76⁰ are possible as Mercury and Venus are never more than this distance apart.

MERCURY – MARS

The Assertive Mind

• **MENTAL AGILITY** • **KNEE-JERK REACTIONS** • **ACTIONS SPEAK LOUDER THAN WORDS** • **HOSTILE CRITICISM** • **BLUNT SPEAKING** • **A SCALPEL MIND** • **FIGHTING TALK** • **IMPATIENT THINKING** • **CONCISE EXPRESSION**

PLANETARY PRINCIPLE

 Mars energizes Mercury giving a lively mentality that knows where it is heading; at best, it can cut to the quick of an issue, and always looks to turn words into deeds.

 Mars can inflame Mercury creating an overly excitable, abrasive and headstrong mind, with a waspish tongue and an irascible temper; at worst, it generates immense mental discord.

IN RELATIONSHIPS

 A bright and breezy approach to relationships; needs a great deal of mental stimulation, preferably sparring partners for lively debate; fearless about speaking the truth.

 Creates conflict through a tendency to speak before thinking; tries to steamroller others' points of view; prone to exaggerating differences; impatient with slower minds.

PSYCHOLOGICAL TRAITS

 A vigorous, practical mind that learns quickly; seeks to initiate ideas with a view to getting things done; forthright views that are upheld by a willingness to act on convictions.

 A restless, impulsive mind given to making rash, premature decisions through poor grasp of details; often adopts a confrontational approach as if expecting to be challenged.

IN DAILY LIFE

 Favours: the cut and thrust of the law courts; aggressive competition; teaching profession; satirical writing; self-employment; any activity requiring good hand-to-eye co-ordination.

 Dangers: stretching mind to the limit; holding one-sided viewpoints; getting stuck on committees; wrangling for the sake of it; intellectual arrogance; spitting sarcasm.

MERCURY – JUPITER

The Expansive Mind

• **BIG IDEAS** • **A FERTILE MIND** • **TALL STORIES** • **SWEEPING GENERALIZATIONS** • **WIDE-ANGLE LENS** • **CONFLICTS BETWEEN REASON AND FAITH** • **A JACK-OF-ALL-TRADES** • **ALL TALK AND NO ACTION**

PLANETARY PRINCIPLE

 Jupiter expands Mercury, giving it a thirst for knowledge and experience, and an awareness of the multi-facetedness of life; at best, it can gain deep insight into the nature of existence.

 Jupiter can inflate Mercury producing hot air in the form of a know-it-all mentality; at worst, it produces an armchair philosopher full of half-baked, rambling ideas.

IN RELATIONSHIPS

 Brings tremendous optimism and a 'big', infectious sense of humour into relationships; can be refreshingly candid; takes a common-sense, constructive approach to clearing the air.

 Indiscrete and unreliable, making grand promises that are never kept; capable of being downright deceitful; misunderstandings arise through not listening to what others say.

PSYCHOLOGICAL TRAITS

 A broad, enquiring mind, with an eye for the 'big' picture; capable of prophetic insight and lofty idealism; a flair for communicating and mixing with people from all walks of life.

 A lazy, disorganized mind, inattentive to detail and thus liable to draw faulty conclusions; a follower of fashionable opinion; the eternal student, with no outlets for applying learning.

IN DAILY LIFE

 Favours: material success through intellectual endeavour; the travel industry; language abilities; opinion forming skills; negotiating business deals; issues concerning justice.

 Dangers: poor judgment in speculative ventures; a gambling habit; dishonest dealings; aimless drifting; not reading the question properly; careless answers.

MERCURY – SATURN

The Structured Mind

- **PRACTICAL IDEAS** • **POWERS OF CONCENTRATION** • **MIND IN A STRAIGHT-JACKET**
- **THE MASTER PLANNER** • **LEARNING THE HARD WAY** • **FORMULA THINKING**
- **SPECIALIST KNOWLEDGE** • **MENTAL BLOCKS** • **GLOOMY THOUGHTS**

PLANETARY PRINCIPLE

 Saturn's gift to Mercury is an organized, disciplined mind, clarity of expression, and mental stamina; at best it is able to plan and master the details of a subject thoroughly.

 Saturn can inhibit Mercury, dulling the mind and imagination, and undermining confidence in mental powers; at worst, it produces a tendency to worry and think the worst.

IN RELATIONSHIPS

 Stony exterior often masks a highly sensitive mind; capable of great honesty and sincerity, provided feelings are not ridiculed; drawn to mature, reliable close friends and partners.

 Can be uncommunicative and unappreciative; finds it awkward to express feelings; takes own position too seriously; may be drawn to relationships in which others do the thinking.

PSYCHOLOGICAL TRAITS

 A serious thinker, with a philosophical bent; values knowledge as a means of getting on in the world; a constructive mind that thrives on overcoming tough problems; practical wisdom.

 A narrow-minded outlook; prone to depression and feeling isolated; learning difficulties can lead to a distrust of intellectuality; can become weighed down by inessential facts and figures.

IN DAILY LIFE

 Favours: organizational and practical skills; any work that involves in-depth research, systematic thinking or a strong sense of form or structure; corporate business; 'academic' interests.

 Dangers: getting stuck in a rut; undervaluing mental abilities; controlling the conversation; shying away from responsibility through a fear of failure; overemphasizing qualifications.

MERCURY – URANUS

The Enlightened Mind

• **A lightning-quick mind** • **Intuitive insights** • **The mental acrobat**
• **Original or progressive ideas** • **Rebel without a cause** • **The absent-
minded genius** • **Scatterbrained thinking** • **Rooting out hypocrisy**

PLANETARY DYNAMICS

Uranus illuminates and accelerates Mercury producing a razor-sharp mind capable of dazzling originality; at best, it gives an intuitive mind that can grasp universal truths in a flash.

Uranus can overload Mercury's circuitry resulting in highly strung and undisciplined mental energy; at worst, this can manifest as incoherent thinking or wildly impractical ideas.

IN RELATIONSHIPS

Mentally stimulating company; quick to understand others' problems from a detached viewpoint; a liberating influence that helps people to see themselves in a different light.

Impatient with slowness of others; tries to force own way of thinking on to friends and partners; a discomfiting influence whose outspoken views have scant regard for others' feelings.

PSYCHOLOGICAL TRAITS

A highly perceptive, progressive mind with the power to influence others through brilliant insights; values independence of thought and freedom of speech and information.

An inability to communicate clearly or effectively; tends to scatter energies and do everything in a rush; cannot bear to be wrong, often bending facts to fit its vision of the truth.

IN DAILY LIFE

Favours: work with like-minded visionaries dedicated to progressive reforms, cutting-edge technologies or communicating broader humanitarian issues; a think-tank mentality.

Dangers: mental stress; having too many irons in the fire; playing the rebel when ideas are ignored or misunderstood; inflexible opinions; lack of courage of convictions.

MERCURY – NEPTUNE

The Inspired Mind

• **INSPIRED SPEECH** • **THINKING IN PICTURES** • **POETIC INSIGHTS** • **HEAD IN THE CLOUDS** • **REFINED PERCEPTIONS** • **MUDDLED THOUGHTS** • **SPIRITUAL YEARNINGS** • **HEARING ONLY WHAT ONE WANTS TO HEAR** • **DELICATE NERVES**

PLANETARY DYNAMICS

 Neptune sensitizes Mercury enhancing receptivity and imagination; at best, the mind is attuned to higher planes of awareness and acts as a conduit for creative or spiritual visions.

 Neptune can confuse Mercury's reasoning powers so that it stumbles between high ideals and a sea-mist of deception and evasion; at worst, it can lead to a total flight from reality.

IN RELATIONSHIPS

 A fluid mentality, able to read other people's thoughts, but also open to ideas; looks for an 'empathy of minds'; capable of sustaining a sense of mystery and romance in relationships.

 Hates to be pinned down; unclear channels of communication create misunderstandings in which fantasy overtakes reality; can be very slippery, twisting words to suit ends.

PSYCHOLOGICAL TRAITS

 A subtle, finely tuned mind, rich in imagery and capable of inspired off-the-cuff solutions, often supported by a persuasive way with words; absorbs information like a sponge.

 A troubled mind that lacks clear boundaries and is prone to dark imaginings; deeply impressionable and thus changeable; may hide sensitivity behind a mask of 'super-rationality'.

IN DAILY LIFE

 Favours: creative thinking in both arts and sciences; 'transcendental' subjects, such as mysticism or the paranormal; acting as a voice for those who cannot speak up for themselves.

 Dangers: susceptibility to other's viewpoints; 'bad' atmospheres; confusion in day-to-day affairs; lack of mental discipline; not listening to what is being said; paranoid thinking.

MERCURY – PLUTO

The Intense Mind

• A penetrating mind • X-ray vision • Dark moods • Black humour • Confidential information • Forbidden knowledge • Mental swordsmanship • Self-knowledge is the path to self-mastery

PLANETARY DYNAMICS

 Pluto sharpens Mercury's perceptions giving a mind that can probe the most impenetrable subject; at best, there is an aptitude for the kind of profound insights that trigger change.

 Pluto can suppress Mercury into checking expression and keeping thought processes on a tight leash; at worst, this can result in a fear of exploring issues buried in the unconscious.

IN RELATIONSHIPS

 Intensely private, only revealing deepest thoughts in a trusting relationship; in turn, can be trusted to act as a confidant(e); once committed, makes a powerful and loyal ally.

 A fatal attraction for mind games; suspects others' motives without good cause; acutely aware of others' blind spots, and may use this knowledge to influence their thinking.

PSYCHOLOGICAL TRAITS

 The ability to see through people and situations; a convincing talker, skilled in the art of suggestion; a fine sense of critical judgment; enjoys intellectual tests of strength.

 A brooding mind, prone to let personal phobias cloud judgment; stirs up trouble by thoughtlessly delving into areas best left alone; puts up smoke-screen out of defensiveness.

IN DAILY LIFE

 Favours: any area concerned with in-depth investigation; the diplomatic service; critical appreciation; public speaking; black humour; working with the mentally disadvantaged.

 Dangers: compulsive pursuits; overestimating mental powers; sly or subversive dealings; over-zealously exploring taboo areas; looking for trouble; poisoned thoughts; acid wit.

VENUS – MARS

A Love of Passion

• **STRIVING FOR LOVE** • **THE PASSIONATE LOVER** • **ROMANTIC IDEALISM**
• **ANIMAL MAGNETISM** • **LOVE-HATE RELATIONSHIPS** • **LOVE OF THE CHASE**
• **SEXUAL HEALING** • **THE PURSUIT OF PLEASURE**

PLANETARY DYNAMICS

 Mars inflames Venus's need for love and the urge to prove herself through creative self-expression; at best, it produces a passionate nature with an endless capacity for enjoyment.

 Mars can coarsen Venus, emphasizing the desire for self-gratification, or causing deep resentments if one's needs are not met; at worst, this can be a mark of low self-esteem.

IN RELATIONSHIPS

 Whole-hearted commitment; strong physical attractions; an exciting sex life; encouraging the best in one's partner; a co-operative approach to problem solving.

 Mistakes sex for love; an inability to sustain early passion; a frustrated sex life; dealing with infidelity and possessiveness; veers between being too demanding and too passive.

PSYCHOLOGICAL TRAITS

 A spontaneous and demonstrative nature; honest about feelings; an innocent charm; the ability to get one's way through co-operating with others; a strong sense of style.

 Competing for attention; insecure about one's desirability; blowing hot and cold emotionally; a confused sexual identity; tempestuous passions; is easily hurt, yet insensitive to others.

IN DAILY LIFE

 Favours: working in public relations; interior or stage design; crafts, working with textiles, fabrics and colours; music; singing; acting, dancing; appreciation of art.

 Dangers: impulsive attachments; frustrated ambitions through lack of initiative; being dominant or dominated; inharmonious relations at work; a lack of social graces.

♀ ♃

VENUS – JUPITER

A Love of Wealth

• PLEASURE IN GIVING • THE IDEALISTIC LOVER • A LOVE OF LUXURY • THE SOCIAL BUTTERFLY • THE PURSUIT OF THE GOOD LIFE • EXCESSIVE VANITY • SPIRITUAL RICHES • EXAGGERATED FEELINGS

PLANETARY DYNAMICS

 Jupiter raises Venus's expectations of life, conferring a streak of idealism, especially in relationships; at best, it instills an unshakable belief in the spiritual power of love.

 Jupiter can inflate the pleasure principle in Venus, producing an extravagant, self-indulgent nature; at worst, this can lead to squandering resources and opportunities.

IN RELATIONSHIPS

 A big appetite for love; an affectionate, honest nature; an infectious sense of romance; a readiness to accept partners' values; an ability to reconcile differences; pleasure in sharing.

 Expects too much from a partner; may choose partners for money or social advantage; refuses to face up to own failings; lack of constancy through an inability to commit.

PSYCHOLOGICAL TRAITS

 Great personal charm; open-hearted generosity; a natural entertainer with a 'big' sense of fun; the ability to handle people from all walks of life; looks on the bright side of life.

 A constant need for approval; a predilection for licentious or amoral living; over-concerned with appearances; a 'help-yourself' attitude; sets impossibly high standards.

IN DAILY LIFE

 Favours: dealing with the public; social functions; teaching; counselling; working with the underprivileged; any 'contemplative' interest, such as philosophy, art or religion.

 Dangers: not delivering promises; excessive materialism; inflated belief in own abilities; an unwillingness to accept responsibility; blind dependence on luck; social climbing.

VENUS – SATURN

A Love of Structure

- THE DENIAL OF PLEASURE • THE DUTIFUL LOVER • SPARTAN TASTES
- TAKING ON OBLIGATIONS • DISAPPOINTMENT IN LOVE • OLDER PARTNERS
- CONTROLLED DESIRES • MEANNESS OF SPIRIT • LOW SELF-WORTH

PLANETARY DYNAMICS

Saturn stabilizes Venus by encouraging greater realism in relationships; at best it confers devotion, loyalty, a strong sense of duty and an ability to give love unconditionally.

Saturn can cause Venus to undervalue herself, and to feel unlovable and unattractive; at worst, this can result in a life-long habit of suppressing desires and affections.

IN RELATIONSHIPS

Prizes loyalty, friendship and long-term commitment above all else; shows endurance in adversity; encourages the best in a partner; takes a commonsense approach to love.

Finds it difficult to express feelings or accept others' affections; demands constant proof of love; may place ambition or duty before love, or avoid intimacy out of a fear of rejection.

PSYCHOLOGICAL TRAITS

A mature outlook; a refreshing lack of vanity; capable of disarming emotional honesty; a strong sense of fair play; the ability to make the best out of any situation.

A melancholy outlook; an awkward manner; distrusts spontaneous shows of affection; an inability to relax and enjoy life; unfeeling and inhibited; highly sensitive to criticism.

IN DAILY LIFE

Favours: the beauty and sex industries; relationship counselling; interior or stage design, crafts, textiles, fabrics; positions of responsibility; working against injustice.

Dangers: working too hard for little reward; taking on too many responsibilities; emotionally draining environments; being uncompromising in the face of opposition.

VENUS – URANUS

A Love of Freedom

• **LOVE AT FIRST SIGHT** • **THE PERFECT LOVER** • **CONFUSING LOVE WITH FRIENDSHIP** • **ABRUPT ENDINGS** • **UNSTABLE AFFECTIONS** • **ILLICIT LOVE** • **EASILY DISSATISFIED** • **UNUSUAL TASTES**

PLANETARY DYNAMICS

 Uranus excites Venus to break 'the rules' of relationship and look for novelty and freedom; at best, it produces an egalitarian approach to love free from the strictures of race or creed.

 Uranus can overstimulate Venus so that the search for love is destabilized by the need for constant excitement; at worst it leads to a totally self-centred gratification of desires.

IN RELATIONSHIPS

 An open, experimental approach to love; capable of genuine emotional rapport; seeks honest and spontaneous expression of feelings; adds spice to sexual relationships.

 Unable to accept love in all its imperfections; cuts off when a relationship turns 'ordinary'; blind to own faults yet overcritical of others'; a reluctance to give up personal freedom.

PSYCHOLOGICAL TRAITS

 An up-beat personality with a buoyant outlook on life; generates an air of excitement and fun; an original sense of style; a love of the unconventional; a wide range of interests.

 Wilfully individualistic, defying convention for the sake of it; emotionally unstable due to powerful unconscious drives; offhand manner masks self-doubt about desirability.

IN DAILY LIFE

 Favours: innovative forms of creative expression, especially in music, art and architecture; any form of work connected with dealing with the public; humanitarian causes.

 Dangers: a low-boredom threshold; bizarre tastes; sexual deviancy; insensitivity to others; neurosis from repressed desires; confusing friendship with love; lack of breathing space.

VENUS – NEPTUNE

A Love of Perfection

• **THE SEARCH FOR ECSTASY** • **THE DREAM LOVER** • **A LOVE OF GLAMOUR**
• **THE DISILLUSIONED ROMANTIC** • **THE SEARCH FOR PERFECTION** • **REFINED**
AESTHETIC TASTES • **LONGING FOR THE UNOBTAINABLE** • **PLATONIC LOVE**

PLANETARY DYNAMICS

 Neptune refines the Venusian principle of erotic love, elevating it to the ultimate ecstatic experience; at best, it symbolizes the search for a spiritual or universal dimension to love.

 Neptune confuses Venus, dissolving the ability to discriminate so that fantasy becomes intermingled with reality; at worst, this results in lust being repeatedly mistaken for love.

IN RELATIONSHIPS

 A capacity for great self-sacrifice in love; the ability to tune into others' feelings; the desire to bring romance into a relationship; subtle powers of seduction; an erotic imagination.

 An inability to accept partners for what they are; drawn to relationships based on the need to save or be saved; promiscuous out of a reluctance to commit to any one person.

PSYCHOLOGICAL TRAITS

 Extremely soft-hearted, with a tendency to look for the best in everybody; the desire to be at peace with the world; a compassionate and caring disposition; a profound love of beauty.

 A hopelessly romantic nature; the urge to escape the harsh realities of life; lack of clear boundaries results in a tendency to deceive or be deceived; a frail grasp of self-worth.

CREATIVE OUTLETS

Favours: creative imagination; the arts; the beauty industry; charitable work; animal welfare; the healing or caring professions; giving oneself to a higher cause.

 Dangers: being seduced by glamour; giving it all away; unrequited love; exposure to suffering; dubious financial deals; lack of application; worshipping false gods.

VENUS – PLUTO

A Love of Power

- **INTENSE ATTRACTIONS** • **TRANSFORMATIVE RELATIONSHIPS**
- **THE DEMONIC LOVER** • **COMPULSIVE LOVES AND HATES**
- **THE POWER OF APPEARANCE** • **CREATIVE POWER**

PLANETARY DYNAMICS

 Pluto intensifies Venus into seeking all-or-nothing emotional involvements; at its best, it represents the desire to experience love as a profoundly transformative experience.

 Pluto can draw Venus into obsessive, all-consuming infatuations which, at worst, can unleash violent, self-destructive passions that often devour others in the process.

IN RELATIONSHIPS

 Capable of great emotional honesty in a trusting relationship; heightened sexuality and a need to express intense emotions can form the basis of a richly rewarding love life.

 Undermines need for emotional security by forming unstable, compulsive attachments; demands constant proof of affections; may withhold love or sex as a means of control.

PSYCHOLOGICAL TRAITS

 Personal magnetism; a flair for dramatic self-presentation; an instinctive awareness of how to use physical assets to personal advantage and how to probe what turns others on.

 A fragile self-worth; an insatiable need for approval; can be obsessed with – and overestimate – own powers of seduction; is unforgiving when rejected or humiliated.

IN DAILY LIFE

 Favours: creative endeavours; occupations that involve breathing new life into anything old or discarded; the rag trade; transforming the appearance of others; relationship counselling.

 Dangers: becoming involved in degrading relationships; misusing money, power or influence; emotional dishonesty; sex without love; invasive charms; too many secrets.

MARS – JUPITER

Self-assertion through Expansion

- **THE HUMAN DYNAMO** • **THE MORAL CRUSADER** • **FORTUNE FAVOURS THE BRAVE**
- **RASH SPECULATIONS** • **THE SEXUAL ADVENTURER** • **DARING ACTIONS**
- **FIRE-AND-BRIMSTONE BELIEFS** • **EXCESS AGGRESSION**

PLANETARY DYNAMICS

 Jupiter expands Mars's energy on the physical and mental level; at best this combination can produce an extremely positive approach to life, and the courage to fight for one's beliefs.

 Jupiter's optimism and Mars's raw power tend to inflate self-belief; at worst this can lead to overhasty action and an almost evangelical conviction that one is always right.

IN RELATIONSHIPS

 When in love, tends to be loyal and generous; approaches romance with irrepressible enthusiasm and a spirit of adventure; an energizing influence with a lusty sex drive.

 Can be extremely competitive; emotionally volatile if desires are thwarted; expects unfettered freedom; sexual overload; anger and possessiveness can be serious issues.

PSYCHOLOGICAL TRAITS

 Likes to lead by example; often takes great pride in physical prowess; the confidence and drive to take the initiative; the will power and discipline to keep goals in sight.

 A full-throttle energy that easily runs out of control; low will to work or succeed; a reckless disregard for authority; a lack of humility; an exaggerated need to do things one's own way.

IN DAILY LIFE

 Favours: the spirit of free enterprise; activities requiring the ability to act fast; sporting contests; preaching to the unconverted; fighting for beliefs; any form of litigation.

 Dangers: taking undue risks; cutting corners; wasting energy and resources on ill-conceived plans; inflammatory remarks; misplaced convictions; lack of moderation and finesse.

MARS – SATURN

Self-assertion through Control

• FEATS OF ENDURANCE • HARD LABOUR • DRIVING FLAT OUT WITH THE BRAKES ON • BOTTLED-UP ANGER • CONCENTRATED WILL-POWER • SUFFERING ABUSE • DELAYED ACTION • FEAR OF VIOLENCE • TROUBLES WITH AUTHORITY

PLANETARY DYNAMICS

 Saturn stabilizes impulsive Mars, teaching it the virtues of patience and measured action; at best it gives the stamina and discipline to lead from the front and achieve one's aims.

 Saturn can stir feelings of insecurity in Mars, which often register as a sense of impotence and a fear of competition; at worst, pent-up frustration can lead to violent outbursts of rage.

IN RELATIONSHIPS

 Love burns with a steady flame; long-suffering, persevering when others would give up; a strong protective streak; a controlled sex drive that often masks a passionate nature.

 A fear of being emotionally vulnerable; passions often blow hot and cold; a tendency to suppress feelings altogether; conflicts over who is controlling whom; an inhibited sex drive.

PSYCHOLOGICAL TRAITS

 The strength to fight doggedly for what one wants; the ability to work under pressure; instinctively enjoys tests of strength; powers of endurance; good sense of timing.

 Inhibited by too much concern for conventional values or what others think; a lack of energy and assertiveness; wilfully obstinate; extreme swings in confidence; an inability to delegate.

IN DAILY LIFE

 Favours: any occupation or activity that involves working in challenging conditions, or where careful planning is paramount; running one's own business; helping others deal with pain.

 Dangers: lack of direction; fear of failure; leaving projects half finished; a defeatist outlook; disputes with authority; over-taxing one's health; accidents due to overexertion.

MARS – URANUS

Self-assertion through Liberation

- **HIGH-VOLTAGE ENERGY** • **FIGHTING FOR LIBERTY AND EQUALITY**
- **A LOVE OF DANGER** • **SEXUAL FIREWORKS** • **UNUSUAL ACTIVITIES**
- **UNPREDICTABLE BEHAVIOUR** • **THE SPIRIT OF REBELLION**

PLANETARY DYNAMICS

 Uranus electrifies Mars producing a highly charged current of energy; at best this is a force for independence and growth, not just on a personal level, but on behalf of others.

 Uranus can incite Mars to the kind of non-conformism that flouts convention just for the sake of being different; at worst, it can engage in a ruthless, even violent, battle of wills.

IN RELATIONSHIPS

 Seeks and provides excitement on all levels; sees love as an expression of freedom as opposed to co-dependency; can help to break down others' sexual inhibitions.

 Affections may be sporadic; brutal frankness; a lack of consideration for others' feelings; an insistence on having everything one's own way; may prefer sex with little emotional content.

PSYCHOLOGICAL TRAITS

 An exciting, irresistible personality with endless reserves of physical energy; mentally alert and inventive; a fierce sense of independence; the courage to achieve extraordinary feats.

 Unfocused energy creates inner tension; swings between extremes of inactivity and restlessness; frustration can trigger violent temper; capable of mindless destruction.

IN DAILY LIFE

 Favours: working in emergencies or dangerous situations; activities that require powers of persuasion; working for the common good; mechanical or engineering skills; new methods.

 Dangers: lack of a cause to fight for; extreme impatience; disruptive atmospheres; wilful trials of strength; allowing oneself to be hemmed in; rash acts; sudden accidents.

MARS – NEPTUNE

Self-assertion through Inspiration

• **FIGHTING FOR IDEALS** • **UNFOCUSED AMBITION** • **DIFFUSED ANGER**
• **CHAMPIONING THE UNDERDOG** • **THE FIGHTING HERO** • **CONFUSED ACTIONS**
• **LIVING IN A FANTASY WORLD** • **INSPIRED INITIATIVES**

PLANETARY DYNAMICS

 Neptune elevates Mars's raw energy to the realm of infinite possibilities – a subtle and complex blend which, at best, gives an ability to turn one's inner vision into reality.

 Neptune can seduce Mars into yearning for the impossible, resulting in frustrated ambition and disillusionment; at worst, this pairing is capable of deceit and depravity.

IN RELATIONSHIPS

 Subtle powers of seduction; a highly romantic approach to relationships; the ability to merge with a partner's feelings; a sensuous and imaginative approach to sex.

 Extremely susceptible to others' desires; conflicts through an inability to admit to negative feelings; can be confused or misled about sexual preferences.

PSYCHOLOGICAL TRAITS

 Heightened sensitivity and compassion; the courage to explore emotional undercurrents; the ability to formulate practical ideals; prefers subterfuge to direct confrontation.

 Lacks the drive and confidence to handle practical affairs; unclear motives; easily defeated; may seek to escape harsh realities of everyday life; sets unrealistic goals.

IN DAILY LIFE

 Favours: creative endeavours; film and photography; the performance arts; working behind the scenes; subtle forms of exercise, such as yoga; charitable work; psychic healing.

 Dangers: Negative atmospheres; constantly shifting objectives; underhand actions; hidden agendas; repressed desires; dishonest people; misdirected energy; psychosomatic disorders.

MARS – PLUTO

Self-assertion through Power

• **THE WILL TO WIN** • **TAKING BY FORCE** • **FEAR OF COMPETITION** • **HIDDEN RESERVES OF ENERGY** • **SEETHING AMBITION** • **BURIED RAGE** • **NUCLEAR POWER** • **VOLCANIC EMOTIONS** • **CONTROLLED SEXUALITY** • **SURVIVAL INSTINCT**

PLANETARY DYNAMICS

 Pluto intensifies Mars's will to win, giving it the drive to overcome any obstacle through decisive action; at best, it can transform the primitive side of Mars into a healing energy.

 Pluto can suppress Mars, undermining the will to succeed; at worst, this creates a deep suspicion of, even revulsion for, Mars-type qualities, such as aggression and anger.

IN RELATIONSHIPS

 Seeks intimacy at a very deep level; has the courage to confront and transmute darkest urges; an intense sex drive which if explored can be immensely rewarding.

 Power struggles in which domination, abuse or violence are an issue; a defiant disregard for other's values; a tendency to suppress desires can trigger explosive emotional outbursts.

PSYCHOLOGICAL TRAITS

 An intense approach to life; seeks to extract the most from a situation; actions are driven by a powerful sense of conviction; an ability to penetrate other peoples deepest motives.

 A tendency to self-destruct through over-reaching; a crude 'have or be had' attitude; alternatively, a reluctance to assert oneself at all through a built-in expectation of failure.

IN DAILY LIFE

 Favours: any activity that demands pushing oneself to the limit, or succeeding against the odds; work that involves exposing social taboos, or exploring the deepest recesses of the psyche.

 Dangers: ruthless drive for power; provoking open rivalries; not being able to forgive and forget; suppressing anger; burying the competitive instinct; sado-masochism.

♃ ♄

JUPITER – SATURN

Growth through Structure

• **Material wealth** • **Lack of opportunities** • **Spartan lifestyle** • **Fear of poverty** • **Controlled expansion** • **Lack of faith** • **Looking for 'God'** • **A fear of taking risks** • **Stifling morality** • **Conservative values**

PLANETARY DYNAMICS

 Saturn checks Jupiter's expansionist tendencies by confining his ambitions within existing social structures; at best, it denotes steady growth through cautious optimism.

 Saturn can cause Jupiter to feel trapped by prevailing cultural values or traditional beliefs; at worst, it can give rise to a profound feeling of emptiness about life.

IN RELATIONSHIPS

 May be drawn to people with strong moral or spiritual beliefs; can inject the lives of others with personal meaning; the ability to help others face their own doubts and fears.

 Difficult dealings with father; restless dissatisfaction with conventional relationships; inclined to impose strict values on family; may lean on others for financial or moral support.

PSYCHOLOGICAL TRAITS

 Hopes and expectations tempered by realism; the ability to persevere through thick and thin; the dogged pursuit of one's objectives; the determination to achieve worldly success.

 Sets impossibly high moral standards; wavers between blind optimism and bleak despair; ambitions undermined by self-doubt and extreme caution; the urge to withdraw from life.

IN DAILY LIFE

 Favours: long-term planning; big business; economics; education; all aspects of the legal profession; the search for spiritual values; philosophy; teaching; heavy responsibilities.

 Dangers: following wild hunches; religious dogma; aimless routine; limiting one's scope in life; gloomy people and environments; laying down the law; meanness of spirit.

♃ ♅

JUPITER – URANUS

Growth through Idealism

• **BIG RADICAL IDEAS** • **ORIGINAL SOLUTIONS** • **SUDDEN CHANGES IN FORTUNE** • **CONTROVERSIAL BELIEFS** • **KNOWLEDGE IS FREEDOM** • **THE ENLIGHTENED REFORMER** • **FLEETING ENTHUSIASMS** • **INDEPENDENCE OF MIND**

PLANETARY DYNAMICS

Uranus excites Jupiter's enthusiasm for insight giving it a flair for grasping 'universal truths'; at best, it denotes a radical thinker with ideas that are often ahead of their time.

Uranus can blind Jupiter with unrealistic ideas; at worst, it indicates a rigid adherence to principles out of a need to be different, rather than through any sense of conviction.

IN RELATIONSHIPS

Broad-minded and tolerant, with a need to share ideals with others; a liberating influence, capable of guiding others to break away from restrictive patterns of relating.

Given to bending others to 'the truth' as one sees it, ignoring that this is often just a personal view; hypocritical, often preaching one set of values while practising another.

PSYCHOLOGICAL TRAITS

An original thinker, with an intuitive grasp of a situation; can point to an ability to speak out for collective issues; a strongly independent streak with a deep sense of a personal mission.

A woolly-minded idealist with a penchant for eccentric beliefs; a contrary nature, given to stubborn non-conformism or, paradoxically, staunchly upholding conventional values.

CREATIVE EXPRESSION

Favours: any area that involves working with progressive ideas or reforms; humanistic studies; social sciences; speculative ventures; also indicates possible interest in metaphysics.

Dangers: seeking novelty for the sake of it; dogmatic views; missed opportunities; speaking one's mind, with no regard for the consequences; clashes with authority.

♃ ♆

JUPITER – NEPTUNE

Growth through Imagination

• INSPIRED BELIEFS • THE MYSTICAL ADVENTURER • A WEALTH OF DREAMS
• DELUSIONS OF GRANDEUR • EXPLORING INVISIBLE REALMS • AN ABUNDANCE
OF COMPASSION • MORAL CONFUSION • THE SPACE CADET

PLANETARY DYNAMICS

Neptune inspires Jupiter to find a 'higher cause' – a philosophy that embraces more than just personal ambition; at best, it denotes the ability to work selflessly for people in need.

Neptune can seduce Jupiter into confusing imagination with reality; at worst, it tends towards excess, self-delusion, misplaced optimism and, ultimately, a loss of faith in life.

IN RELATIONSHIPS

Compassionate and gentle, with an ability to give love generously; seeks relationships to share hopes and ideals; can have an intuitive understanding of other's spiritual needs.

Highly impressionable and vague, with a tendency to be easily seduced or to mislead others; tends to idolize people, especially loved ones; can lack sincerity of purpose.

PSYCHOLOGICAL TRAITS

Extremely idealistic with a strong altruistic streak; sensitivity to suffering with a powerful need to make the world a better place; the ability to turn hunches into reality.

Lives in an unreal world; an 'anything-goes' approach to life; can be extremely gullible and woolly minded; clash between worldly and spiritual beliefs can lead to escapism.

IN DAILY LIFE

Favours: artistic ability, especially in the area of visual arts and rhythm; playing the stock market; traditionally linked with sailing; possible interest in mysticism or spiritualism.

Dangers: taking blind risks; believing one's luck to be infallible; dishonest speculations; becoming embroiled in scandal; squandering fortunes; a fatal attraction to glamour.

24 ♇

JUPITER – PLUTO

Growth through Transformation

• **SPIRITUAL REBIRTH** • **SECRET AMBITIONS** • **ENLIGHTENED DESPOT** • **REPRESSED** **HOPES** • **MISSION IMPOSSIBLE** • **UNTAPPED POWER** • **BURIED TREASURE** • **ROOT-AND-BRANCH REFORM** • **THE BLACK MARKET ECONOMY**

PLANETARY DYNAMICS

 Pluto intensifies Jupiter's search for hidden meaning and power; at best, it confers the ability to discern the profound truths that come through personal crises and suffering.

 Pluto can distort Jupiter's search for meaning, so that personal beliefs are mistaken for universal truths; at worst, it produces a greed for power and self-gratification.

IN RELATIONSHIPS

 Looks for passionate and intense involvements; can direct insights to help partners unearth hidden talents; financial benefits through partners.

 Seeks to dominate in relationships; conflicts through trying to impose personal beliefs on others; unwilling to make concessions; an obsession with sex.

PSYCHOLOGICAL TRAITS

 Approaches goals fearlessly and with a strong sense of conviction; seeks self-improvement through transformative experiences; can act as a transmitter of collective beliefs.

 Arrogant belief in one's right to power and influence; dogmatic outlook on life; rebellious attitude to authority; lack of enterprise through fear of change; intolerant of opposition.

IN DAILY LIFE

 Favours: working for social change; handling large sums of money; exploring the workings of the psyche; regenerating or recycling waste; possible interest in the occult.

 Dangers: lust for wealth; devious financial dealings; surrounding oneself with cronies; being over-confrontational; lack of humility; inflated self-confidence; megalomania.

♄ ♅

SATURN – URANUS

Structured Ideals

• GRADUAL REFORM • CONTROLLING OR OPPRESSIVE BEHAVIOUR • CHALLENGING AUTHORITY • PRO- VERSUS ANTI-ESTABLISHMENT • FEAR OF THE NEW • BREAKING WITH CONVENTION • PRACTICAL IDEALS

PLANETARY DYNAMICS

 Uranus stimulates Saturn into incorporating new ideas within the established order; at best this pairing produces a cautious approach to reform, combining originality with practicality.

 Uranus can challenge Saturn, creating immense inner frustration; at worst, it leads to a stalemate in which the need for freedom and new growth is undermined by a fear of change.

IN RELATIONSHIPS

 Thoughtful and open-minded, often willing to change attitudes to relating; may look for relationships that break with tradition; is capable of shouldering huge responsibilities.

 Unfeeling due to an inability to accept own emotional needs; can be extremely touchy; extreme restlessness from a tendency to get stuck in deeply conventional relationships.

PSYCHOLOGICAL TRAITS

 A forceful, authoritative personality; shows great will power in the face of opposition; the strength of character to face and overcome one's own inhibitions; leadership potential.

 Strong principles often mask inner uncertainty; an inability to alter a course of action when necessary; a tyrannical insistence that one is always right; an inability to face the truth.

IN DAILY LIFE

 Favours: practical or scientific endeavours; revitalizing old traditions; working in new technologies; ideas that benefit group welfare; studying 'mind over matter' subjects.

 Dangers: anarchic behaviour; promoting cranky or unrealistic ideas; bending the rules to suit one's goals; inflexible expectations; autocratic methods; lack of scruples.

ħ Ψ

SATURN – NEPTUNE

Structured Visions

• **TRANSCENDING LIMITATIONS** • **GLAMORIZING AUTHORITY** • **FEAR OF LOSING CONTROL** • **THE SOCIAL MISFIT** • **LACK OF GUIDANCE** • **LESSONS IN 'LETTING GO'** • **PSYCHOSOMATIC ILLNESSES** • **LIFE IS BUT A DREAM**

PLANETARY DYNAMICS

Neptune can inspire Saturn to transcend worldly ambition and find a higher cause to serve; at best this combination can work selflessly to make spiritual visions a reality.

Neptune can inflate Saturn's desire for worldly success or confuse its grip on reality; at worst, this can lead to total disillusionment with or the urge to withdraw from the material world.

IN RELATIONSHIPS

Willing to sacrifice own needs to fulfil demands of others; sympathetic to other's suffering; capable of honouring the most arduous commitments.

Tends to see rejection where none is intended; need for privacy can override desire for intimacy; finds commitment a burden; may be drawn to victim-saviour relationships.

PSYCHOLOGICAL TRAITS

Capable of great wisdom and insight; strong awareness of personal boundaries; the need to become one's own authority; can act as a mouthpiece for expressing collective fantasies.

Inclined to think the worst; tormented by self-doubt and guilt; confidence eroded by feelings of despair; feels 'all at sea' in the face of adversity; inclined to flee from harsh reality.

IN DAILY LIFE

Favours: artistic inspiration; working for a higher cause; voluntary work; plumbing the emotional depths; ecological issues; 'visionary' work; mystical pursuits; ascetic lifestyle.

Dangers: being submerged in others' problems; impractical ideals; living in clutter; a messianic complex; losing sight of one's dreams; lack of humility; dealing in treachery.

♄　♇

SATURN – PLUTO

Structured Power

• **POWER WITH RESPONSIBILITY** • **FEAR OF ANNIHILATION** • **TEARING DOWN DEFENCES** • **CONTROLLED USE OF FORCE** • **DEATH AND REBIRTH** • **NO GAIN WITHOUT PAIN** • **FEATS OF SURVIVAL** • **REPRESSIVE AUTHORITY**

PLANETARY DYNAMICS

 Pluto intensifies Saturn to tear down anything that restricts the creative use of power; at best, it is capable of uprooting outworn structures and clearing the way for new growth.

 Pluto can corrupt Saturn's desire for power, encouraging fanatical beliefs and a climate of suspicion and fear; at worst, it can produce a police state mentality of the 'enemy within'.

IN RELATIONSHIPS

 Believes in intense commitment; capable of profound intimacy; unconsciously seeks relationships that initiate a challenging process of self-realization and growth.

 Tends to repress feelings and desires; uses sex as a means of emotional control; intolerant of others' weaknesses; inclined to be suspicious of others' motives; can be extremely defensive.

PSYCHOLOGICAL TRAITS

 Self-transformation through mastering powerful emotions; a capacity for great achievements through self-denial; the courage to probe one's motives; a ruthless survival instinct.

 Deep feelings of inadequacy; fearful of expressing one's own power; an obsession with maintaining control or order; intensely introverted; depression through loss of purpose.

IN DAILY LIFE

 Favours: working on behalf of the victims of society; any activity that requires a killer instinct; demolition and salvage work; psychotherapeutic processes.

 Dangers: extreme ambition; making powerful enemies; restrictive practices; abuse of power; rigid principles; control by force; too much austerity; cloak-and-dagger intrigues.

URANUS – NEPTUNE

Idealized Visions

- DREAMS OF A BRAVE NEW WORLD • ALTERED STATES OF CONSCIOUSNESS
- INSPIRED REFORMS • STRANGE NEW IDEAS • NEW AGE BELIEFS
- THE RIGHT TO SELF-DETERMINATION • MASS DELUSION

PLANETARY DYNAMICS

 Neptune inspires Uranus to explore the realm of collective ideas and emotions; at best, it can acts as a trigger for social revolution or revolutionary leaps in consciousness.

 Neptune can distend Uranus so that the intuitive faculties are clouded by confused utopian ideals which, at worst, can result in a tendency to extremism or escapism.

IN RELATIONSHIPS

 A willingness to make major adjustments in love; drawn to relationships that enhance spiritual awareness; experiencing emotional intensity through sexual expression.

 Disappointments in love through over-idealizing partners; frustrated need for excitement; drawn to people who are erratic or who are in some way unavailable.

PSYCHOLOGICAL TRAITS

 Extremely intuitive; feels driven to work for the benefit of mankind; able to tap into the public's wishes for sweeping changes in society; the ability to seize the moral high ground.

 Lost in a sea of apathy and inertia; emotional and psychic turmoil; prone to sudden and strange ideas; espousing ideals that serve naked self-interest; not practising what one preaches.

IN DAILY LIFE

 Favours: improving the human condition; working to expose corruption and greed; new forms of music and art; a renaissance in the areas of mysticism and the occult.

 Dangers: appealing to the lowest common denominator; populist nationalism; a resurgence of racism; the drug culture; the pursuit of indiscriminate change.

URANUS – PLUTO

Idealized Power

• Radical reforms • Collective responsibility • Remarkable new technologies • Sudden annihilation • Retrieval of buried knowledge • Tapping into hidden power • Underground revolution

PLANETARY DYNAMICS

 Pluto intensifies Uranus's drive to raise the level of group consciousness; at best, it symbolizes a radically new approach to life through transforming the established order.

 Pluto can corrupt Uranus, bringing out the destructive energies of both planets; at worst, it leads to anarchy and subversion – in short, violent upheaval and destruction on all levels.

PSYCHOLOGICAL TRAITS

 Remarkable energy; the desire to make radical improvements in quality of life both on a personal and collective level; the urge to live and express oneself to the fullest.

 Obsessive urge for freedom without regard for other people's rights; exploiting resources without responsibility; motivated purely by the desire for profit; fanatical views.

IN RELATIONSHIPS

 Sudden and powerful infatuations; the ability to explore and transform one's motives for intimacy; relationships that draw out hidden talents or that revolutionize one's lifestyle.

 Destructive or violent relationships that focus on the issue of domination; stubborn refusal to give ground or co-operate; extreme impatience with others; rapacious sexual appetites.

IN DAILY LIFE

 Favours: earth sciences and environmental issues; renewable sources of energy; new insights into the laws of matter; sub-particle physics; the arcane arts; radical politics.

 Dangers: over-ambitious objectives; violent aggression; acts of subversion; environmental destruction; nuclear holocaust; economic collapse; sexual abuse (often with Mars).

NEPTUNE – PLUTO

Visions of Transformation

- **SUBTLE TRANSFORMATIONS** • **HIDDEN FORCES OF CREATION** • **THE POWER OF THE SUPERNATURAL** • **THE INTERFACE BETWEEN MIND AND MATTER** • **INVISIBLE DIMENSIONS** • **THE COLLECTIVE UNCONSCIOUS**

PLANETARY DYNAMICS

 Pluto intensifies Neptune's attunement to the mysteries of inner and outer space; at best, it offers a gradual deepening of humankind's understanding of reality and consciousness.

 Pluto can suppress Neptune's otherworldly yearnings; at worst, it leads to a denial of the existence of a spiritual realm – or any other reality apart from the physical universe.

IN RELATIONSHIPS

 Self-transformation through sacrificing personal needs for the welfare of others; refining one's attitude to relationships through self-exploration; spiritually based unions.

 Seduced into giving one's power away to others; frustrated quest for the ideal partner; deep-seated mistrust of others' motives; unfulfilled or repressed sexual fantasies.

PSYCHOLOGICAL TRAITS

 The search for alternative realities; the need for spiritual insight; widening one's sense of connectedness with the forces of nature; the urge to explore one's psychological foundations.

 Self-torment through the disintegration of old certainties; dissatisfaction with the daily concerns of mundane reality; confusion about the meaning or purpose of existence.

IN DAILY LIFE

 Favours: redefining one's understanding of God; exploring the paranormal and the hidden powers of the mind; the search for hidden knowledge; nuclear fusion.

 Dangers: casual experimentation with the occult; uncontrolled hallucinatory experiences; false prophets; spiritual pride; morbid fears and neuroses; drug and alcohol abuse.

CHAPTER 6

ASPECTS TO THE
ANGLES

In Chapter 4, we discussed the significance of the Angles – the Ascendant–Descendant and the MC–IC axes. Because they symbolize our moment of arrival on this planet, astrology invests them with enormous significance. For instance, any planet conjunct the Ascendant (a common practice is to allow an 8⁰ orb) will manifest the traits associated with both planet and sign with great force, to the extent that it can dominate the chart. In fact, although conjunctions to the Ascendant are regarded as extremely powerful, all aspects to the Angles are important.

When interpreting these aspects, it is essential to remember that each Angle is a point at the end of an axis, so that any planet aspecting the Ascendant or MC will automatically aspect its opposite point – the Descendant or IC. For example, people with Mars on the Ascendant may be characterized as spontaneous and impatient, with an almost exaggerated need to impose their will on everything they do. But, apart from considering any other planetary aspects to

Mars, this assessment must also be balanced by the fact that Mars is opposite the Descendant – how the world responds to the individual. The opposition to the Descendant suggests that Mars's impulsive energy will be met with resistance, highlighting the need for restraint and co-operation.

Similarly, aspects from planets to the MC – the 'conscious self' – shape how we set about achieving our goals in life, whereas the same aspects to the IC – the 'innermost self' – show the motives behind our ambition, what subconsciously drives us. As our conscious aims are strongly shaped by childhood conditioning, aspects to the MC–IC axis are also believed to shed light on our parental influence, or those responsible for our upbringing.

Given that the Angles move so fast – on average one degree of the Ecliptic every four minutes – the aspects they form to the planets on any one day change very rapidly. So, if the time of birth is uncertain, any aspects to the Angles should be treated cautiously.

SUN • ANGLES

The Need to be Recognized as Unique

• **STRENGTH OF PERSONALITY** • **FINDING A MISSION IN LIFE** • **BECOMING AN AUTHORITY** • **SEEKING THE LIMELIGHT** • **FULFILMENT THROUGH CAREER** • **PUTTING ON AN IMPRESSIVE FRONT**

ASCENDANT

 A radiant personality, with a strong measure of self-belief and charm; seeks to be master of own destiny; motivated by a need to be seen as special; often has a flair for self-promotion.

 Self-respect undermined by misplaced confidence; powerful personality clashes with others; tries to boost self-confidence by being pushy or boastful; personality may lack depth.

MIDHEAVEN

 Projects a strong sense of vocation and a clear vision of aims; seeks honour and recognition in work; possible leadership qualities; career is often strongly influenced by father figure.

 Dreams of fame and fortune without developing necessary talents to achieve them; clashes with authority figures; frustrated objectives; lacks direction for want of parental guidance.

DESCENDANT

 A strong desire to find oneself through close involvements with others; can feel uncomfortable in the limelight; often has the ability to 'empower' other people.

 Tends to lionize partners at expense of self-esteem; can rely too much on others for guidance; brittle self-confidence; needs to strive for equality in relationships.

IMUM COELI

 Ambitious, but with a strong awareness of the need to balance career with home life; values privacy more than stardom; often becomes an authority in some area later in life.

 Conflict between professional and private life; motives are often unclear; plans frustrated through over-ambitious goals; can be arrogant, expecting success as a matter of right.

MOON • ANGLES
The Need to Fit In

• **THE ABILITY TO FIT IN** • **FINDING A SENSE OF BELONGING** • **POWERFUL REACTIONS** • **ATTACHMENT TO THE PAST** • **VULNERABLE FEELINGS** • **FINDING SECURITY** • **PERSONAL MAGNETISM**

ASCENDANT

A highly receptive nature that adapts easily to surroundings; often seeks to provide and protect, although needs reassurance in return; values long-term close relationships.

Can be extremely moody and changeable; finds it hard to break habits; difficulties with separating from family, especially mother; is easily slighted and harbours petty resentments.

MIDHEAVEN

Projects a caring, feeling image; highly attuned to public opinion; often entertains a deep longing for public acclaim; strong parental (mother) influence on career.

Attaches too much importance to public image; inner needs not fulfilled by career or home; complications in personal relationships; career marred by indecision and many changes.

DESCENDANT

Highly receptive to the needs of others; often arouses strong protective instincts in partners; when secure, can be easy-going, sympathetic and helpful; good contacts with women.

Needs to develop greater self-reliance in relationships; is prone to over-reacting in a childish way; can be extremely disharmonious; struggles to see own behaviour objectively.

IMUM COELI

Strongly pulled by the past, especially by the family and its history; can have a very sound emotional footing; needs home as a place of retreat; strong bond with parent(s).

Finds it difficult to let go emotionally of objects and people; family 'pushes' choice of career, causing much resentment; can indicate frequent changes in residence or life direction.

MERCURY • ANGLES
The Need to Communicate

• **INQUISITIVE MIND** • **MENTALLY ATTUNED TO SURROUNDINGS** • **THE ABILITY TO ANALYSE** • **PASSION FOR LEARNING** • **RESTLESS SPIRIT** • **SUPERFICIAL KNOWLEDGE** • **MENTAL GYMNASTICS** • **THE ABILITY TO IMITATE**

ASCENDANT

A youthful personality, with a constantly changing identity; often articulate with a flair for languages or mimicry; stimulating and witty company; innumerable social contacts.

Can be extremely restless and impatient; often misunderstood; tries to dominate conversations; superficial contacts; can be woundingly critical; a fondness for idle gossip.

DESCENDANT

Looks for a 'meeting of minds' in close relationships; often skilled at handling people and holding an audience's attention; can denote the ability to listen.

May feel insecure about mental abilities; often shows poor judgment, saying the wrong thing at the wrong time; inhibited self-expression through not knowing one's own mind.

MIDHEAVEN

Projects an 'educated' image; wants to be respected for mental abilities; frequently well-connected; acts as a 'junction box' for people and ideas; can indicate a skilled mediator.

A reputation for dishonesty, which at best manifests as a gift of the gab; overestimates mental powers; lacks self-criticism; may feel disadvantaged through lack of education.

IMUM COELI

A highly sensitive or intuitive mind; a powerful urge to study and/or to communicate; often suggests a background where education is valued; possible interest in genealogy.

May feel ill-equipped mentally to deal with the outside world; feels undermined by people who are articulate or well-informed; can be narrow minded; an inability to relax.

VENUS · ANGLES
The Need for Harmonious Surroundings

• MAKING THE RIGHT IMPRESSION • THE IMPORTANCE OF APPEARANCES
• A LOVE OF LUXURY • PERSONAL CHARM • AN ARTISTIC TEMPERAMENT
• AN EMPHASIZED NEED FOR RELATIONSHIP

ASCENDANT

 Indicates great charm, youthful vitality and an ability to make people feel at ease; motivated by the desire for harmony; often displays impeccable manners, taste and dress sense.

 The entire approach to life may be dominated by the pursuit of pleasure; is often over-concerned about appearance and popularity; can be insincere, frivolous and rivalrous.

MIDHEAVEN

 Projects an open, sociable image; an accommodating manner; fortunate contacts in career; a strong aesthetic sense; can often be an indication of great public appeal.

 Highly image conscious; often attaches great importance to status; desire for public approval above close relationships may lead to loss of friends; can be extremely superficial.

DESCENDANT

 A strong need for relationship is matched by a willingness to find the common ground with partners; has a talent for making others feel attractive; often seeks an artistic environment.

 May look to others to supply glamour in relationships; finds it difficult to deal honestly with relationship problems; can be vulnerable to being exploited by others' desires.

IMUM COELI

 Like Venus on the MC, often denotes a desire to be in the public eye, although modified by a strong need for a loving, fulfilling home life; often points to a supportive upbringing.

 Suggests there is a conflict between personal desires and the demand of home; may be uncertain about attractiveness; can sometimes signify a rivalrous relationship with a parent.

MARS · ANGLES

The Need to Impose Oneself on One's Environment

• **VIGOROUS MANNER** • **HIGHLY GOAL CONSCIOUS** • **BATTLES WITH AUTHORITY**
• **TAKING THE INITIATIVE** • **MISPLACED AGGRESSION** • **EARNED SUCCESS**
• **FIGHTING FOR RESPECT** • **PREMATURE ACTION**

ASCENDANT

 An assertive, energetic personality, usually with a strong physical presence; is often passionate and emotional; invariably keen to get on with the job in hand; leadership potential.

 Views environment as competitive or unsafe and thus often acts provocatively, as if spoiling for a fight; often tries to force its own way; may harbour fears about being ineffectual.

MIDHEAVEN

 Projects an enterprising, decisive image with a strong sense of purpose; often thrives in a competitive environment; a tough negotiator; an individualist, who likes to run the show.

 Masks underlying feelings of weakness through aggressive behaviour; may feel pressurized by family expectations into being competitive; likely to experience conflicts with superiors.

DESCENDANT

 Has the strength to find a balance between compromise and self-assertion; brings passion and enthusiasm to relationships; often drawn to fight on behalf of the downtrodden.

 Sees the world as a constant battleground; instinctively seeks competitive relationships as a means of expressing will power; may be attracted to people who like to dominate.

IMUM COELI

 A powerful urge to be 'one's own person'; can have huge reserves of energy; an energetic home-maker; intensely protective of family; often motivated to act out of a sense of outrage.

 Can suffer from periodic bouts of low energy or drive; feelings of anger may be linked to a family history of conflict; may vent frustration on family; domineering in the home.

4

JUPITER • ANGLES

The Need to Expand One's Environment

• SEARCHING FOR A FAITH • EXPLORING NEW HORIZONS • SELF-INFLATED IMPORTANCE • IMMENSE CHARM • EXTRAVAGANT HABITS • INSPIRED OPPORTUNISM • GOOD FORTUNE • EXPANDING WAISTLINE

ASCENDANT

A larger-than-life personality, with a big appetite for life; a gift for inspiring others; a philosophical outlook; a strong sense of vision; the ability to land on one's feet.

Suffers from inflated self-importance; lacks the discipline to follow through ideas; can be supremely arrogant and dismissive; tends to be ferociously judgmental; the arch-hypocrite.

MIDHEAVEN

Projects an enthusiastic, optimistic image; keen to make an impression; strong sense of drama; often denotes popularity, even public acclaim; possible leadership material.

Lack of inner faith or ideals can create feeling of emptiness, even if successful in career; projecting a false image of optimism; frustrated desire to be important; over-ambitious goals.

DESCENDANT

Endlessly fascinated by other people, with a talent for finding the common ground; looks to partners to broaden horizons; loves to give advice; generous with time and energy.

Expects too much of relationships; beliefs may be at variance with projected image; misplaced generosity; extravagant to the point of self-indulgence; likes to lord it over others.

IMUM COELI

Fortunate or privileged background; often has a strong sense of inner contentment based on strong moral, religious or spiritual certainty; likes to play the generous host at home.

A conflict between inner expectations and what life actually delivers; may reject family belief system or values, but struggle to find a replacement; misplaced self-confidence.

SATURN • ANGLES

The Need to Structure One's Environment

• **TAKING ON RESPONSIBILITY** • **A FEAR OF REJECTION** • **OVERCOMING HARDSHIP**
• **INHIBITED EXPRESSION** • **INFERIORITY COMPLEX** • **SLOW PROGRESS**
• **FRUSTRATED AMBITIONS** • **BLEAK OUTLOOK** • **SUSTAINED EFFORT**

ASCENDANT

A serious, self-contained personality with a cautious manner; a fine sense of timing and an eye for taking the appropriate course of action; often takes on responsibility from an early age.

Often indicates an unsupportive environment; lacks spontaneity; keeps emotions on a tight leash, appearing callous; confidence eroded by feelings of loneliness and inferiority.

MIDHEAVEN

Projects a self-reliant, responsible personality; indicates success through hard work and discipline; a flagbearer for the status quo; craves respectability and material security.

May feel straight-jacketed by responsibility; actions inhibited by slavish adherence to tradition or fear of failure; an under-achiever; carries the weight of parental aspirations.

DESCENDANT

Often takes on the father role in relationships or looks for a partner to do the same; can shoulder enormous responsibility; has the staying power to build lasting relationships.

Tends to project own failings and inadequacies on to partners; may stay in a relationship for fear of being alone; difficult relationships; may unconsciously seek to control partners.

IMUM COELI

Often denotes the need to conquer self-doubt in order to realize ambitions; learns from hard experience to be self-sufficient; marked powers of endurance; a late developer.

An emotionally or materially impoverished background; feels greatly misunderstood by the world; inclined to pessimism; can be cold and unloving; difficulties with putting down roots.

URANUS · ANGLES

The Need to Be Free to Choose One's Environment

• **BEING SEEN AS DIFFERENT** • **UNCONVENTIONAL LIFESTYLE** • **NERVOUS ENERGY**
• **EXCITING RELATIONSHIPS** • **SPIRIT OF REBELLION** • **OUTSPOKEN VIEWS**
• **ORIGINAL IDEAS** • **UNORTHODOX METHODS** • **RADICAL CHANGES**

ASCENDANT

 A highly charged, exciting personality with an energy that sets it apart from others; values independence and the right to do as it pleases; adept at galvanizing others into action.

 Prone to scatter energies erratically and to suffer from periodic nervous strain; conflict between the need to express one's individuality and a fear of standing out from the crowd.

MIDHEAVEN

 Projects an energetic, individualistic image; willing to take risks; unusual career; success through intuitive, ground-breaking ideas; unafraid to challenge conventional wisdom.

 A rebellious attitude to work, often seen as too temperamental and unreliable; fanatical pursuit of goals; chequered career; finds it difficult to work for others; dislikes routine.

DESCENDANT

 Looks for unpredictable relationships unhampered by traditional social values; relationships that awaken one's 'radical' potential; a preference for unusual partners.

 Unstable, compulsive attractions which end abruptly; intractable when feels freedom is threatened; may cultivate an air of eccentricity as a means of drawing attention.

IMUM COELI

 Powerful need for independence as a result of early conditioning; sees life as a voyage of self-discovery; rebelling against (stifling) family tradition; putting down new roots.

 Sudden shocks or disruption in early life – possibly frequent changes in residence; prone to hasty action; inability to settle; upheavals at home; can signify 'the family outcast'.

NEPTUNE • ANGLES

The Need to Merge with One's Environment

• LOOKING FOR SALVATION • SPIRITUAL IDEALS • SENSITIVE TO SURROUNDINGS • SLIPPERY IMAGE • UNFOCUSED GOALS • ARTISTIC INSPIRATION • WITHDRAWING FROM LIFE • A GLAMOROUS FRONT

ASCENDANT

 A subtly elusive and beguiling personality that can act as a hook for others' fantasies; exceptionally sensitive to atmospheric moods; strong need to 'rescue' people in need.

 Self-image at odds with what others see; problems caused by vagueness and confusion in personal dealings; highly impressionable, even gullible; addicted to glamour.

MIDHEAVEN

 Projects a glamorous, romantic image; may seek to serve others' needs; is capable of sacrificing personal ambitions to a higher cause; can denote the ability to capture the public imagination.

 Lack of progress or luck in career due to ill-defined goals; unrealistic ambitions; may not gain recognition for efforts; easily deceived; often lacks drive; finds it hard to work alone.

DESCENDANT

 Tends to idealize relationships and to glamorize partners; has an ability to act as a mirror to others; is often prepared to sacrifice own needs to help others; highly intuitive feelings.

 An inclination to immerse oneself in a partner at one's own expense; dishonesty in relationships out of a lack of clear boundaries; often finds relationships disillusioning.

IMUM COELI

 Sees home as a refuge for recharging batteries or as a source of inspiration; seeks a focus for for creative or spiritual needs; may become reclusive later in life.

 Often feels like a fish out of water; tends to romanticize early childhood; great uncertainty about family background; can signify weak or absent parent(s); strong escapist urges.

PLUTO • ANGLES

The Need to Control One's Environment

- DEPTH OF PERSONALITY • IMPENETRABLE MOTIVES • POWERFUL CONVICTIONS
- COMPULSIVE ATTRACTIONS • POWER COMPLEX • MANIPULATIVE METHODS
- FULFILMENT THROUGH POWER • REBUILDING SELF-IMAGE

ASCENDANT

 An intriguing, complex personality that gives little away, creating a veil of inscrutability; adept at drawing others out of their shell; controls emotions with an iron will.

 Feels the world is somehow unsafe; can be intensely self-conscious through a fear of exposure; the need to express power occasionally leads to violent disputes.

MIDHEAVEN

 Projects an intense, fascinating image; can focus single-mindedly on goals; has an eye for the main chance; capable of huge feats of endurance; often describes a controlling parent.

 Intolerant of others' weaknesses; a ruthless killer instinct; has a knack of making powerful enemies; crises triggered by pushing one's luck too far; craves power without responsibility.

DESCENDANT

 Attracts strong-minded partners; is drawn to deep relationships that have a transforming effect; helping others through times of crisis; instinctively knows how to please partners.

 Power struggles in relationships; can use sex as a way of controlling partners; may find it difficult to form intimate relationships and thus avoid close involvements altogether.

IMUM COELI

 Strong survival instinct; a renewed sense of self through starting own family; may feel driven to explore origins; possible interest in psychotherapy; marked need for privacy.

 Uses underhand methods to control environment; feelings of betrayal and abandonment about one's upbringing; finds it difficult to trust and show feelings.

CHAPTER 7

ASPECT PATTERNS
AND
CHART SHAPES

Often, an aspect between two planets does not occur in isolation, but links up with one or more planets in the chart to form a network of planetary contacts known as an aspect pattern. These patterns are considered to be extremely important because they point to dynamic, complex and often contradictory traits within our psychological make-up. Frequently, they provide the key that unlocks the rest of the chart.

An aspect pattern may consist of a number of aspects belonging to the same aspect group – for example, a series of interconnecting conjunctions or squares – or a blend of groups, such as three interlinking trines joining up with an opposition. Aspect patterns can also involve the Ascendant or MC at one end of the configuration instead of a planet – for instance, two planets in opposition both square the Ascendant. In this case, the Ascendant is treated as if it were a planet, because it acts as a funnel through which the energies of the other planets are 'discharged'.

It is also not uncommon for a chart to have more than one aspect pattern. Sometimes two aspect patterns are linked by one or more planets, setting up an extremely powerful flow of energies. When this happens, a chart is said to be well integrated because it connects several facets of the psyche. A chart with few interlinking aspects, on the other hand, suggests difficulties with finding an inner sense of unity.

The more planets involved in an aspect pattern, the more dominant its overall effect is likely to be. This is especially true when the orbs between the aspects in the pattern are close. However, it is usual to allow wider-than-normal orbs in aspect patterns, because the complex of planets magnifies the aspects' sphere of influence. As a rule, you should allow 2^0 more than the orbs suggested for the individual aspects (*see box on page 108*).

Strictly speaking, very few charts are devoid of aspect patterns, as any two planets in aspect that also link up with other planets set up a flow of energy. It is not unusual, however, for none of the recognized aspect patterns to appear in a chart. This does not mean that the individual concerned has a 'weak' chart – it is simply that the focus of planetary energies is less localized, and therefore less intense. As we shall see later on in the chapter, in the section covering 'chart shapes', a chart's basic dynamics can be determined as much by the overall pattern created by the positions of the planets as by any particular aspect configuration.

ASPECT PATTERN DYNAMICS

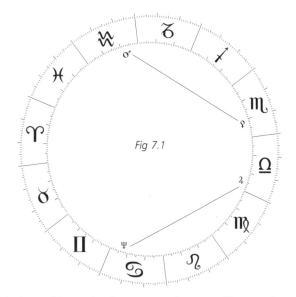

Fig 7.1

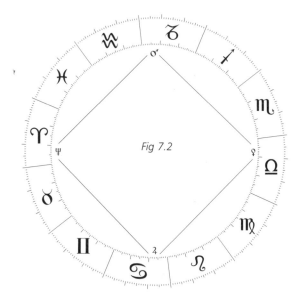

Fig 7.2

A chart with a pair of unconnected squares *(figure 7.1)* can generate a great deal of energy, but because there is no 'bridge' between the aspects this dynamism tends to be unstable. When the squares are all linked, as in the aspect pattern called a Grand Cross *(figure 7.2)*, the flow of energy is amplified, but it is also stabilized, and is therefore less dynamic.

The Stellium

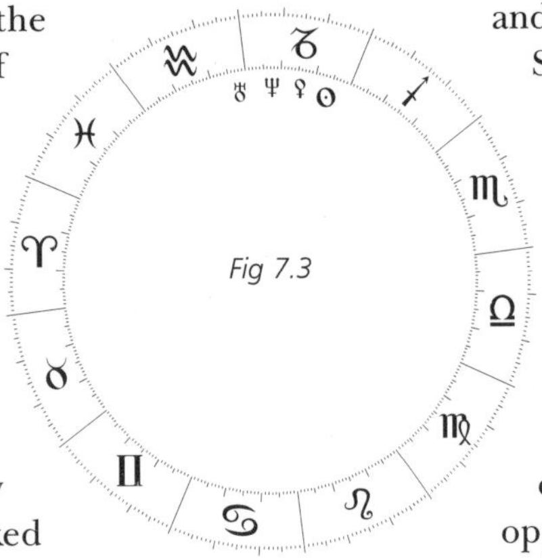

The Stellium, also known as the Satellitium, meaning 'cluster of stars', is a fairly common aspect pattern consisting of a minimum of three – some astrologers insist on four – or more planets in a chain of interconnecting conjunctions. Even if the first and last planet in the Stellium are technically 'out of orb' – that is, too far apart to be in conjunction – they still must be considered as linked through the conjunctions they make to the planet(s) in between *(figure 7.3)*.

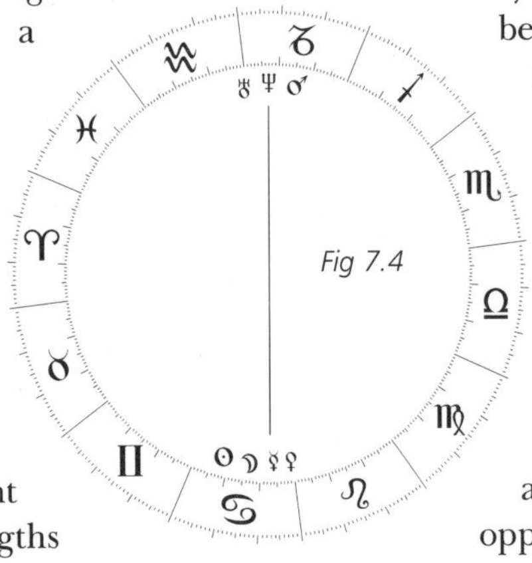

Because the planetary energies operate in concert, the Stellium is a particularly intense aspect pattern. When positively channelled, such a powerful concentration of energies can produce remarkable results. But the down side is that it can prove extremely difficult for people with this configuration to consider any standpoint other than their own. To determine which planet is the more dominant force, establish the relative strengths

Fig 7.3

Fig 7.4

and weaknesses of each planet in the Stellium. Also, check whether any other planets or one of the Angles is in close aspect to one of the planets in the Stellium, as this will modify the overall expression of the pattern.

A somewhat less common variation on this theme is the 'see-saw' pattern or multiple opposition, where one Stellium opposes another *(figure 7.4)*. This pattern blends the intensity of the conjunction with the conflict of the opposition in a way that can be extremely dynamic. But, because of the subjective quality of the conjunction and the unconscious projection of energies that invariably occurs with the opposition, there is a tendency to swing uncontrollably from one extreme to another. When handled constructively, however, this aspect pattern bestows the ability to see both sides of an issue and to strike a happy balance between opposing interests and activities.

The Grand Cross

As its name suggests, the Grand Cross incorporates four planets in square to one another on the arms of a cross, usually in signs of the same Quality. This is undoubtedly the most stable of the challenging aspect patterns, as it imparts tremendous strength and rootedness in the face of considerable frustration. If and when people with this configuration learn to get on top of their formidable energies, they are often capable of exceptional achievements.

The way in which the energies of a Grand Cross are likely to make themselves felt is coloured by the Quality of the signs in which the pattern falls. A Cardinal Grand Cross (*figure 7.5*), for instance, signifies enormous drive which is invariably frustrated by the conflicting demands of everyday life. While people with this type of Grand Cross may blame others for the resistance they encounter, much of it is self-induced for – initially, at least – they seldom plan or think carefully before acting, and compound matters by insisting on doing everything their own way, often at break-neck speed. Those with a Fixed Grand Cross (*figure 7.6*), by contrast, are inclined to do everything within their powers to keep things just as they are, so that when change inevitably comes, it is usually dramatic and sudden. Once they put their minds to it, they have the determination and strength to overcome the most difficult obstacles; the problem is, however, making the initial move.

People with a Mutable Grand Cross (*figure 7.7*) have little difficulty accepting change – in fact they positively thrive on it. But when faced with unwanted situations, they are inclined to change course in the vain hope that this will somehow avert the problem. The reality is that they often make matters worse, for their conflicts ultimately arise from within, out of immense restlessness and a lack of consistency.

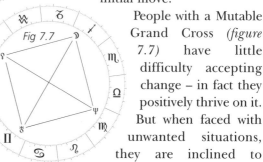

The T-Square

The T-Square is identical to the Grand Cross, except that one of the 'arms' of the cross is missing – the pattern forms a T-shape, with two or more planets in opposition both squaring a third *(figure 7.8)*. As with the Grand Cross, a T-Square typically involves planets in signs of the same Quality. The exception to this rule is discussed at the end of the chapter *(see page 179)*.

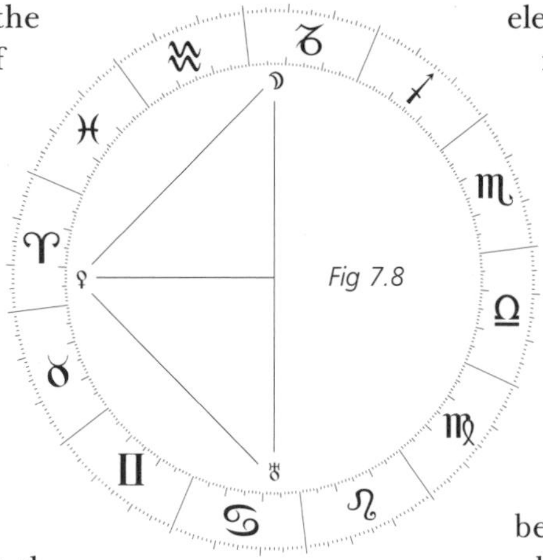

Some astrologers maintain that the missing arm of the T-Square softens the 'hemmed-in' effect of the Grand Cross. According to this line of thinking, the degree of the sign at the end of the missing arm offers an escape route for the energies locked in the T-Square, effectively making it easier for the tension created by the planets involved to be resolved *(figure 7.9)*.

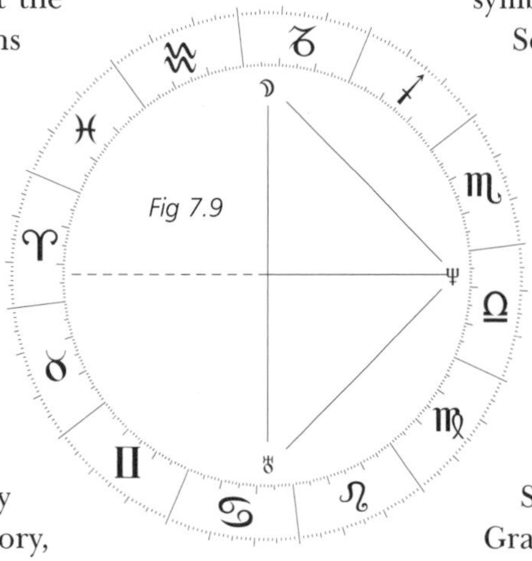

In the opinion of many astrologers, however, this theory,

Fig 7.8

Fig 7.9

elegant though it sounds, is simply not borne out by experience. The consensus is that, rather like cutting a leg off a four-legged chair, the empty quarter has a destabilising effect, making the T-Square more volatile than the Grand Cross.

All the same, this is an undeniably powerful aspect pattern, because it demands considerable strength of purpose before the potential benefits symbolized by the planets in the T-Square can be reaped. It is only when the issues at stake are avoided or suppressed that the tension generated by this aspect pattern causes serious problems – usually in the form of events which the individual feels are totally beyond his or her control. The same sort of dilemmas apply to the different Quality T-Squares as to the those of the Grand Cross.

The Grand Trine

The Grand Trine consists of three planets, 120⁰ apart, forming an equilateral triangle, usually in signs of the same Element. This aspect pattern signifies an abundance of free-flowing energy that finds its expression through natural-born talents and aptitudes. But, benign though these energies are, they can be something of a mixed blessing. The reason for this is that the abilities indicated by the planets in aspect come so naturally that, unless there are challenging aspects tapping into the Grand Trine, there is little motivation to develop them further. As a result, the easy-come-easy-go attitude that often characterizes this aspect pattern can become counterproductive.

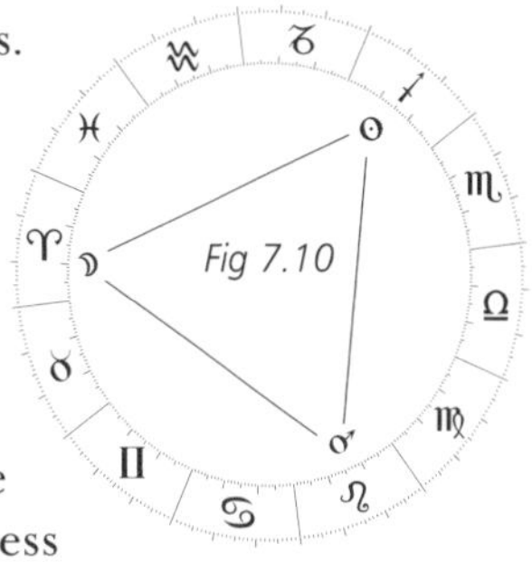

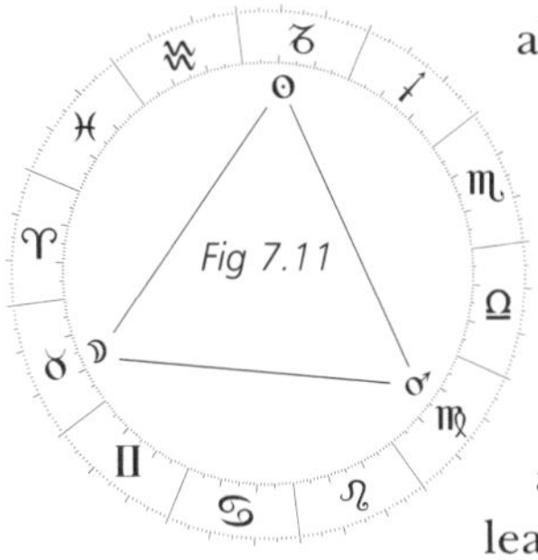

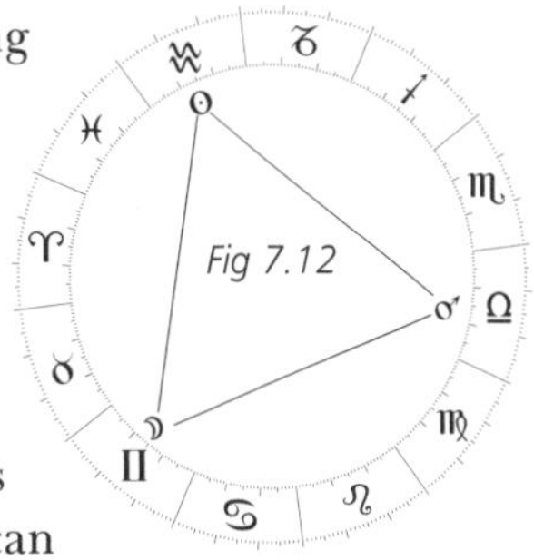

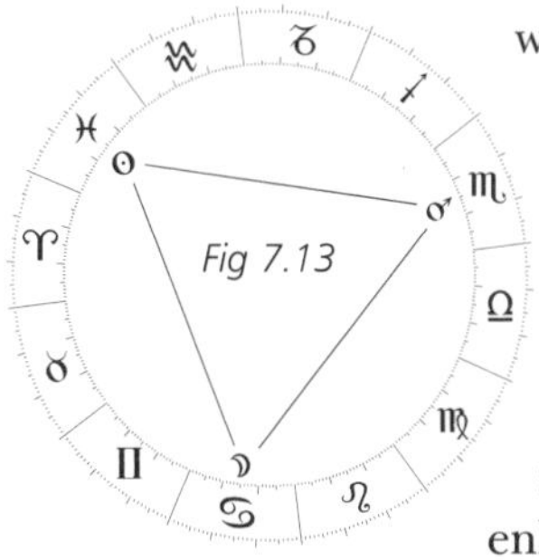

People with a Grand Trine in Fire *(figure 7.10)*, often produce impressive results through sheer confidence, especially in their own capabilities. But their blind faith in their powers can work against them when expectations fail to materialize. Those with a Grand Trine in Earth *(figure 7.11)*, may display an instinctive touch with all things practical, but they can become so absorbed in taking care of their material needs that they lose sight of what ends these needs are supposed to serve.

With a Grand Trine in Air *(figure 7.12)*, there is a natural facility for learning and thinking, which, if it is properly harnessed can produce original ideas. When discipline is lacking, however, the likely outcome is a butterfly mentality. A Grand Trine in Water *(figure 7.13)* enhances a person's intuition and sensitivity to emotional atmospheres. However, this receptivity needs to be made conscious, and directed outwards, if it is not to become a source of inner emotional turmoil.

Fig 7.10

Fig 7.11

Fig 7.12

Fig 7.13

The Minor Grand Trine

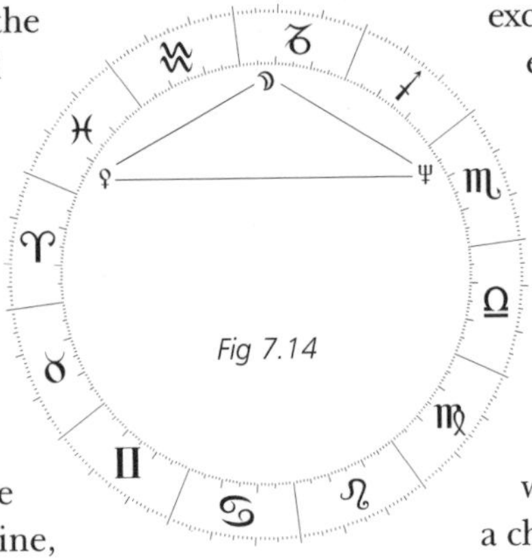

A slightly more dynamic version of the Grand Trine is the Minor Grand Trine *(figure 7.14)*. This occurs when two planets trine each other and sextile a third, usually combining energies in signs that belong to mutually 'sympathetic' Elements – Air and Fire or Earth and Water.

An extremely common aspect pattern, the Minor Grand Trine is similar in its effects to its more expansive cousin, the Grand Trine,

Fig 7.14

except that the sextile introduces an element of tension, or at least conscious effort, that would otherwise be lacking. All the same, because the energies in this configuration flow harmoniously and free from challenging aspects, the same kind of difficulties can arise as with the Grand Trine – notably, a reluctance to change one's ways, especially in circumstances where a change of attitude is called for.

The Kite

The Kite occurs when planets forming a Grand Trine link up with another planet which opposes one apex of the triangle and sextiles the other two *(figure 7.15)*. In theory, this aspect pattern offers the best of both worlds – the balanced flow of energy of the Grand Trine is stiffened by the presence of the opposition, which challenges the inclination towards complacency of the soft aspects.

Fig 7.15

Although the Kite is more dynamic pattern than the Grand Trine, it requires careful handling. Given that the Kite contains only one opposition, it is possible to skirt around the issues symbolized by the challenging aspect and remain within the relative comfort of the trines and sextiles. But if the conflicts shown by the opposition are faced head on, the potential for greater self-awareness is high.

The 'Mystic Rectangle'

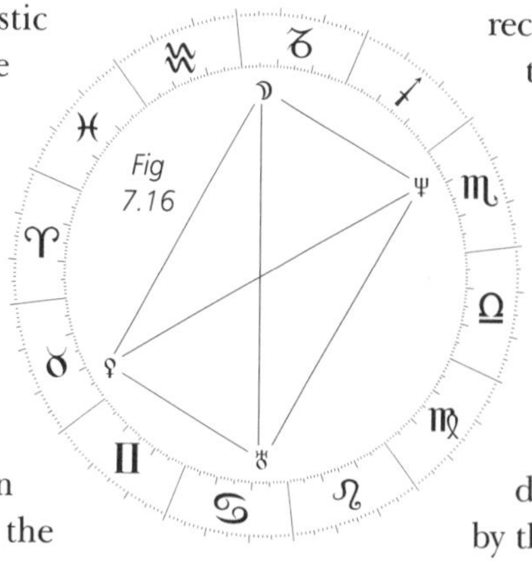

The glamorously named 'Mystic Rectangle' is in fact a slightly more complex modification of the Kite. It consists of two oppositions both ends of which form sextiles and trines to each other (*figure 7.16*).

The additional opposition makes this a more forceful planetary formation than the Kite, but because of the Mystic Rectangle's shape, the planetary energies can simply circuit the perimeter of the

Fig 7.16

rectangle, gliding effortlessly between the flowing aspects – the pair of sextiles and trines – and missing out the two oppositions altogether. However, if the oppositions are integrated, the blend of challenging and flowing aspects can result in the kind of constructive dynamism that enables individuals with this configuration to develop the natural abilities indicated by the planets concerned to the full.

The Grand Sextile

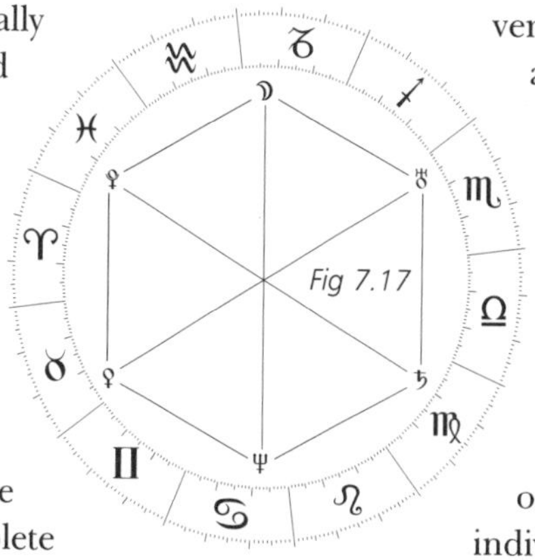

One of the rarest and most visually striking aspect patterns is the Grand Sextile. As its name implies, planets in this complex are connected by a string of sextiles and oppositions. With a complete Grand Sextile, this involves six sextiles and three oppositions (*figure 7.17*), or two Grand Trines in perfect sextile to one another, which explains why it is so rare – the planets seldom oblige by lining up in this way. Incomplete

Fig 7.17

versions of this aspect pattern, however, are much more common.

Despite its rarity value, the Grand Sextile does not appear to produce particularly outstanding individuals. But what it does create is a potent 'push-me-pull-you' energy flow. On the one hand, the sextiles indicate problems with self-motivation, while on the other, the oppositions drive the individual to make a sustained effort.

The Yod/Finger of Fate

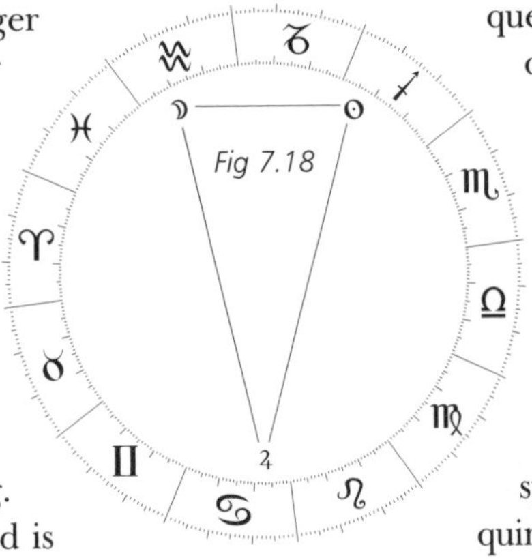

The Yod – sometimes called the Finger of Fate or God – occurs when two or more planets that are sextile each other make a quincunx to another planet, which forms the tip of the 'finger' *(figure 7.18).*

The Yod, meaning 'blessed' in Hebrew, is reputed to have a quality of fate about it in the sense that the planets involved point to a certain direction or vocational calling. Although the 'fated' quality of the Yod is questionable, the presence of two quincunxes in the pattern means that this is not an easy configuration to work with, even though it is mitigated by a sextile. This aspect pattern seems to generate a great deal of restless energy, and denotes issues that will not go away unless they are acted on. In this respect, the Yod is potentially a more positive symbol of transformation than a quincunx on its own.

Fig 7.18

Dissociate Patterns

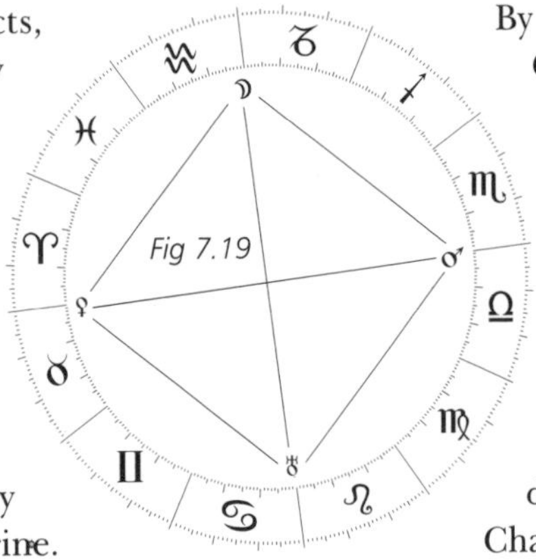

Just as with dissociate aspects, dissociate aspect patterns can only happen when the planets concerned fall near the end or the beginning of their respective signs. A dissociate Grand Trine, for instance, occurs when one planet in the triangle falls in a different Element from the other two. Because it occupies an incompatible sign, the flow of energy is less stable than a 'pure' Grand Trine.

By the same token, dissociate Grand Crosses and T-Squares are softer versions of their pure forms, toning down the overall level of tension. In the case of a Grand Cross, two of the 'arms' can fall in signs of a different Quality *(figure 7.19).* The same principle applies to a dissociate Stellium, which spans neighbouring signs. Interpreting dissociate aspects is discussed in Chapter 5 *(see page 114).*

Fig 7.19

CHART SHAPES

The Splay

The Splay is one of the most common and least clearly defined chart shapes, because the planets are spread unevenly around the chart *(figure 7.20)*. At the very least, there must be one cluster of two or three planets, with the rest distributed randomly, but it is not unusual for there to be up to three such clusters, which may also be linked to each other in an aspect pattern such as a Grand Trine or a T-Square.

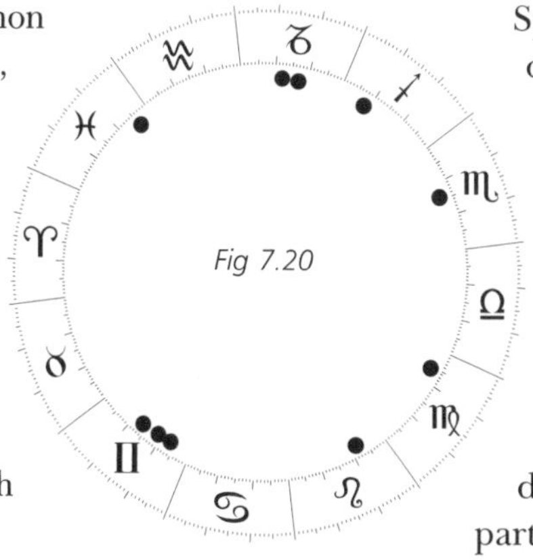

Fig 7.20

Splay types tend to be very much their own people, and have problems adapting to the demands of others. Typically, they hold on to their views tenaciously and give little ground to people who disagree with them. Often motivated by a strong need for freedom, Splay types are likely to be extremely self-sufficient. However, a dislike of discipline and routine can prove to be particular stumbling blocks.

The Splash

In contrast to the Splay, the Splash shape has an even distribution of planets around the chart – ideally with few or no conjunctions and as many signs occupied as possible *(figure 7.21)*. The Splash personality is also less focused and entrenched than the Splay type, as this chart shape indicates a more open-minded approach to life and a correspondingly wider range of abilities and interests.

Fig 7.21

The keywords for Splash types are adaptability and versatility. While these qualities give them an ability to slot into almost any environment, their all-rounder mentality can result in a lack of direction, the effects of which can be seen in their tendency to scatter their energies and spread their talents too thinly. However, aspects from planets to the Ascendant and MC will help to mollify this weakness.

The Bowl

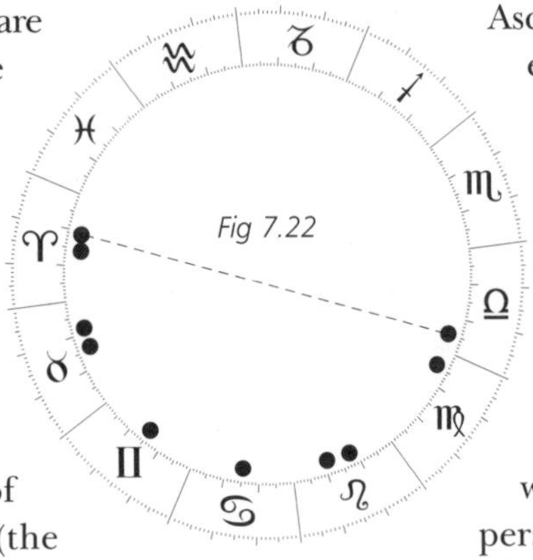

With the Bowl shape, all the planets are concentrated within one half of the chart – sometimes 'sealed' by an opposition (*figure 7.22*). Reflecting the shape of this pattern, Bowl types are said to be immensely self-contained and resourceful. But they also tend to be 'one-sided', so their life's challenge is to integrate the empty half of the chart.

Bowl types with a majority of planets above the horizon (the

Fig 7.22

Ascendant axis) generally take a more extroverted or objective approach to life; below the horizon, the tendency is towards introversion and a more subjective viewpoint; to the east, or left, of the MC axis, the emphasis is on establishing social outlets for personal initiatives; to the west, or left, the individual is primarily concerned with finding a balance between personal and relationship needs.

The Bucket

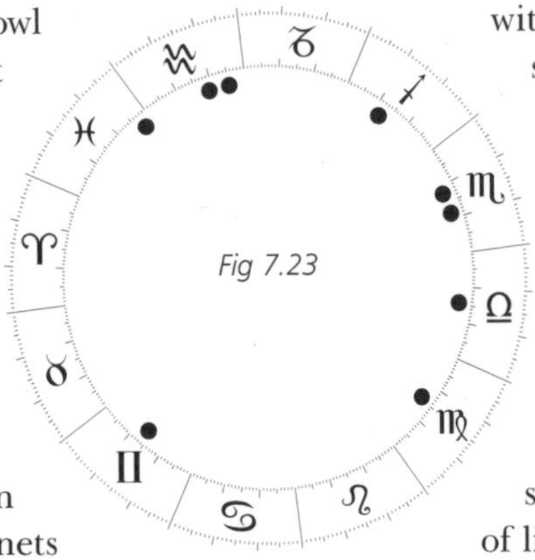

The Bucket shape is similar to the Bowl except that one planet, or at most two planets in a conjunction, forms a 'handle' – otherwise known as a singleton – outside the main chart pattern (*figure 7.23*). As the only presence in the empty half of the chart, the singleton acts as a counterbalance to the remaining planets, and is often the conduit through which the other energies in the chart are channelled. Any planets

Fig 7.23

within the bowl that aspect the singleton will also modify the nature of the energy flow.

Bucket types are characterized as 'goal-fixated', because they are capable of concentrating their considerable energies on achieving specific aims with single-minded determination. The sign and house position of the singleton show how and in what area of life this effort is likely to be directed.

The Locomotive

The Locomotive shape is an extended version of the Bowl, with the planets more or less evenly spread over two-thirds of the chart, or the equivalent of nine consecutive signs *(figure 7.24)*. Locomotive types are dynamic, sometimes irresistibly so, and apply their energies to challenges signified by the houses in the tenanted area. However, the vacant section of the chart represents an area of life that is not fully experienced, or at least is felt to be missing, and often indicates a vulnerable part of the personality that needs careful handling.

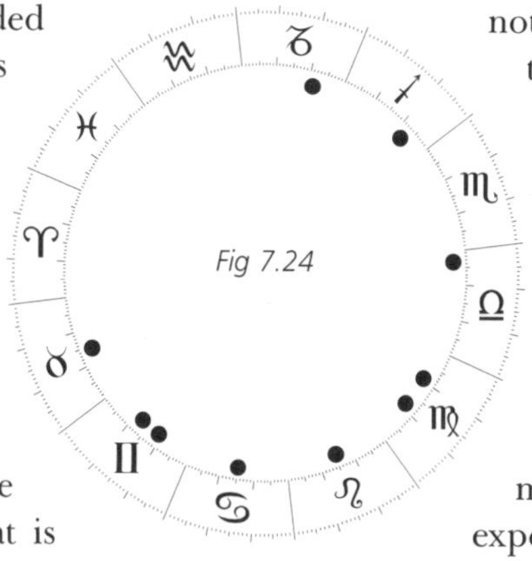

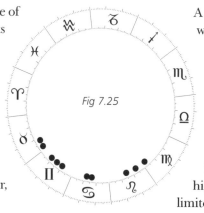

Fig 7.24

The planet 'leading' the others in a clockwise direction around the chart is the driving force of this shape which, together with its house position, will show which part of the personality is the motivating force and what kind of experiences it is likely to seek out.

The Bundle

The Bundle shape is the polar opposite of the Locomotive, with all the planets grouped within one-third of the chart *(figure 7.25)*. Although rare, this shape reflects a narrowness of vision and experience. Bundle types tend to channel their energies into issues related to the occupied section at the expense of the rest of the chart. This shape describes the specialist in his or her field or, negatively, the obsessive personality.

Fig 7.25

A variation of the Bundle is the Sling, which has one planet or a conjunction outside the main bundle. With this shape, the planet forming the Sling's handle acts as a channel for the bundled planets, often producing a highly focused individual who is driven by a vocational calling. Both Bundle and Sling types can be highly effective operators within their limited field of experience

FURTHER CONSIDERATIONS

Evaluating Aspect Patterns

**The Birth Chart of
Diana, Princess of Wales**

Minor Grand Trine. In this chart, the Sun and Mercury trine Neptune on the Ascendant with both points forming a sextile to Mars–Pluto. This would normally be considered an 'easy' aspect pattern, were it not for the fact that it is 'challenged' by the Jupiter square to Neptune, the Moon opposition to Mars and the sesquiquadrate from the Sun to the Moon.

Stellium. Under any circumstances, this is a very strong aspect pattern, but it is made even more powerful by the fact that Mars and Pluto are also involved in the Yod, and Uranus lies at one end of the T-Square. This is a very unusual link-up of energies and gives the chart a very 'driven' quality.

Yod. This is a highly significant aspect pattern, because the five planets involved – the Sun, Mercury, Mars, Jupiter and Pluto – draw in all the other planets in the chart, as well as the Ascendant and MC.

T-Square. Some of the instability generated by a T-Square can be mitigated by soft aspects from other planets. In this case, however, the three planets concerned, the Moon, Venus and Uranus, are besieged by a volley of hard aspects. The only exception is a stabilizing trine from Venus to Saturn.

Aspect patterns are extremely important focal points of energy, which can dominate a chart. But it is all too easy to look at them out of context and ignore other aspects that key into them. These 'satellite' aspects are critical, because they can strongly modify the flow of energies within the aspect pattern itself. For instance, the 'relaxed' quality of a Grand Trine can benefit enormously from the dynamism of a hard aspect, such as a square or opposition, while the instability of a T-Square can profit from the soothing 'influence' of a trine or sextile. To illustrate this point, we have chosen the chart of the late Diana, Princess of Wales (*above*), which has no less than four interlinking aspect patterns.

183

CHAPTER 8

BIRTH CHART
INTERPRETATION

Learning the language of astrology is a fascinating challenge. At first, the strangeness of the symbols along with the sheer volume of information can seem daunting, but that is only to be expected. For those new to the art of interpretation, the secret lies in breaking down the chart into its component parts, then reassembling them into manageable categories. The process gets easier with practice, and you will soon develop your own system of chart interpretation.

The procedure described over the following pages is designed to help you analyse a birth chart one step at a time, using the information you have gathered working through the previous chapters. Accompanying each step is a sample breakdown of the chart of the late Diana, Princess of Wales. The point of organizing the information in such a systematic way is to isolate all the details and place them in their proper context. This way there is less risk of underestimating or overlooking them. There is a blank 'check list' of key points at the end of the book, which you can either photocopy or use as a template for your own version (see page 222).

As you progress, some of the information may appear contradictory. There is nothing unusual in this, for no one is entirely one thing or the other. But there are times when the contrast will seem extreme; for example, one planetary aspect may suggest an extrovert, easy-going personality while another hints at someone who is shy and intensely private. The main point to remember, however, is that these contradictions do not cancel each other out. They can either pull the individual in different directions, causing much inner tension, or one set of characteristics may appear outwardly more dominant and so camouflage the existence of the other. The 'golden rule' in these circumstances is to keep an open mind – the chart takes you beyond the outer mask of the personality, so you can expect the inner landscape to be different.

Finally, as you break down a chart, you will find that certain astrological 'themes' crop up time and again. These are precisely what you are looking for, as they show you where the main emphasis of the chart lies, and act as signposts guiding you to the heart of the individual.

SAMPLE CHART

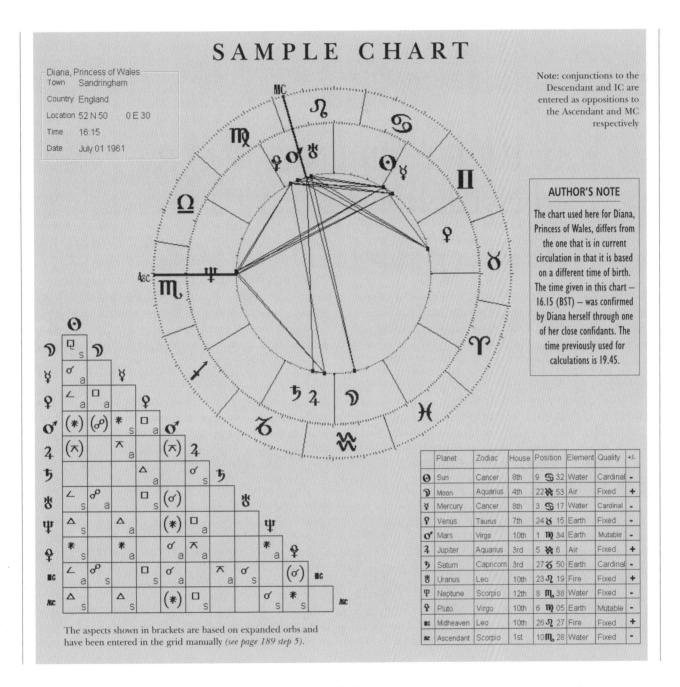

Diana, Princess of Wales
Town — Sandringham
Country — England
Location — 52 N 50   0 E 30
Time — 16:15
Date — July 01 1961

MC

Note: conjunctions to the
Descendant and IC are
entered as oppositions to
the Ascendant and MC
respectively

AUTHOR'S NOTE

The chart used here for Diana,
Princess of Wales, differs from
the one that is in current
circulation in that it is based
on a different time of birth.
The time given in this chart —
16.15 (BST) — was confirmed
by Diana herself through one
of her close confidants. The
time previously used for
calculations is 19.45.

The aspects shown in brackets are based on expanded orbs and
have been entered in the grid manually *(see page 189 step 5).*

Planet		Zodiac	House	Position	Element	Quality	+/-
☉	Sun	Cancer	8th	9 ♋ 32	Water	Cardinal	-
☽	Moon	Aquarius	4th	22 ♒ 53	Air	Fixed	+
☿	Mercury	Cancer	8th	3 ♋ 17	Water	Cardinal	-
♀	Venus	Taurus	7th	24 ♉ 15	Earth	Fixed	-
♂	Mars	Virgo	10th	1 ♍ 34	Earth	Mutable	-
♃	Jupiter	Aquarius	3rd	5 ♒ 6	Air	Fixed	+
♄	Saturn	Capricorn	3rd	27 ♑ 50	Earth	Cardinal	-
♅	Uranus	Leo	10th	23 ♌ 19	Fire	Fixed	+
♆	Neptune	Scorpio	12th	8 ♏ 38	Water	Fixed	-
♇	Pluto	Virgo	10th	6 ♍ 05	Earth	Mutable	-
MC	Midheaven	Leo	10th	26 ♌ 27	Fire	Fixed	+
Asc	Ascendant	Scorpio	1st	10 ♏ 28	Water	Fixed	-

PREPARING FOR INTERPRETATION

Before looking at specific details, establish the chart's general features – its overall shape and any aspect patterns (*see Chapter 7*). The aspect patterns in Diana's chart are also discussed on page 183:

CHART SHAPE: *Diana's chart has a Splay shape with an emphasis of planets above the horizon.*
ASPECTS PATTERNS: *There are four aspect patterns – a Fixed T-Square involving the Moon, Venus and Uranus; a Yod, or Finger of Fate, with Sun-Mercury, Mars-Pluto and Jupiter; a Stellium consisting of Uranus, Mars and Pluto clustered around the MC; a minor Grand Trine embracing Sun–Mercury, Mars–Pluto and Neptune–Ascendant.*

First Impressions:
• The Splay shape of Diana's chart is well spread out, with all the planets and the Angles linking up, suggesting reserves of strength and will power – in short, someone who should not be underestimated.
• The powerful energies straining at the leash in the Fixed T-Square indicate enormous stubbornness,

determination and a refusal to be coerced or cowed.
• The Yod is a powerful aspect pattern in this chart as it involves five planets, including the all-important Sun. Jupiter in Aquarius, at the configuration's apex, suggests a need to find a humanitarian cause for all these pent-up energies.
• With the Stellium, the combination of Mars, Uranus and Pluto is a powerful cocktail of volatile energies that can suddenly erupt.
• A technical point: Mars and Uranus in the Stellium are just 'out of orb', but because both planets are conjunct the MC, there is a strong case for expanding the normal orb here. The same applies to the Sun and Mars in the Yod. Both are out of orb to Jupiter but are drawn into the picture by their respective conjunctions to Mercury and Pluto.

Next, look at the balance of the Elements, Qualities and Polarities (*see Chapter 2*). When assessing their relative strengths and weaknesses, 'weigh' the signs in which the planets, Ascendant and MC fall according to their importance. A helpful way of

doing this is to use a simple points system. Award four points each to the Sun, Moon and Ascendant, as these constitute an individual's basic astrological 'signature'; three points each to the MC, Mercury, Venus and Mars; two points apiece to Jupiter and Saturn, and one point each to the 'generational' planets, Uranus, Neptune and Pluto:

ELEMENTS: *Earth – Venus, Mars, Saturn and Pluto; Water – the Sun, Mercury, Neptune and the Ascendant; Air – the Moon and Jupiter; Fire – Uranus and the MC.*
QUALITIES: *Fixed – the Moon, Venus, Jupiter, Uranus, Neptune, the Ascendant and MC; Cardinal – the Sun, Mercury and Saturn; Mutable – Mars and Pluto.*
POLARITIES: *Negative – seven planets and the Ascendant; Positive – three planets and the MC.*

First Impressions:
• Water is the dominant element in this chart, with Earth in strong support, implying sensitivity and resilience. Even with the Moon in Aquarius, Air is not particularly strong – the Moon is not generally at home in Air signs. Although Uranus in Leo on the MC hints at a fiery public persona, the absence of Fire elsewhere suggests a fragile self-confidence.
• Of the Qualities, the Fixed signs vastly outweigh the Cardinals (self-assertion) and Mutables (adaptability), so the emphasis in this chart is overwhelmingly on resistance to change.
• The emphasis of Negative signs echoes the prominence of Water and Earth in the chart, suggesting a tendency to introversion and subjectivity.

STEP 3

Next, note the Ascendant and MC signs and their rulers – together with the rulers' signs and houses. Repeat the process for the Sun and Moon. Check also whether the Sun and Moon are in aspect, as this gives an indication of the basic balance between the 'male' (active, objective, conscious) and 'female' (passive, subjective, instinctive) sides of the individual. If there is no aspect, look at the the Sun and Moon's compatibility by sign:

ASCENDANT SIGN: *Scorpio.*
CHART (ASCENDANT) RULER: *Pluto in Virgo in the*

tenth house; co-ruler Mars also in Virgo in the tenth.
SUN SIGN AND HOUSE: *Cancer, eighth house.*
SUN SIGN RULER: *The Moon in Aquarius in the fourth house.*
MOON SIGN AND HOUSE: *Aquarius, fourth house.*
MOON SIGN RULER: *Uranus in Leo in the eleventh house.*
MC SIGN: *Leo.*
MC RULER: *The Sun in Cancer in the eighth house.*
SUN/MOON INTER-ASPECT: *Sesquiquadrate.*

First Impressions:

• The hard aspect between the Sun and Moon shows a conflict between the emotions and the will. With the Sun in a feminine sign and the Moon in a masculine one, there is also confusion between the 'male' and 'female' sides of the psyche, which is further muddied by the Moon being the ruler of the Sun's sign.

• The Scorpio Ascendant and the strong showing of the chart rulers – Mars and Pluto – on the MC add intensity and a very strong element of compulsion to the emotional nature.

• Uranus, the ruler of the Moon sign, hints at an instinctive wilfulness and difficulties with handling emotional undercurrents. This turbulence is amplified by the fact that Uranus is also conjunct Mars–Pluto on the MC.

STEP 4

Next, look at the planetary strengths. Under this section you should include: planets in their natural sign or house; planets that are Angular – that is, conjunct the Angles (*see Chapter 6*); planets with the most aspects; any unaspected planets. Also make a note of the most elevated planet (nearest to the MC) as this shows the most consciously directed energies in the chart. Finally, check the planetary Exaltations, Detriments and Falls:

PLANET(S) IN OWN SIGN/HOUSE: *Venus (Taurus); Saturn (Capricorn); Moon (fourth); Venus (seventh); Neptune (twelfth).*
PLANET(S) CONJUNCT THE ANGLES: *Neptune (Asc); Mars–Uranus–Pluto (all MC); the Moon (IC).*
PLANET(S) WITH MOST ASPECTS: *The Sun.*
ELEVATED PLANET(S): *Mars, Uranus and Pluto.*
EXALTATIONS, DETRIMENTS AND FALLS: *Uranus (Detriment).*

First Impressions:

• The Moon is in a dominant position in its own house, and underpins the whole chart. As it opposes the Stellium on the MC, it indicates that Diana was driven by deep and powerful subconscious urges.

• The Sun aspects all the planets except Saturn, suggesting a lack of anchoring, or grounding, to stabilize all the turbo-charged solar energy.

• Neptune conjunct the Scorpio Ascendant points to an elusive magnetism which can act as a channel for other people's fantasies. It also suggests a distinctly manipulative personality.

• The number of angular planets – five – underlines what an exceptionally powerful chart this is, especially as three of them are 'generational'. This chart is a very good example of how the outer planets can become a focus, or channel, for issues that affect the lives of many, not just the individual concerned.

STEP 5

Assess the main aspect type, and whether there are any types of aspect missing, as these show whether the chart is stable or dynamic, or a mixture of both. Look at the closest aspects as these will stand out most sharply. (What constitutes a close aspect is a matter of judgment; in this case, given the abundance of close aspects, a 'cut-off' orb of 2^0 for the major aspects and 1^0 for the minor aspects has been used, but in a chart with mostly wide aspects you can extend the orbs. If you do so, enter the aspects by hand in the aspect grid, as the orbs in the software are preset.) Finally, look at other aspects to the Angles besides conjunctions:

ASPECTS TO THE ASCENDANT: *Sun–Mercury form a trine; Jupiter a square; Mars–Pluto a sextile.*

ASPECTS TO THE MC: *The Sun makes a semisquare; Venus a square; Saturn a quincunx.*

MAIN ASPECT TYPE(S): *Conjunction.*

MISSING ASPECT(S): *None.*

CLOSE CONJUNCTION(S): *Neptune–Ascendant (1^0 49).*

OTHER CLOSE ASPECTS: *Sun semisquare Venus (0^0 16); Sun trine Neptune (0^0 53); Sun trine Ascendant (0^0 56); Moon square Venus (1^0 21); Moon opposite Uranus (0^0 26); Mercury sextile Mars (1^0 42); Venus square Uranus (0^0 55); Jupiter quincunx Pluto (0^0 55); Neptune conjunct Ascendant (1^0 49).*

TIGHTEST ASPECT(S): *Sun semisquare Venus; Moon opposite Uranus.*

First Impressions:

• The plethora of conjunctions confirms Diana's instinctive nature. Normally, this effect can be offset by the presence of oppositions, which encourage greater objectivity. But in Diana's case, the three oppositions all involve the Moon on the IC, and therefore serve to reinforce her subjectivity.

• The tight aspects between the planets involved in the T-Square (the Moon, Venus and Uranus), show this to be a particularly significant pattern, which focuses on the conflicting needs for intimacy, support and independence.

• The Sun aspects both the Ascendant and MC, and reflects a desire to be noticed and to be in the public eye. This contrasts sharply with Diana's intense dislike of having her privacy invaded, reflected by her Scorpio Ascendant and fourth house Moon.

STEP 6

Now work through the meanings of the planets in the signs and houses (*see Chapters 2, 3 and 4*). A useful way to begin your interpretation is to build up a personality profile using keywords and phrases, remembering to include both positive and negative descriptions. For example:

• *Sun in Cancer in the eighth house: Sensitive, protective, nurturing, vulnerable, moody, defensive, over-emotional; derives sense of identity through close emotional ties; expresses emotions through caring or, if displaced, through possessiveness; sensitive to criticism; seeks to become immersed in intense, transformative relationships; needs to purify or let go of the darker side of the emotions...and so on.*

STEP 7

Finally, repeat the same process for the aspects (*see Chapter 5*). Note the type of aspect, but give priority to the planets involved. With Sun–Neptune aspects, for instance, there is always confusion about one's self-identity in some way or another, no matter what the aspect. Remember to look at the accidental rulers for each house – the planet ruling the sign on the cusp of a house (*see page 106*). The aspects to these rulers will also have a bearing on the relevant houses, even if other planets are present.

Diana's chart check list

1. CHART OVERVIEW
Chart Shape: Splay
Aspect Pattern(s): Stellium; Fixed T-Square; Minor
Grand Trine; Yod
Strongest Element: Water (Earth)
Weakest Element: Fire (Air)
Strongest Quality: Cardinal
Weakest Quality: Mutable
Strongest Polarity: Negative

2. 'SIGNATURE' DETAILS
Ascendant Sign: Scorpio
Chart (Ascendant) Ruler: Pluto (co-ruler Mars)
Chart Ruler Sign and House: Virgo; 10th
Sun Sign and House: Cancer; 8th
Sun Ruler: Moon
Sun Ruler Sign and House: Aquarius; 4th
Moon Sign and House: Aquarius; 4th
Moon Ruler: Uranus (co-ruler Saturn)
Moon Ruler Sign and House: Leo; 10th (Capricorn; 3rd)
MC Sign: Leo
MC Ruler: Sun
MC Ruler Sign and House: Cancer; 8th

3. PLANETARY STRENGTHS
Planet in Own Sign: Venus (Taurus); Saturn (Capricorn)

Planet in Own House: Moon (4th); Venus (7th),
Neptune (12th)
Planet conjunct the Angles: Neptune (Asc); Moon (IC);
Mars, Uranus, and Pluto (all MC)
Most Aspected Planet(s): Sun
Unaspected Planet: None
Exaltations, Detriments and Falls: Uranus (Detriment)

4. ASPECTS
Sun/Moon Inter-aspect: Sesquiquadrate
Remaining Aspects to the Angles: Sun trine the Asc,
semisquare the MC; Mercury trine the Asc; Venus
square the MC; Mars sextile the Asc (wide); Jupiter
square the Asc; Saturn quincunx the MC; Pluto
sextile the Asc
Main type of Aspect(s): Conjunction
Absent Aspect(s) type: None
Close Conjunctions: Neptune–Ascendant
Other close Aspects: Sun semisquare Venus (0^0 16);
Sun trine Neptune (0^0 53); Sun trine Ascendant (0^0 56);
Moon square Venus (1^0 21); Moon opposite Uranus (0^0
26); Mercury sextile Mars (1^0 42); Venus square Uranus
(0^0 55); Jupiter quincunx Pluto (0^0 55); Neptune conjunct
Ascendant (1^0 49)
Tightest Aspect(s): Sun semisquare Venus (minor
aspect); Moon opposite Uranus (major aspect)

PUTTING IT ALL TOGETHER
SAMPLE READING

The symbols contained within a birth chart are essentially a code to the psyche. Once these symbols have been decoded, the next step is to arrange them into something resembling a coherent 'story' – in other words, a recognizable profile of the individual.

There are many ways of synthesizing this decoded information. For the beginner, perhaps the simplest is to let yourself be guided by the chart itself. If one or two planets stand out against the rest, you might consider beginning your interpretation here. When there are no obvious focal points, a safe bet is to start with the three most important factors in the chart, the Sun, the Moon, and the Ascendant – many astrologers would add the chart ruler to this list – and build your interpretation around their respective strengths and weaknesses.

Another method is to begin with an overview of the individual, looking at basic psychological traits, such as mental and emotional temperament. Then you can move on to examine more specific areas of experience, such as relationships, career and so on.

In essence, it does not really matter which approach you use, so long as you look at the chart 'holistically' – from the point of view of the individual as a whole.

Finally, in the sample reading that follows, the astrological symbols which correspond to the personality traits under discussion have been added as footnotes. The notation is mostly self-explanatory, except that when planets are shown in brackets, such as [☉☌☿in ♋] △ [♆☌Asc♏], it means that the aspect shown outside the parentheses is made to all the planets inside them. Written out in full, the example above reads: the Sun and Mercury conjunct in Cancer trine both Neptune and the Ascendant conjunct in Scorpio.

Overview

Looking at the Sun–Moon–Ascendant complex, the strong position of the Moon, together with Neptune in watery Scorpio on the Ascendant and the Sun in Cancer[1] show this to be a chart in which the emotions rule supreme. There is great depth of feeling and compassion indicated, and in particular an instinctive ability to empathize with other people's suffering on a very personal level[2]. Yet, there is an equally strong flow of energy in the opposite direction.

Whereas Diana's Sun and Ascendant show a need to personalize the feelings, the Moon in emotionally aloof Aquarius seeks to depersonalize them. Moreover, the ruler of Diana's Moon sign – the distinctly unemotional Uranus – forms a highly charged opposition to the Moon, a combination that can waver erratically between the extremes of emotional dependence and detachment. This is an immensely testing aspect under any circumstances, but, because it falls on the MC–IC axis, it represents a titanic struggle between conscious and unconscious elements of the psyche. All this, compounded by an extremely foggy self-image[3], shows a deep-rooted conflict in Diana's personality between the urge to distance herself from her emotions and the need to hold onto them. It is a contradiction that was to influence every aspect of her life.

Emotional Temperament

The hard aspects to Diana's Moon[4] reveal a split in her emotional make-up between the warm and caring side of her popular image and the off-hand[4] and defensive[5] side of her nature that often afflicted her personal relationships. A natural tendency to blow hot and cold emotionally[6] makes for huge inconsistencies; on the one hand there is a craving for affection and emotional support[7], while on the other there is an almost pathological desire for independence[8].

It is a common characteristic of sensitive Water types that, for all their receptivity to others' feelings, the issue they feel most thin-skinned about is themselves. This is often seen in a tendency to exaggerate slights[9], or to suspect others' motives for no apparent good reason[10]. It can also make them

1 ☉ in 8th; ☽ ☉ in 4th ☍ MC 2 [☉ ☌ ☿ in ♋] △ [♆ ☌ Asc ♏] 3 ☉ △ [♆ ☌ Asc] 4 [☽ ☍ ♂ ☌ ♅] □ ♀ 5 [☉ ☌ ☿ ♋ △ Asc ♏] ⚹ [♂ ☌ ♀] 6 ☽ ☍ ♅; ♂ □ ♀ 7 ☽ □ ♀ 8 ☽ ☍ ♅ 9 ☉ in ♋ ∠ ♅ in ♌; ☉ ⚼ ☽; ☽ ☍ ♂ 10 [☿ in ♋ △ ♆ ☌ Asc in ♏] ⚹ [♂ ☌ ♀]

liable to misconstrue offers of advice as personal criticism. This certainly appeared to be true in Diana's case. As one of her confidants observed, 'If she sensed that people were not fully behind her she would often strike first by rejecting them – and she could do it quite ruthlessly[11]'. But how could someone so sensitive at the same time be so callous? Part of the answer lies in the Moon–Uranus opposition.

Hard contacts between these planets involving the fourth house often indicate an early emotional shock. In Diana's case, this could relate to the break-up of the family. The emotional 'cut-out' associated with this aspect is a way of anaesthetizing pain, but when it happens to a child it can often set up an unconscious expectation of rejection and abandonment. So while a fourth house Moon points to a childlike neediness, the opposition to Uranus implies that, as a result of her parents' acrimonious divorce, Diana was forced to become emotionally independent at a painfully tender age. With the chart rulers, Mars–Pluto keying into this opposition[12] – a potentially violent combination, signifying seething rage – it is quite easy to see how Diana might unconsciously have turned the emotional hurt of her parents' divorce inwards and vented the fury on herself, as her subsequent bulimia might suggest. Add the self-protective side of her 'watery' nature[13], and it becomes clear why she developed the perverse habit of biting the hand that fed her[14] – she had instinctively learned not to allow anyone to come too close for fear of being abandoned again. Maybe, too, this is why she found it easier to express her compassion 'universally'[15] than through her personal adult relationships[16].

Mental Temperament

Diana's chart shows that she had an imaginative, intuitive and deeply impressionable mind which was strongly coloured by her moods[17]. The same complex of planets also reveals a highly romanticized and idealistic view of life, which initially found its expression through a high-minded though largely impractical humanitarianism.[18] The ring leader of all this diffuse mental energy is Jupiter

[11] ♂ ☌ ♅ ☌ ♀ [12] ☽ ☍ [♂ ☌ ♅ ☌ ♀] [13] [☉ ☌ ☿ in ♋] △[♆ ☌ Asc in ♏] [14] ☽ ☍ ♅ [15] ☽ and ♃in ♒ [16] [☽ ☍ ♅] □ ♀
[17] [☉ ☌ ☿ in ♋] △ [♆ ☌ Asc in ♏]; ♃ □ ♆; ☿ ⚻ ♃ [18] ♃ □ [♆ ☌ Asc]

in Aquarius in the third house where, if his tendency to excess is not checked, he can behave with all the responsibility of an intractable, rebellious child.

The antidote to a wayward Jupiter, Saturn, is in Capricorn – its own sign – and conjunct Jupiter. Potentially, this placement promises great mental discipline, but because one of Saturn's function is to delay, his presence in the third house is often a sign of late mental development. Apart from the conjunction, Saturn is weakly aspected, which suggests that Diana had to battle against extreme swings between self-indulgence and self-control, blind optimism and bleak despair, before she could tame the wildly erratic and impulsive mental energies indicated by the string of hard aspects to Jupiter[19].

Relationships

With Venus in its own house – the seventh – there is a strong need for relationship. But here again, there is enormous conflict between the desire for intimacy and the need to plough a lone furrow[20]. This is intensified by the combination of a Taurus Descendant and a Venus–Saturn[21] aspect (Venus, remember, rules Taurus), which looks for security through conventional relationships, whereas Venus's involvement with Uranus[22] seeks excitement and has a deep horror of stifling commitments. To complicate matters further, Jupiter–Neptune[23] indicates wildly unrealistic expectations of relationships which, when added to the contrariness of the Moon–Uranus opposition, makes it clear why Diana found this area of life so difficult to handle. One side of her looked to immerse herself body and soul in a relationship[24], but in so doing became too compliant[25]. From this perspective she endured a loveless marriage[26] until her rebellious spirit broke rank[27]. But one wonders, given all the volatile energy locked up in the T-Square, whether Diana was really capable of sustaining a truly intimate relationship at all.

Public Life

Uranus on the MC in Leo – the sign associated with royalty – perfectly describes Diana's public role as

---

[19] [☉ ☌ ☿ ✶ ♂ ☌ ♀] ⊼ ♃; ♃ □ [♆ ☌ Asc]   [20] ♀ □ ♅   [21] ♀ △ ♄   [22] [☽ ☍ ♅] □ ♀   [23] ♃ □ ♆   [24] ☉ in the 8th △ ♆; ♃ □ ♆
[25] Venus 7th; ☉ ∠ ♀   [26] ♀ △ ♄   [27] [☽ ☍ ♅] □ ♀

the headstrong princess who defiantly refused to toe the establishment line. It also describes the bold show-woman in her[28] and her reckless spirit of adventure[29]. What is more, it is fairly clear that the glamorous nature of her role fed her love of excitement[30]. But she paid a heavy price for her individualism, in that her privacy was sacrificed to the nation – her life effectively becoming public property. Here we see Neptune at work, weakening the boundaries between the 'self' and 'others', so that the demarcation lines between her personal and public affairs became blurred.

This reveals yet another paradox in Diana's deeply complex nature. Her Neptune–Ascendant[31] in Scorpio and her fourth house Moon show a deep yearning to withdraw into herself and find an inner peace. But such periods of withdrawal were never likely to last for long, for Neptune loves glamour, and the Moon is in a sociable sign, the ruler of which sits squarely on the MC in the public glare. In other words, Diana was pulled in opposite directions by the lure of the limelight and the desire to hide under a rock. Given the humanitarian bias of her Moon–Uranus, which also happens to pull at her Sun – symbol of the essential self[32] – it seems that the only way Diana could deal with the immense conflict of interests between her private and public lives was to channel her personal feelings of suffering into her concern for others.

Although it would be overstating the case to suggest that Diana had made peace with the warring factions of her psyche by the time she died, the astrological indicators suggest that she had at least understood the significance of her public role. Perhaps the most lucid example of this was the way she used her considerable influence to draw attention to the victims of violence and suffering, especially children, as if she was finally making a conscious acknowledgement of her own childhood pain. Nowhere did her actions more clearly reflect the positive expression of her astrological symbolism than in her involvement in the anti-landmine campaign. For, aside from festering anger, what else can Mars–Pluto signify? Explosives (Mars) buried underground (Pluto).

---

28 ♀ □ [♅ ♂ MC]   29 ♂ ♂ ♅   30 ♀ □ ♅; ♆ ♂ Asc   31 ♆ in the 12th;   32 ☉ ∠ ♅; ☉ □ ☽

CHAPTER 9

THE ART OF CHART COMPARISON

When trying to evaluate success or failure in personal relationships, the birth chart alone is of limited value. It may show what we seek in the world, and how we set about finding it, but it cannot reveal the other side – what the world seeks in us. Astrology's solution to this dilemma is both simple and effective. By comparing the charts of the people involved in a process called *Synastry*, it becomes possible to build up a picture of the unique qualities of their relationship.

There are several techniques for comparing the astrology between two or more people. Fortunately, for the beginner, the most commonly used method of synastry also happens to be the easiest. Using the program supplied with this book, simply follow the instructions to calculate two birth charts and an aspect bi-grid *(see How to Run the Program on pages 6–14)*. Then prepare the ground as if you were interpreting a birth chart, except that you must also look at where the planets of one person fall in the chart of the other (and vice versa); then you need to check the cross-aspects – or 'contacts' as they are often called – formed between both parties' planets and Angles *(see pages 204–218)*.

In theory, any two charts can be compared – between friends, business partners, parents and children, teacher and pupil, boss and employee, even, if you feel so inclined, between a pet and its owner – provided, of course, the pet's time of birth is known. Not surprisingly, however, the greatest demand for synastry tends to come from would-be lovers, or people in long-term relationships.

How to Use Synastry

Synastry is a symbolic language which shows how people 'talk' to each other on many different levels – some of them conscious, some of them not. It can highlight areas of mutual attraction or tension, and open up ways of resolving problems, but it cannot reveal whether a relationship is 'meant to be', or even how long it will last; that rests on how much the two people involved want the relationship to work.

Bearing this caveat in mind, we shall look at the synastry of 'George' and 'Louise' *(see page 198)* to see how chart comparison works.

Birth chart wheels of Louise and George with aspect bi-grid

Louise

Town	Wallsend
Country	England
Location	55 N 00 1 W 31
Time	5:7
Date	August 07 1966

George

Town	Kempsey
Country	England
Location	52 N 11 2 W 13
Time	23:47
Date	February 28 1963

Bi-Grid – Louise and George

Louise

George

PREPARING FOR INTERPRETATION

Before looking at a couple's synastry, establish the main astrological features in their birth charts. Then start your comparison by assessing the main points of focus between the charts. In particular, make a note of the balance of Elements, Qualities and Polarities between the charts. These show at a very basic level what two people tend to look for in each other to compensate for qualities they lack in themselves. This is especially true when either chart shows a relative emphasis or weakness in one or more Elements or Qualities (*see Chapter 2*).

GEORGE

ELEMENTS: *George has an emphasis of planets in Earth and Water; Fire is weak, with only Mars in Leo.*
QUALITIES: *The Fixed signs are strongly represented, while the Cardinal signs, with only Venus in Capricorn are weak; the Mutable signs are well balanced.*
POLARITIES: *The Negative signs prevail.*

LOUISE

ELEMENTS: *Fire is the strongest Element, with Water in*
strong support. Earth is fairly weak and there are no planets in Air.*
QUALITIES: *There is an abundance of planets in Fixed signs and strength in the Cardinal signs; the Mutable signs are weak, with no personal planets occupying them.*
POLARITIES: *There is a balance between Positive and Negative signs.*

First Impressions:

Even at this early stage of comparison, the basic dynamics of the attraction are beginning to show:
• The combination of Fire (Louise) and Earth (George) is not a particularly easy one as these Elements are essentially antagonistic. Fire can scorch Earth, which in turn can smother Fire. On the other hand, Fire can give Earth some much-needed sparkle and spontaneity, while Earth's gift to Fire is solidity and reliability. With Water also strong in both charts, there are powerful emotional undercurrents. This suggests mutual strength of feeling, although with this combination playing second fiddle to Fire and Earth, care is needed to ensure that each respects the sensitivities of the other.
• With the Qualities, Louise supplies the Cardinal 'push' that is missing in George's chart, while

George has a good spread of planets in Mutable signs that makes up for the weakness of this Quality in Louise's chart. This blend of Qualities suggests that, even if Louise was not the dominant partner, she would have enjoyed taking the lead. Revealingly, it was Louise who made the first move and asked George out for a date. However, both George's and Louise's charts are heavily 'Fixed', implying tremendous strength of purpose when they pulled together and a strong resistance to each others' viewpoints when they did not.

STEP 2

Next, compare the signs and house positions of the personal planets – the Sun, the Moon, Mercury, Venus and Mars – and the contacts they make to each other's chart. These represent the basic thrust of the relationship and show how, and in what area, the emotional and mental attitudes of one party influence those of the other. Venus and Mars in particular hold the key to how the relationship works on the physical level.

While the respective positions and cross-aspects of Mercury reveal the level of mental compatibility – an important consideration in any relationship – strong contacts between both sides' 'male' planets, the Sun and Mars, and 'female' planets, the Moon and Venus, are traditionally one of the clearest weather-vanes of sexual attraction. For an affair of the heart to get off the ground, it helps if there are some cross-aspects between the male and female planets, irrespective of whether these are hard or soft. In addition, pay attention to the male–female balance between a couple's Suns and Moons, as this reveals the basic dynamics of the relationship.

You should also look at any contacts between the personal and outer planets. These signify deep and powerful emotional responses within the relationship, which can sometimes be compulsive. In fact, the way issues thrown up by these particular planetary energies are handled will often determine whether the relationship stands or falls by the wayside.

Finally, make a special note of any planets from one person's chart that fall in the other's seventh or eighth house. Although neither house should be considered on its own, both have a bearing on what we seek in a relationship. As it is not possible here to look at all the procedures outlined above, we will concentrate on the synastry between George's and Louise's Suns and Moons:

GEORGE

• *George's Sun in Pisces falls in Louise's seventh house, trines her Mars and opposes her Uranus–Pluto conjunction in Virgo.*
• *George's Moon in Taurus falls in Louise's ninth house, sextiles her Venus–Mars–Jupiter Stellium in Cancer, opposes her Neptune and trines her Uranus-Pluto conjunction in Virgo.*

LOUISE

• *Louise's Sun in Leo falls in George's tenth house, squares his Moon and Neptune–Ascendant, opposes his Mercury–Saturn and is conjunct his Mars.*
• *The Moon in Aries falls in George's 6th house, sextiles his Mercury–Saturn and squares his Venus.*

First Impressions:

• One of the most striking features here is that George's Sun and Moon fall in feminine signs, while Louise's occupy decidedly masculine ones. This suggests a switch in traditional 'gender roles', with George acting as the protective, nurturing influence and Louise in many ways 'wearing the trousers'. This crossover of masculine–feminine energies is implied elsewhere in their synastry, for example, by the fact that Louise's Sun squares George's Moon, her Mars opposes his Venus and her Fire–Cardinal emphasis is a much more forceful combination than his strong showing in the Earth–Water–Fixed signs. In fact, George had a habit of falling for 'strong' women, but in Louise's case the aspects from her Sun to his Mars and Saturn (which sits on her Descendant) suggests that he was never likely to be comfortable with her tendency to take the leading role.

• Another significant factor is that Louise's Sun falls on the vacant 'arm' of George's Moon–Mercury–Saturn–Neptune T-Square. Here, the Sun can either act as a positive influence, by helping to shed light on the issues symbolized by the planets in the partner's T-Square, or merely accentuate the conflicts and insecurities. With George and Louise, the presence of his Saturn in this planetary complex – opposite her Sun – suggests potential difficulties. Sure enough, the first signs that the relationship was beginning to flounder emerged when George's pessimistic and critical Saturn began to take control.

STEP 3

Repeat the same process in Step 2 for the remaining planets – Jupiter to Pluto. Look in particular at any contacts between Jupiter–Jupiter and Jupiter–Saturn. Jupiter in synastry can bring mutual enjoyment and a shared outlook, but both hard and soft contacts to this planet can greatly magnify problems elsewhere in the relationship, unless the restraining influence of Saturn is near to hand.

Aspects between one person's Jupiter or Saturn to the other's outer planets are not critical unless their positions in one or other of the charts is especially powerful, for example, conjunct or ruling the Ascendant. Even so, these contacts should not be ignored, as they can sometimes throw light on issues that arise as a result of age differences.

STEP 4

The next stage is to look at both sides' Angles and see where they fall in each other's charts. It is safe to say that, in astrological terms, a relationship's potential is greatly strengthened by cross-aspects from one person's planets to the other's Angles, and this applies to both the Ascendant–Descendant and the MC–IC axis.

Cross-aspects between the chart rulers are also important, as they give additional information about the nature of the couple's attraction. Finally, contacts between a couple's Angles – for example, when the Ascendant of one is conjunct the Ascendant or MC of the other – are also significant, as these reflect similarities of outlook:

GEORGE
• *George's Ascendant squares Louise's Sun–Ascendant and trines her Venus–Mars–Jupiter.*
• *His Virgo MC trines Louise's MC in Taurus.*
• *The co-ruler of George's chart, Mars, is conjunct Louise's Mercury and her chart ruler, the Sun.*

LOUISE
• *Louise's Ascendant keys into George's Fixed T-Square, involving his Moon, Mercury–Saturn and Neptune–Ascendant, and also forms a quincunx to his Jupiter.*
• *Her MC sextiles his Sun, trines his Uranus and squares his Venus and Mars.*

• *Her Ascendant ruler is the Sun (which, as it is also in Leo makes her a 'double' Leo) and, like her Ascendant, contacts George's Fixed T-Square.*

First Impressions:

• The numerous contacts from both George's and Louise's Ascendants and chart rulers to the other's planets confirm that their relationship was initially based on a very strong attraction.

• The cross-aspects from Louise's MC to George's planets show that to some extent she saw him as a reflection of her own ideal image. This is reinforced by the fact that Louise's Sun forms a square to George's Neptune.

STEP 5

Next, check whether a couple have the same planets in aspect in their birth charts – the type of aspect is less important here. These 'duplicate' aspects are extremely important, especially if they are echoed in the synastry, as they represent similar issues that a couple bring into the relationship – albeit usually from a different perspective. For example:

GEORGE
• *His Sun trines Neptune–Ascendant.*
• *His Moon opposes Neptune–Ascendant and trines Pluto.*

LOUISE
• *Her Sun squares Neptune and conjuncts the Ascendant.*
• *Her Moon is quincunx Neptune and Pluto, and trines the Ascendant.*

First Impressions:

• The aspects involving the Sun–Neptune–Ascendant in both their charts and their synastry imply that George and Louise had an extremely confused image of themselves and therefore of each other. The attraction appears to have been inspired by an idealized view of love, which was bound to lose its gloss when the relationship came down to earth.

• With both of them also having Moon–Neptune–Pluto aspects in their birth charts, there are a number of unresolved issues about power and control lurking in the basement (Pluto).

George and Louise's story is summarized at the end of the chapter. The next step, however, is to use the 'directory' over the following pages to see how the planetary energies between two people combine.

THE SUN IN SYNASTRY

In synastry, the Sun is a vitally important agent in the 'glue' of a relationship. But that does not mean one partner's Sun has to be in a compatible sign to the other's for the relationship to be a binding one. Admittedly, it helps if the two Suns make soft aspects to one another or, failing that, fall in mutually harmonious signs (Air-Fire or Earth-Water). But if they don't, it by no means signifies a disastrous relationship.

Equally important are the aspects made between a couple's Suns and the other planets in their charts. The Sun of one person 'vitalises' the planets it aspects in another person's chart, and it is these cross-aspects, or contacts, that can give a relationship its sense of direction. In most cases, a smattering of hard contacts involving both Suns – to keep the balance even – may be exactly what is required to give a dynamic edge to a relationship. Conversely, too many hard contacts can create constant friction which in time may become unbearable.

By contrast, a relationship with mostly soft solar contacts will radiate a sense of ease, but may also lack a strong sense of purpose. Even though the attraction is likely to be strong, there may not be enough dynamism to make it hold together. A healthy allocation of hard and soft contacts between both Suns and the other planets, therefore, means that there is room for the kind of growth that will help both sides to adjust to the relationship with confidence.

Signs of Compatibility

As in birth chart interpretation, it is advisable to tread cautiously when following these guidelines. For example, the traditional – and most valued – sign of compatibility is when a man's Sun aspects a woman's Moon, preferably by conjunction. If the woman's Sun also contacts the man's Moon, this is held to be a match made in heaven.

The danger of following this principle to the letter, however, can be seen in the combination of a Sun-Leo, Moon-Scorpio man with a Sun-Scorpio, Moon-Leo woman – or vice versa. Even if these planets are not square each other either in the respective birth charts or in the couple's synastry, they are still square by sign. As both Leo and Scorpio are Fixed signs, they constitute a formidable cocktail of energies, and may well indicate a relationship that is overshadowed by intense emotional friction.

SOLAR CONTACTS

TO THE SUN (☉-☉): The conjunction can either be an indication of harmony, or denote the kind of friction that emerges when two people of similar temperament spend too much time in each other's company – there simply may not be enough contrast. Occasionally, when one of the natal Suns is afflicted, the partner may be able to shed light on those areas where the conflict is most testing. But as often as not, the conjunction can fail to 'spark' the relationship.

Soft contacts between Suns blend most easily, and point to a match in which, if other contacts in the synastry concur, both sides feel mutual respect, and are able to accommodate one another's aims. The square, by contrast, often denotes a personality clash. Again, unless other factors in the synastry indicate otherwise, this battle of wills can be positively channelled. But, as often as not, this contact demands a great deal of breathing-space and substantial concessions on both sides about who does what, when and how.

Perhaps, surprisingly, the opposition is not as difficult a contact as might be expected. Frequently, the relationship profits from the balanced viewpoint this contact offers, with each side bringing something of value into the relationship that the other lacks, making this contact a stimulating match. However, the complementary nature of this contact may offer few comforts if either Sun is under siege from a series of challenging natal aspects, in which case there can just as easily be open hostility.

TO THE MOON (☉-☽): Traditionally, this is the classic indicator of compatibility for marriage, as well as friendship. The conjunction is considered to be especially favourable – with the soft aspects not far behind – as the lunar partner can tune in instinctively and adapt to the Solar partner's motives. With the hard aspects, the attraction is still there, although there is considerably more tension. The initial pull may begin to fade if the Sun becomes too overbearing, while the Moon may come across as indecisive and moody, particularly with the square.

TO MERCURY (☉-☿): A stimulating mental rapport with many interests in common, especially with the conjunction and, to a lesser extent, the soft contacts. Differences of opinion implied by the hard contacts can become a problem if neither side is willing to hear the other out, but in general they do not signify serious long-term discord.

TO VENUS (☉-♀): Traditionally, an excellent omen of sexual attraction and kindred spirit, especially if the woman's Sun contacts the man's Venus. Of the hard aspects, only the square and quincunx indicate possible tension in the relationship, particularly if Venus plays hard-to-get with the Sun. The opposition suggests that the relationship might benefit from an occasional brief separation.

TO MARS (☉-♂): Action-packed and fiery, this

☉

combination is not for the faint-hearted. In love, all contacts inflame sexual desire, although the hard contacts can also inflame the nerves. In business, Mars supplies the drive for the Sun's vision. The soft contacts encourage co-operation; the hard contacts, however, need more careful handling as they can highlight competition and possible power struggles.

To Jupiter (☉-♃): All aspects point to opportunities to learn from one another. There is congeniality and mutual tolerance with the soft contacts, whereas more effort is required to establish trust with the hard aspects. Often seen as a sign of a fortunate union.

To Saturn (☉-♄): At best, this is a steadying combination, with the emphasis on commitment and shared responsibilities. With the hard aspects, sombre Saturn can flatten the Sun's exuberance, while the Sun can run rings around Saturn's insecurities. Both sides, however, are likely to have to swallow some painful truths. With patience, the Sun can lighten up Saturn and learn self-discipline in return.

To Uranus (☉-♅): A magnetic, exciting attraction that needs plenty of room to breathe. Never likely to be dull, Uranus can open up the Sun partner to a whole new way of looking at life, although the hard contacts point to a potentially serious clash of wills. If both sides refuse to give up their independence the liaison is likely to be sporadic or short-lived.

To Neptune (☉-♆): The Sun may idealize and be beguiled by Neptune, the spell breaking only when reality forces both sides to face up to more worldly matters. There is a risk of both sides slipping into saviour-victim roles, particularly with the square, where either party may fail to read the other's motives or intentions clearly. On the other hand, there can be a tremendously strong rapport with these contacts, as if both sides are psychically attuned to one another.

To Pluto (☉-♇): Pluto can either raise the Sun's confidence levels or, with the hard contacts in particular, undermine it by indulging in subtle power games. Change on a deep level is likely with this contact, although it may be resisted if secretive Pluto is not clear about his intentions. In love, this combination often signifies a powerful, even compulsive sexual attraction.

To the Ascendant (☉-Asc/Desc): A combination that is likely to have a marked impact, with both sides finding much to appreciate in the other. Even though this is one of the classic signs of compatibility, with the hard contacts each may blame the other for joint failures.

To the Midheaven (☉-MC/IC): The Sun often identifies powerfully with issues that relate to the partner's MC-IC axis, and may become a guiding influence in these areas. With the hard contacts, however, the Sun may try to hog the limelight.

THE MOON IN SYNASTRY

The Moon symbolizes our instinctive emotional response to other people. Our 'gut' feelings when we first set eyes on someone, or the type of person that we naturally feel drawn to, convey a great deal about our own lunar personality – information that is possible to glean from the birth chart. But the astrological reasons as to why a relationship seems to 'make' a couple behave in a particular way – sometimes completely out of character – only starts to become clear when the positions and aspects of their respective Moons charts are compared.

As in natal interpretation, it is worth bearing in mind that the Moon has both a light and a dark side. As it also tends to reflect the nature of any planet it contacts in another person's chart, there will be times when it is virtually impossible to figure just who is triggering what response in whom. As a guide, however, soft contacts and the conjunction between one person's Moon to the other's suggest a powerful emotional bond, founded on an intuitive understanding of each other's needs. This is often accompanied by an urge to protect and nurture one another, particularly in times of difficulty.

Generally, these contacts are reckoned to favour long-term relationships, but they can also encourage compulsive habits – often connected with unconscious patterns of behaviour from the past – especially if these are indicated in either birth chart. The only serious problem with the conjunction, though, is that both parties may feel that they are cut from the same emotional cloth, which can sometimes be too close for comfort.

Inhibited Feelings

Hard contacts point to areas in the relationship where feelings of inhibition or rejection are likely to surface, or where emotional responses to situations conflict, causing an undercurrent of resentment. The intense feelings these emotions tend to stir up means that there is no easy way out – sooner or later these issues will have to be faced and resolved.

Finally, remember that the same guidelines for interpreting the Moon in natal astrology applies to synastry. In a woman's chart, it shows, among other things, her attitude to her own sex, and her role as a mother; in a man's, it reveals his image of the ideal woman. In synastry, however, strong contacts to a man's Moon may stir feelings in him that he may be unaccustomed to expressing openly.

LUNAR CONTACTS

TO THE MOON (☽-☽): Contacts between Moons are like tuning into an emotional frequency. The soft contacts and the conjunction show that the signals between both sides are being clearly received, and there is usually a strong emotional rapport. There is often some 'interference' with the opposition in the form of irritating misunderstandings that arise out of a failure to adjust to one another's different ways of reacting. On the other hand, these differences can also be highly stimulating. The square, however, is often a difficult contact to handle. At a deep level, something may be felt to be missing, with neither side ever feeling truly 'at home' with the other.

TO MERCURY (☽-☿): With these planets there is often an instinctive mutual understanding and an ability to voice and resolve grievances. Hard contacts may generate tension if the Moon feels Mercury is being too rational, or Mercury cannot cope with the Moon's moods.

TO VENUS (☽-♀): Unless the Moon or Venus is afflicted in either birth chart, contacts between these planets should bring a soothing hand to soften any friction elsewhere in the synastry. With the square, however, the infatuation may be compulsive. In the synastry between women, especially mother and daughter, the hard contacts can sometimes be an indication of rivalry.

TO MARS (☽-♂): Highly strung and hot-blooded, this volatile combination often signifies a tempestuous relationship in which the crockery is likely to fly. Sexual energy is also extremely high with all contacts, but it may not be enough to offset the explosive conflicts of the hard aspects – especially if Mars repeatedly tries to get the upper hand. In friendship or business, the hard contacts can be a source of niggling disagreements.

TO JUPITER (☽-♃): These two planets usually enjoy each other's company and contacts between them can bring generosity of spirit together with mutual support and protection. The hard contacts, however, suggest a need for space as there is a tendency to make mountains out of molehills and to exaggerate differences – although, unless other factors dictate otherwise, these should not be serious enough to undermine the relationship.

TO SATURN (☽-♄): Often an indicator of emotional barriers, contacts between the Moon and Saturn are not usually exciting or cheerful. Saturn tends close up the Moon and make it feel criticized and rejected, while the Moon often comes across as too flighty and changeable for Saturn. Emotional stability is valued above all else which, with the soft contacts, can produce a lasting relationship based on loyalty and shared responsibility – although in synastry these two planets will not explain the initial attraction. At worst, this combination produces stalemate, with each side stubbornly refusing to consider the possibility of change. Contacts between these planets can also dredge up unresolved childhood issues to do with emotional rejection, with the Moon partner often looking for Mother and the Saturn partner taking on a – possibly heavy handed – fatherly role. This can be a particularly difficult contact to deal with when both sides' Moons contact the others' Saturn, because each is instinctively looking for signs of rejection from the partner.

TO URANUS (☽-♅): A magnetic attraction which may prove too highly charged and erratic after the initial pull begins to weaken, or proves too much to handle. At the outset, at least, the Moon is likely to experience Uranus' unorthodox approach to life as a breath of fresh air. But the unpredictable nature of Uranus, especially in the hard contacts, can come across as a lack of consideration for the Moon's comparatively delicate sensibilities. Whatever the contact, the 'on-off' quality of the relationship should make this a stimulating but exhausting combination.

TO NEPTUNE (☽-♆): As both these planets emphasize receptivity, contacts between them tend to activate the imagination on both sides. Moreover, the sensitive Moon is easily won over by Neptune's idealism, sense of aesthetic beauty and spirituality, while Neptune finds a sympathetic and compassionate friend in the Moon. With the hard contacts, however, both sides may misinterpret the emotional signals that the other gives off, and are as likely to get lost in a fog of illusory or unrealistic demands as they are to fulfil each other's dreams.

TO PLUTO (☽-♀): This planetary duet intensifies the emotions, often to an uncomfortable degree. With the conjunction and, less obviously, the soft contacts, there is often an intuitive understanding on a deep level, which if sympathetically handled promises hidden riches. But because Pluto often operates on an unconscious level, the Moon's influence here can symbolize a journey into unchartered waters, bringing deeply buried fears to the surface. With the hard contacts, Pluto's habit of exploiting others' weaknesses can lead to possessiveness and emotional blackmail.

TO THE ASCENDANT(☽-Asc/Desc): This contact is often a sign of a hypnotic physical attraction, although the emotional bond is also strong, with the Moon able to tune into the partner's deepest feelings. Occasionally, this contact stirs strong feelings of *déjà vu*, even with the square.

TO THE MIDHEAVEN (☽-MC/IC): The Moon on a partner's MC can offer much-needed support career-wise. With the conjunction to the IC, both sides may 'click' from first meeting, and often display a telepathic understanding of each other – as if moulded from the same clay. The square suggests possible family interference in the relationship or, just as likely, that the conflicting demands of work and home are a source of tension.

MERCURY IN SYNASTRY

In synastry – just as in natal astrology – the Sun and Mars and the Moon and Venus are respectively viewed as symbols of archetypal 'male' or 'female' energies, with hapless Mercury consigned to the sidelines as a genderless or 'neutral' planet. But this is misleading – for the Messenger of the Gods is certainly no eunuch when it comes to romantic or sexual encounters.

In Greek mythology, Mercury's counterpart, Hermes, was in fact androgynous, containing both male and female characteristics in one person – qualities that psychology asserts we all inherently have, to some degree or other. This suggests that Mercury's role as the symbol of the mind is anything but asexual. Moreover, his greatest conquest was Aphrodite, the Greek equivalent of Venus, goddess of physical love – and his romantic liaison with her, symbolizing a union between the mind and physical desire, shows just how important Mercury's role is in affairs of the heart. The brain is the largest erogenous zone in the human body, and when two people's minds are not engaged, nothing much is likely to happen on the physical level.

In fact, Mercury invariably makes his presence felt from the moment Cupid's arrow strikes its target. He is 'responsible', among other things, for the oily charms of the seducer, and it is he who is mysteriously absent when we open our mouths only to be lost for words.

Mental Compatibility

In other respects, Mercury contacts in synastry reveal what kind of mental rapport a couple will have, the mutual interests they might enjoy and, most importantly of all, whether they share the same sense of humour – arguably the greatest aphrodisiac of all. Soft contacts, and particularly the conjunction between both Mercurys may also signal an unspoken understanding, as if either side knows what the other is thinking or going to say.

Even without this intuitive understanding, these contacts show that a relationship is unlikely to break down due to poor communications – and as long as couples talk, there is always a chance that problems can be sorted out. Hard aspects from one Mercury to another, however, often come into sharper focus once the physical side of the relationship has settled down. It is at this stage of the relationship that people really start to find out whether there is anything of lasting value to build on.

MERCURY CONTACTS

TO MERCURY (☿-☿): Soft aspects and the conjunction show a strong mental affinity and compatible interests outside the bedroom. The opposition produces objectivity and the potential to learn from the different ways each other's minds work; the square and quincunx may resort to cutting remarks, and can also test resolve when it comes to everyday decisions or listening to one another's viewpoint.

TO VENUS (☿-♀): This planetary pairing shows a natural urge to express affection and to be sensitive to one another's feelings. There may be a tendency to suppress grievances, although less so with the hard aspects.

TO MARS (☿-♂): Sparks are likely to fly, as Mercury and Mars both enjoy mental arm wrestling and letting off steam. With the hard aspects, passionate conflicts early on may prevent a relationship from flowering.

TO JUPITER (☿-♃): Usually a strong indication of mental compatibility. Even when they do not see eye to eye, these planets are capable of complementing one another perfectly: Mercury handles the details; Jupiter likes to take the overview.

TO SATURN (☿-♄): Saturn can either add substance to Mercury's ideas in the form of practical advice, or trample them into the ground by being overly critical. Mercury, by contrast, may find Saturn too slow for his tastes. With the hard contacts and the conjunction, Saturn can strip away any romantic illusions.

TO URANUS (☿-♅): Mentally, this is the equivalent of being connected to a live wire. Both planets stimulate each other to question and challenge accepted beliefs. Although exciting, the hard aspects may generate differences of opinion just for the sake of it.

TO NEPTUNE (☿-♆): Rational Mercury is easily overwhelmed by Neptune's formless, unfathomable world. Communication may be almost telepathic, and the exchange of ideas inspired. But just as often there is impracticality, confusion or downright deception.

TO PLUTO (☿-♇): At their best, Pluto and Mercury combine to unearth what makes a relationship tick. With the hard aspects, old prejudices and patterns of thinking may have to be faced. It is important that both sides learn to accept the other's views.

TO THE ASCENDANT (☿-Asc/Desc): With these contacts, a couple may think as one, but they can also be drawn to the kind of healthy disagreements that stimulate debate – although with the square, there is a danger of Mercury becoming overly analytical.

TO MIDHEAVEN (☿-MC/IC): A positive combination for business. In love, life is likely to be stimulating and, with the square, possibly controversial. Other factors will show if differences of opinions are likely to be serious.

VENUS IN SYNASTRY

In synastry, Venus shows how we set about creating and maintaining the checks and balances that keep a relationship on an even keel. But she does not do this out of any sense of altruism; her interest in keeping the peace is basically self-serving, so that she can get what she wants by appearing to appease the partner. The cross-aspects that she makes between a couple's charts are the keystone to understanding how the relationship works on this level.

Some traditional textbooks talk about the need for 'passive' Venus to contact a would-be partner's 'active' planets – traditionally the Sun or Mars – for an initial attraction to develop into something more substantial than a mere fluttering of hearts. Aspects from Venus to a partner's Ascendant were also thought to be a sign of a powerful attraction. While these are undoubtedly significant contacts, astrologers now take a broader view.

For instance, cross-aspects from one or both partner's Venus to the other's Uranus, Neptune and Pluto are also considered to be powerful love magnets. Moreover, these aspects frequently involve an element of 'projection', whereby the Venusian partner tends to indulge in wishful thinking, attributing qualities to the other half that have more to do with Venus herself. There is no doubt that these contact can deliver something out of the ordinary, but they also demand that both sides be absolutely clear about their motives.

Fatal Attractions

Soft contacts from Venus to a partner's planets or Angles show that the couple enjoy each other's company, and share similar tastes and values. If Mars is involved, sexual compatibility is implied. A surfeit of hard contacts to Venus is often found in love affairs that have a 'fated' quality about them. The attraction tends to be much stronger than with the soft contacts – in fact it can often be compulsive, pushing one, if not both, partners to behave completely out of character. On the positive side, relationships as intense as these offer us the opportunity to gain a deeper level of self-awareness.

Apart from the sexual dimension, Venus in synastry shows how two people – be they close friends, family or even work colleagues – get along together. More specifically, she shows how both sides adjust to each other's needs, as well as their expectations of each other.

212

♀

VENUS CONTACTS

TO VENUS (♀-♀): The conjunction and soft contacts find each other's company soothing. While the hard contacts may not share the same values, the attraction is still likely to be strong. The differences sign-posted by hard Venus contacts rarely threaten the relationship unless other factors point in this direction.

TO MARS (♀-♂): Mars arouses Venus' desires, and together these contacts reveal how a relationship functions physically. With soft contacts, the physical and emotional side of relationship will be well balanced. With the hard aspects, the sexual atmosphere will be steamier – perhaps compulsively so at times.

TO JUPITER (♀-♃): All these contacts promise great warmth and affection, although with the conjunction and soft contacts there is a tendency to accept things as they are. The hard aspects can put backbone into the relationship in a way that is mutually beneficial.

TO SATURN (♀-♄): The classic 'going steady' relationship – cool and reliable. Feelings are genuine but largely inhibited. Hard aspects often hint at 'bad timing'; the attraction is there but somehow the relationship never gets off the ground. This combination can also show great commitment.

TO URANUS (♀-♅): Unpredictable Uranus can wreak havoc with Venus' sense of values – often in a thrilling way. This planetary pairing brings a spirit of exploration to a relationship, but no cosy routine. The unexpected ups and downs, particularly with the hard aspects, may be too much for some.

TO NEPTUNE (♀-♆): These are generally highly idealistic contacts, indicating a search for the 'beautiful partner'. There can be much compassion and tenderness, but unless both sides see each other clearly, with both hard and soft aspects, there is a strong tendency to confuse physical attraction for love, leading to disillusionment on both sides.

TO PLUTO (♀-♇): There is nothing lightweight about these contacts. Venus and Pluto are both adept at playing power games in love, and a relationship with this pairing often has a compulsive love-hate or manipulative side to it. With the soft aspects, the compulsion is often more subtle, if not unconscious.

TO THE ASCENDANT (♀-ASC/DESC): Traditionally, this is one of the most propitious signs of compatibility. Both sides will feel encouraged to be affectionate and to give what the other needs. With the square, there may be minor irritations, although both sides should still enjoy each other's company.

TO THE MIDHEAVEN (♀-MC/IC): The conjunction to the MC often shows people who look good together in public. With Venus on the partner's IC, the emphasis is likely to be more on relaxing together in private.

MARS IN SYNASTRY

As in natural astrology, Mars in synastry represents the reverse side of the coin to Venus. Corresponding to the archetypal male principles of aggression and will power, Mars stands at the opposite end to Venus and her search for compromise and balance. On a psychological level, Mars also shows how much we like to take the lead and be our own person, whereas Venus symbolizes the desire to link up with someone else. In synastry, the balance between these two forces is critical in deciding whether the relationship is likely to be harmonious or unstable.

In love, Mars and Venus are also the classic significators of the physical side of the relationship. The traditional ideal was that the male's Mars should contact the female's Venus – but that is now seen as a crude stereotype. Not all men look for passive women, and by no means all women are attracted to dominant men. Besides the reverse situation – a woman's Mars contacting a man's Venus – does not diminish a man's masculine powers or a woman's femininity. In fact, it can enrich both sides' image of the opposite sex. What is important, though, is that there is a balance of Venus–Mars contacts in the synastry. When Mars contacts predominate, the chances are that one or both sides will be more concerned with looking after their own interests than supporting the other. On the other hand, few or no contacts to either side's Mars suggests a lack of passion and motivation in the relationship. In all cases, however, contacts between these planets are in no way a guarantee of a lasting relationship.

Sexual Compatibility

Soft contacts from Mars to the partner's chart imply that the couple are temperamentally well suited and have compatible sex drives – especially if Venus and Jupiter are in the picture. With the possible exception of contacts to Saturn or Neptune, both sides should gain individually from being together.

Hard aspects – and with Mars, this usually includes the conjunction – do not mean that the relationship will be a rocky one, but it is vital that the energies of Mars are not suppressed, otherwise the pressure may become intolerable. Often, sexual energy is extremely high, and may serve as an outlet for bottled-up feelings. However, there is also a risk that passions may run out of control, or simply be 'out of synch'.

MARS CONTACTS

To Mars (♂-♂): The impulsive energies of Mars can prove quite a handful in synastry. The hard aspects often point to stormy emotions and a spirit of confrontation. Sexual passions run high, but there is often a lack of tenderness. With the soft aspects – and to a lesser extent the conjunction – passions are still easily stirred, but with less abrasiveness on both sides.

To Jupiter (♂-♃): These contacts generate physical energy, as well as a mental rapport. Jupiter shows faith in Mars' ambitions, while Mars can make Jupiter more dynamic and active, and find outlets for their combined energies. Sexually, this can be an extremely raunchy combination, regardless of the cross-aspects.

To Saturn (♂-♄): Feelings of frustration are emphasized here, together with a sense that both hot and cold taps are running at once. Saturn may think Mars is too self-centred, while Mars can find Saturn harsh and obstructive. With all the aspects, both sides need plenty of space if the relationship is to prosper.

To Uranus (♂-♅): This combination is often found in people who are seeking – consciously or otherwise– to break away from previous relationship patterns. The attraction is often instant, extremely physical and off-beat – but for many it can prove too hot to handle over time. This pairing in synastry may signify a once-in-a-lifetime affair that has a lasting effect in that it opens the door to a new way of relating.

To Neptune (♂-♆): These are difficult energies to work with. Mars gets befogged by Neptune's other-worldliness, while Neptune finds it hard to appreciate Mars's go out and prove yourself' approach. The combined effect is rather like a hall of mirrors in which the relationship becomes distorted through a total lack of mutual understanding.

To Pluto (♂-♇): This combination can frequently produce an unconscious power struggle, in which Pluto seeks to dominate Mars, who in turn tries to get Pluto to show his cards. Both sides have to prove themselves right, although less compulsively with the soft contacts. At times the relationship may resemble a battlefield, in which case the strong sexual attraction may not be strong enough to sustain it.

To the Ascendant (♂-Asc/Desc): These aspects tend to magnify other factors in the chart. The effect on the relationship depends on whether the couple see themselves as a team or, especially with the square, as individuals. These contacts may prosper in a working relationship where disagreements can be contained.

To the Midheaven (♂-MC/IC): Mars can either help the MC-IC partner to make it in the world or be fiercely competitive. Similarly, home may be a stimulating environment, or a cauldron of arguments and dissent. Never likely to be dull, this combination demands that compromises be made.

4

JUPITER IN SYNASTRY

In synastry, expansive, enthusiastic Jupiter brings his philosophical insights and positive outlook to bear. In so doing, he can either help a partner or friend make optimum use of their resources, or he can take a *laissez-faire* attitude, tolerating levels of behaviour that any other relationship would be unable to withstand. This can create serious problems when a situation calls for a firm hand on the tiller.

Contacts between Jupiter and a partner's outer planets can have the effect of raising the relationship's expectations. With the conjunction and soft contacts, Jupiter's encouragement and optimism can help keep the relationship on an even keel, particularly in times of stress. Hard contacts to the outer planets may encourage Jupiter's extravagant, self-indulgent side to prevail.

Jupiter cross-aspects to the Angles usually promote a mutual spirit of generosity, but hard contacts can denote recklessness and over-indulgence.

JUPITER CONTACTS

TO JUPITER (♃-♃): These contacts usually encourage well-being and mutual understanding. Even hard contacts are likely to broaden both sides' outlook.

TO SATURN (♃-♄): Despite symbolizing the opposite principles of expansion and restriction, these planets often balance each other out. With the hard contacts, though, there may be a lack of mutual appreciation.

TO URANUS (♃-♅): Hard contacts should be watched in a business relationship as Jupiter can be tempted into over-reaching himself, though soft contacts and the conjunction may point to a telepathic link.

TO NEPTUNE (♃-♆): Denotes great sensitivity. Good for sharing material aspirations or spiritual goals, but the hard contacts can lead to a breakdown of trust.

TO PLUTO (♃-♇): Relationships with this pairing often have a deep level of understanding, and a capacity for exploring hidden potential; the hard contacts may point to a lack of co-operation.

TO THE ANGLES (♃-ASC/MC): Whatever the outcome, these contacts generally bring good humour and valuable opportunities for growth. With the hard contacts Jupiter may be guilty of misplaced generosity.

♄

SATURN IN SYNASTRY

For all his gloomy reputation, Saturn's presence in synastry is vital. Whereas the personal planets, together with Jupiter, tend to reflect our hopes and desires, Saturn brings us face to face with the realities of love. His great strength is to bring a relationship down to earth and to teach some important lessons about living together – the kind of lessons that many of us need to learn from time to time. Without Saturn's discipline and perseverance, most relationships would probably lack the staying power to hold together when the going gets tough.

On the other hand, Saturn can overdo it; when prominent in synastry there is a danger that duty will inhibit romantic feelings to such an extent that both sides end up feeling little warmth or sympathy for each other. At his most extreme, Saturn contacts with the personal planets in particular can have the unfortunate habit of bringing out deep-seated feelings of inadequacy and rejection.

SATURN CONTACTS

TO SATURN (♄-♄): Soft contacts and the conjunction often reveal shared ambitions and a willingness on both sides to deal responsibly with each other's inhibitions and insecurities. Hard contacts may test these weak spots to the limit.

TO URANUS (♄-♅): This combination usually indicates tension through Uranus being too progressive and Saturn too conservative for each other's liking. The conjunction can be particularly unstable as each side tries to outwit the other.

TO NEPTUNE (♄-♆): Slippery Neptune is usually too elusive for Saturn, who in turn can be too rigid for Neptune. The conjunction, however, has the potential for Saturn to turn Neptune's dreams into reality.

TO PLUTO (♄-♀): Although Saturn can feel undermined by Pluto, and Pluto distanced by Saturn, this pair can survive (and sometimes create) great hardship. Hard contacts can trigger deep feelings of mutual suspicion.

TO THE ANGLES (♄-ASC/MC): Saturn can either be a restrictive influence or bring a much-needed sense of structure and stability to the partner's life. On the MC-IC axis, Saturn may take on the role of teacher.

THE OUTER PLANETS IN SYNASTRY

Because the outer planets – Uranus, Neptune and Pluto – move so slowly through each sign of the zodiac, most couples either have them in the same or the neighbouring sign. As a result, contacts between them are often ignored in synastry. Yet, although aspects between the slower moving planets may have little to say about how a relationship gets off the ground, they can sometimes reveal something about what keeps it together or pulls it apart.

OUTER PLANET CONTACTS

URANUS TO URANUS (♅-♅): The sextile represents a fourteen-year gap and the square twenty years. Therefore these contacts signify the contrasting ways different generations take new ideas on board.

URANUS TO NEPTUNE (♅-♃): An unstable, highly strung combination: Neptune may be able to inspire Uranus's radicalism with the conjunction, but the hard contacts often produce nervous tension and unrealistic ideals.

URANUS TO PLUTO (♅-♃): A revolutionary duo, especially with the conjunction where both planets strive to replace outmoded systems with something vibrant. The hard contacts may encourage fanaticism.

URANUS TO THE ANGLE(♅-Asc/MC): This planet tends to disrupt any attempt to settle into a conventional relationship; an unstable influence with the square.

NEPTUNE TO NEPTUNE (♆-♀): Only the conjunction is significant here, so Neptune's effect depends on other planetary contacts it makes in either chart.

NEPTUNE TO PLUTO (♆-♀): Together these planets can raise awareness, intensify fantasies and fears and encourage unusual, possibly mystical, interests.

NEPTUNE TO THE ANGLES (♆-Asc/MC): Neptune contacts to the Ascendant or MC can indicate an inspired, spiritual bond, or an affair which loses itself in a web of illusion, false hopes and deception.

PLUTO TO PLUTO (♀-♀): ♀Likely to manifest as compulsive likes or dislikes, depending on other contacts.

PLUTO TO THE ANGLES (♀-Asc/MC): Deep, intense and fascinating, Pluto usually acts on an unconscious level as an agent of transformation or destruction.

SAMPLE READING

George and Louise were drawn to each other from the moment they met. For a brief spell, they both felt they were soulmates, yet within two years, elation had turned to disillusionment, and the relationship ended in bitterness. From their synastry, it is not hard to see why they were so attracted to each other. With Water the common Element between them, they seemed to have an intuitive understanding of each other's emotional needs, and the attraction was reinforced by Louise providing the Fire–Cardinal spark that George lacked, who in turn supplied the Air missing from her chart. Moreover, mutual contacts between their Angles and personal planets point to a very strong sexual chemistry.

Looking at the planetary themes, one feature immediately catches the eye: Louise's Sun–Ascendant falls on the missing arm of George's Fixed T-Square, pulling her Neptune into the planetary complex[1]. This makes the strong Neptune influence in both their birth charts even more powerful in their synastry. But, because it is such an unfocused energy, Neptune in synastry can be extremely slippery, the main challenge being to keep the channels of communication clear in order to steer clear of the typical Neptunian pitfalls of confusion, misinformation and outright deception.

Emotionally

To begin with, Louise was totally beguiled by the gentle, sensitive Neptunian side of George's personality. Her Sun square his Moon–Neptune opposition on the Ascendant axis is a spell-binding, though potentially hypersensitive, combination. In Louise, George found someone he could instinctively protect and nourish[2]. She, as a Sun Leo, was happy to be adored. But while his Saturn on her Descendant initially gave the relationship an air of emotional stability, it was not enough for George. It also proved too restrictive for Louise[3].

The main source of controversy was George's possessiveness[4]. Louise was a fiercely independent woman, who insisted on the right to make her own choices as and when she pleased[5] – although, she maintained, she was also passionately loyal when in love[6]. But George saw it rather differently – and with good reason. Louise had a bewitching catch-me-if-you-can quality that drove a lot of men wild[7], and at the time she met George, she had many male admirers in tow. In the first few months of their relationship, what George came to call Louise's 'tomcat posse' all but disappeared. But, gradually, her admirers began to re-emerge. It was at this stage that the complex of insecurities symbolized by George's Fixed T-Square began to surface.

At the centre of it all was George's fear of rejection[8]. It was an old pattern: he would fall in

---

[1] His [☽ ☌ ♆ ☌ Asc] □ [☿ ☌ ♄] contacts her [☉ ☌ Asc] □ ♆   [2] His ☽ ⚹ her [♀ ☌ ☌ ♂ ♃], ☍ her ♆ and □ her Asc   [3] [[♀ ☌ ♂ ☌ ♃] △ ♆] ⚹ [♅ ☌ ♀]
[4] ☽ in ♉ ☍ Asc   [5] ☽ in ♈ △ ☊ Asc; Cardinal emphasis   [6] ♀ in ♋; ☉ in ♌   [7] [☉ ☌ Asc] □ ♆; [♀ ☌ ♂ ☌ ♃] △ ♆   [8] ☽ □ ♄

love with women who were either unavailable, or could not reciprocate his feelings for them[9]. And when they duly left him, stifled by his possessiveness and unable to live up to his impossibly high expectations, he felt rejected. Louise was no exception. With the trine from her Uranus to George's Moon mirroring the quincunx between these planets in her own chart, she eventually felt driven to break away from what she felt to be her lover's suffocating emotional demands.

Mentally

Initially, George and Louise believed they had a great deal to offer each other. The trine between their Jupiters – also linked by trine to both their Neptunes – shows much common ground in their outlook on life, including a strong idealistic streak. But there was plenty of stimulating contrast as well[10]. Over time, however, a darker side began to surface. They began to quarrel – mostly over George's possessiveness, or at least his refusal to admit it[11]. Then, the deception began[12]. She began to lie about who she was seeing, and inevitably George found out that it was another man – 'just a friend', she claimed. But by then, the quarrelsome, destructive side of the relationship had already begun to dominate[13], and the differences of opinion became too much for Louise to bear.

Physically

To begin with, the physical side of the relationship was very strong[14], with the Water emphasis between them revealing much tenderness and consideration for each other's needs, and Venus, Mars and Jupiter adding the spice. But Louise's fiery nature sits uncomfortably beside her planets in self-protective Cancer. When George started to play manipulative games by using sex as a measure of her love for him[15] her passions began to blow more cold than hot[16]. When the relationship finally fell apart, Louise did precisely what George had always feared she would do – she left him for another man. But the question is, with Neptune so strong in their birth charts and their synastry, who really pushed whom?

---

9 ☽ ☍ ♆   10 Her ☿ ☌ his ♂; his ☿ ☍ her ☉   11 ☿ ☌ ♄ in ♒   12 His ☿ □ her ♆   13 Her [♀ ☌ ♂ ☌ ♃] ✶ ♅ ♀ ⚻ his ☿ ☌ ♄; her ☉ ☍ his ♄; his ☉ ☍ her ♀   14 His ♀ ☍ her [♀ ☌ ♂ ☌ ♃] △ his ♃; his ☽ ✶ her ♂; her ☉ ☌ his ♂   15 ☉ in ♓; ☉ ☌ ♀♀; ☽ in ♉; ♀ in ♋   16 ♀ ☌ ♂

CHART CHECK LIST

1. CHART OVERVIEW
Chart Shape:
Aspect Pattern(s):

Strongest Element:
Weakest Element:
Strongest Quality:
Weakest Quality:
Strongest Polarity:

2. 'SIGNATURE' DETAILS
Ascendant Sign:
Chart (Ascendant) Ruler:
Chart Ruler Sign and House:
Sun Sign and House:
Sun Ruler:
Sun Ruler Sign and House:
Moon Sign and House:
Moon Ruler:
Moon Ruler Sign and House:
MC Sign:
MC Ruler:
MC Ruler Sign and House:

3. PLANETARY STRENGTHS
Planet(s) in Own Sign (Rulers):
Planet(s) in Own House:
Planet(s) Conjunct the Angles :

Most Aspected Planet(s):
Unaspected Planet(s):
Exaltations:
Detriments:
Falls:

5. ASPECTS
Sun/Moon Inter-aspect:
Remaining Aspects to the Angles:

Main Type of Aspect:
Absent Aspect(s) Type:
Close Conjunctions :
Other Close Aspects :

Tightest Aspect(s):

FURTHER READING

Reference and Data Books

Clifford, Frank C. *British Entertainers – The Astrological Profiles*. London: Flare Books, 1997

Rodden, Lois. *Astrodata I (Profiles of Women)*. Tempe, AZ: American Federation of Astrologers, 1979

——. *Astrodata II (American Book of Charts)*. Tempe, AZ: American Federation of Astrologers, 1980

——. *Astrodata IV*. Tempe, AZ: American Federation of Astrologers, Inc 1986

Shanks, Thomas S. *The American Atlas (Revised Fourth Edition)*. San Diego, CA: ACS Publications (also available on CD-ROM)

——. *The International Atlas (Expanded Fifth Edition)*. San Diego, CA: ACS Publications (also available on CD-ROM)

General

Arroyo, Stephen. *Astrology, Psychology and the Four Elements*. Reno, NV: CRCS Publications, 1975

——. *Astrology, Karma & Transformation*. Sebastopol CA: CRCS, 1978

Braha, James. *How to be a Great Astrologer*. Longboat Key FL: Hermetician Press, 1992

Davidson, Ronald C. *Synastry*. New York: Aurora Press, 1983

——. *Astrology*. Sebastopol CA: CRCS, 1979

Greene, Liz. *Relating*. London: Coventure, 1977

——. *The Astrology of Fate*. London: Mandala 1984

Hand, Robert. *Horoscope Symbols*. Gloucester, MA: Para Research, 1981

Harvey, Charles & Suzi. *Sun Sign, Moon Sign*. London: Thorsons, 1994

Marks, Tracy. *The Art of Chart Interpretation*. Sebastopol CA: CRCS, 1979

Sasportas, Howard. *The Twelve Houses*. London: The Aquarian Press, 1985

Tompkins, Sue. *Aspects in Astrology*. Shaftesbury, Dorset: Element Books, 1989

Mail Order Address

All the above books may be ordered through:

Midheaven Bookshop
396 Caledonian Road
London N1 1DN
Tel. 0171 607 4133 Fax. 0171 700 6717
e-mail: 106063.420@compuserve.com

ACKNOWLEDGEMENTS

The authors wish to thank Dr James and Dominique Colthurst, Jill Davies, Mary Dowton, Roland Greig, Ray Leaning and Martin Preston for all their help and encouragement along the way on what has been a long, hard journey. Special thanks go to Yolande for her love and support beyond the call of duty, to Terry Chandler for his programming genius, to Nick and Ian at Eddison Sadd for steadfastly believing in this project, and to Brazzle for his scintillating Mac skills.

THE AUTHORS

FELIX LYLE, who devised this package, has been practising and teaching astrology for seventeen years, and for the last eight years has been a professional astrologer based in London. Between 1989 and 1991 he acted as chief consultant on the best-selling partwork *Zodiac*, during which time he pioneered new ways of bringing serious astrology within the grasp of the amateur through extensive use of colour graphics and imagery. He has recently worked on the highly successful partwork *The X Factor*.

BRYAN ASPLAND has been interested in astrology for twenty-five years, and a practising astrologer for the last ten years. He has also been involved in the world of computing since the birth of the PC in the early 1980s. Since then he has spent a great deal of time in combining these two interests to make astrology available to all.

EDDISON•SADD EDITIONS

Editorial Director: Ian Jackson
Project Editor: Liz Wheeler
Editor: Felix Lejac
Proof Reader: Slaney Begley

Creative Director: Nick Eddison
Art Director: Elaine Partington
Mac Designer: Brazzle Atkins
Line Illustrator: Anthony Duke

Production: Karyn Claridge and Charles James

The photograph on page 192 is from JS Library International, and that on page 219 is from Roy McMahon/The Stock Market